THE ACCOUNTANT'S HANDBOOK OF FRAUD AND COMMERCIAL CRIME

SUBSCRIPTION NOTICE

This Wiley product is updated on a periodic basis with supplements to reflect important changes in the subject matter. If you purchased this product directly from John Wiley & Sons, we have already recorded your subscription for this update service.

If, however, you purchased this product from a bookstore and wish to receive (1) the current update at no additional charge, and (2) future updates and revised or related volumes billed separately with a 30-day examination review, please send your name, company name (if applicable), address and the title of the product to:

Supplement Department
John Wiley & Sons, Inc.
One Wiley Drive
Somerset, NJ 08875
1-800-225-5945

The Accountant's Handbook of Fraud and Commercial Crime

G. Jack Bologna
Robert J. Lindquist
Joseph T. Wells

John Wiley & Sons, Inc.
New York   Chichester   Brisbane   Toronto   Singapore

This text is printed on acid-free paper.

Copyright © 1993 by John Wiley & Sons, Inc.

This publication is designed to provide accurate and authoritative information in regard to the subject matter covered. It is sold with the understanding that the publisher is not engaged in rendering legal, accounting, or other professional services. If legal advice or other expert assistance is required, the services of a competent professional person should be sought. *From a Declaration of Principles jointly adopted by a Committee of the American Bar Association and a Committee of Publishers.*

Library of Congress Cataloging-in-Publication Data:

Bologna, Jack.
    The accountant's handbook of fraud and commercial crime / G. Jack
  Bologna, Robert J. Lindquist, Joseph T. Wells.
        p.   cm.
    Includes bibliographical references and index.
    ISBN 0-471-52642-8
      1. Auditing, Internal.   2. Managerial accounting.   3. Fraud.
  4. Commercial crimes.   I. Lindquist, Robert J.   II. Wells, Joseph
  T.   III. Title.
  HF5668.25.B65   1992
  657′.458—dc20   92-14510
                                                   CIP

Printed in the United States of America

10 9 8 7 6 5 4 3 2 1

About the Authors

G. Jack Bologna, BBA, CFE, JD, is President of Computer Protection Systems, Inc., Plymouth, Michigan, and Assistant Professor of Management, Siena Heights College, Adrian, Michigan. He has authored numerous works on the subject of fraud and is editor of the monthly newsletters *Forensic Accounting Review* and *Computer Security Digest*.

Robert J. Lindquist, CFE, FCA, is Chairman of Lindquist Avey Macdonald Baskerville, Washington D.C. and Toronto, a leading forensic and investigative accounting firm. He has two decades of experience in forensic accounting, has written books and articles on the subject and given numerous seminars to accountants and law enforcement personnel. He is President of the Canadian Chapter of the National Association of Certified Fraud Examiners, Toronto, Ontario.

Joseph T. Wells, CFE, CPA, is Chairman of the National Association of Certified Fraud Examiners, Austin, Texas, which offers a certificate program to accountants, police, government officials and other white-collar crime investigators. He previously spent ten years as an FBI Agent documenting embezzlement, corruption, and fraud cases. He writes, researches, and lectures on white-collar crime issues.

Preface

This is a book about business fraud—not how to do it, but how to enhance one's awareness of it, how to prevent it, and if necessary how to deal with it.

Fraud is a major concern for professional accountants, business, and society generally. Since the 1970s the media has been enamored with the "megafrauds." More recently they have reported on Boesky, Milken, the Savings and Loan scandal, the Maxwell pension funds, and BCCI. Large frauds in the millions of dollars also receive extensive front-page attention in local media when they occur: an assistant bank manager and compulsive gambler defrauds a major bank of $10 million, losing most of it in Atlantic City; a trust company employee and an ex-police officer collude to defraud the trust company of $6 million, make off for Europe, and are later caught living in a London hotel suite.

However, the "glamorous" frauds are only the tip of the iceberg. Search through the local stories in any major newspaper over a given week, and you will likely find several references to small- and medium-size frauds involving thousands, tens of thousands, and even hundreds of thousands of dollars—no small piece of change for those being victimized.

Fraud holds a special significance for accountants. As employees in industry and government, they are expected to minimize the potential for fraud. In public practice, they are often the first to be criticized—and sued—when they fail to detect fraud. And yet the reality is that many accountants have had little practical exposure to the subject. An overlying structure—fraud knowledge, an investigative mentality, rules of evidence—is never built. It is hoped that *The Accountant's Handbook of Fraud and Commercial Crime* will provide accountants in industry, government, and public practice with the basic tools and raw materials required to build that structure.

Finally, it should be noted that fraud is a human problem which becomes a business problem. The first step in addressing this aspect of business is to recognize that fraud is a body of knowledge with its own distinctiveness and expertise.

Plymouth, Michigan	G. Jack Bologna
Toronto, Canada	Robert J. Lindquist
Austin, Texas	Joseph T. Wells

October 1992

Acknowledgments

This book is the result of considerable effort on the part of many. The authors would especially like to thank:

Tedd A. Avey, BComm, CA, Managing Partner of Lindquist Avey Macdonald Baskerville, Forensic and Investigative Accountants in Toronto for his significant contribution to this book.

John Wiley & Sons, Inc., New York, and in particular **Jeff Brown** and **Sheck Cho**, who are responsible for overseeing the development and publication.

Lindquist Avey Macdonald Baskerville, Toronto, for their contribution in drafting and reviewing various portions of the material.

Tony Walsh, CA, Toronto, who was instrumental in the development of the Handbook and did much of the work in managing its production.

Tim Leech, CA, of **Multiplex Consulting Services Inc.**, Toronto, for his contribution during the planning stage.

Sun Life Assurance Company of Canada, Toronto, for their permission to reprint the Code of Business Conduct in Chapter 3.

The Guarantee Company of North America, Toronto, and **Craig Malcolm**, for their contribution in drafting Chapter 4.

Coopers & Lybrand, Toronto, and in particular **David A. Griffiths**, BSc, C&L Partner-In-Charge of Computer Security Services, for their contribution during the planning stage and in drafting Chapter 5.

Macmillan Publishing Company, New York, for their permission to use material which forms the basis of Chapter 8.

Acknowledgments

The National Association of Certified Fraud Examiners, Austin, Texas, for their permission to use material that forms the basis of the glossary.

The National Commission on Fraudulent Financial Reporting, for their permission to reprint material appearing in the appendix.

The American Institute of Certified Public Accountants, for their permission to reprint material appearing in the appendix.

Kathie Green and Jim Ratley of the National Association of Certified Fraud Examiners, who lent their expertise in developing the manuscript.

Contents

PART I   **UNDERSTANDING FRAUD**

   Chapter One   Introduction   3

PART II   **PREVENTION: GENERAL TECHNIQUES**

   Chapter Two   Managing the Risk of Fraud   15
   Chapter Three   Promoting an Ethical Environment   45
   Chapter Four   Risk Financing and Fidelity
      Insurance   59
   Chapter Five   Computer Security and System
      Recovery   83

PART III   **PREVENTION: SPECIFIC TYPES OF FRAUD**

   Chapter Six   Asset Misappropriation from Within   119
   Chapter Seven   Frauds Perpetrated by Outsiders   145
   Chapter Eight   Computer Crime and Computer
      Criminals   173
   Chapter Nine   Commercial Crime   205

PART IV   **CRISIS MANAGEMENT**

   Chapter Ten   Dealing with a Known or Suspected
      Fraud   231

Bibliography   249

Glossary   251

Appendix: Professional Studies and Pronouncements   291

Index   327

PART I

Understanding Fraud

CHAPTER ONE

Introduction

§1.1 **The Nature and Extent of Fraud**
  (a) Definition
      (i) Criminal Deception
      (ii) Financial Benefit
  (b) Magnitude of the Threat
  (c) Sources of the Threat
      (i) Internal Sources
      (ii) External Sources

§1.2 **About This Handbook**
  (a) Prevention: General Techniques
      (i) Managing the Risk of Fraud
      (ii) Promoting an Ethical Environment
      (iii) Risk Financing and Fidelity Insurance
      (iv) Computer Security and System Recovery
  (b) Prevention: Specific Types of Fraud
      (i) Asset Misappropriation from Within
      (ii) Frauds Perpetrated by Outsiders
      (iii) Computer Crime and Computer Criminals
      (iv) Commercial Crime
  (c) Crisis Management-Dealing with a Known or Suspected
      Fraud
  (d) Back Matter

Introduction

"The Lord said to Moses, . . . you shall not defraud or rob your neighbor."—Leviticus 19:1,13

"Officials of the Bank of Credit and Commerce International were indicted yesterday on criminal charges for running 'the largest bank fraud in world financial history' . . . The best estimates indicate at this time that upward of $5 billion has been lost . . ."—Reuter, July 30, 1991

Even after more than 3,000 years, it seems that there are still many sinners among us. This Handbook is about keeping them away from your money, your organization's money, and your clients' money.

§1.1 The Nature and Extent of Fraud

(a) Definition

The key word used in most dictionaries to define fraud is *deception*. In the broadest sense of the word *fraud,* this definition may be sufficient. However, in the context of this Handbook, a slightly more restrictive definition is appropriate: fraud is *criminal deception intended to financially benefit the deceiver*. Both of the qualifiers in this definition are necessary, i.e., the deception must be *criminal* in nature and involve *financial benefit*. Each of these is described below.

(i) Criminal Deception. The qualifier *criminal* is necessary in order to exclude certain deceptions, which may financially benefit the deceiver, but which we are not interested in examining in this Handbook—for example, the mild overstatement of one's skills on a job application. While such an overstatement could be labeled *fraudulent* in the broadest sense of the word, it is the kind of transgression that can hardly be described as criminal.

It should also be noted that, for purposes of this definition, the word *criminal* is not used in a strictly legal sense. Rather, it refers to any seriously "wrong" action taken with malicious intent. Thus, even if perpetrators of fraud are able to avoid successful criminal prosecution—for example, because a particular jurisdiction has lax laws or enforcement, or because of some legal technicality—their actions are still considered criminal for purposes of this handbook.

(ii) Financial Benefit. The characteristic of *financial benefit* is necessary in order to exclude certain types of criminal deception, which we do not commonly think of as fraud and are therefore not dealt with in this Handbook—for example, a bigamist failing to disclose a previous marriage.

The financial benefit, which results from an action need not be direct for that action to be considered fraudulent. Indirect financial benefits are also possible, for example, the environmental criminal who avoids higher disposal costs by dumping toxic waste in a river.

(b)   Magnitude of the Threat

Since the essence of fraud is deception, determining its prevalence is problematic. Many frauds go undetected—probably more than 75 percent—and many that are detected do not get reported. It is virtually impossible to compile reliable statistics under these circumstances.

Simply based on the largest reported frauds—e.g., the Savings & Loan scandal, BCCI, Boesky and Milken—it is safe to say that fraud in the United States and Canada runs in the billions of dollars. If one assumes that fraud represents about 2 percent of GNP—conservative by some estimates—then the total cost in the United States and Canada would be well over $100 billion.

Macrostatistics are not particularly meaningful, however, even if accurate statistics could be obtained. The fact is that the threat of fraud depends largely on the circumstances, i.e., the environment in which it takes place. The reason for this starts with a view of personal integrity, such as the one depicted in Figure 1.1.

There are many views of personal integrity, and the percentage figures shown are not definitive. Some views suggest a more even split between the three categories, while others state that the honest and dishonest categories may be as low as 10 percent each. However, all of these views point to one important conclusion: exclusive reliance on the honesty of individuals is the surest way to be victimized. Well over half the population—and probably more than two-thirds—are quite capable of committing dishonest acts in the right (or should we say wrong?) environment.

The importance of creating an environment that discourages fraud brings us back to the question "What is the magnitude of the threat?" Answer: *the threat of fraud is as big as one allows it to be.*

Figure 1.1

ONE VIEW OF PERSONAL INTEGRITY

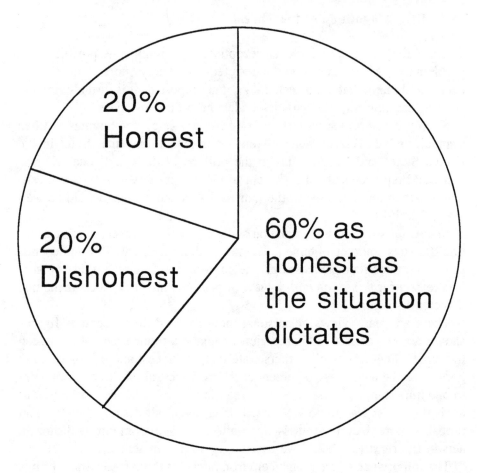

(c) Sources of the Threat

The magnitude of the fraud threat is only one dimension contributing to the extent of the problem. The breadth of the fraud threat—i.e., the various sources of fraud—must also be considered. A truly comprehensive prevention strategy must address the full spectrum of fraud sources.

The sources of the fraud threat can be classified as either internal or external. Each of these classifications is briefly described below.

(i) Internal Sources. Internal opportunities to commit fraud differ from company to company. Some typical examples that illustrate the broad nature of these opportunities include:

- Officers of a company may issue false financial reports to improve their own performance measurement;

- Managers may receive kickbacks from suppliers or inflate their expense accounts;

- Other employees may commit fraud such as embezzlement, cash skimming, or accounts receivable lapping; and

- Corporate directors may defraud a company and its shareholders through stock market manipulation and insider trading.

(ii) External Sources. Typical examples of external opportunities to commit fraud include:

- Suppliers can falsify or duplicate invoices;

- Competitors can victimize a company through industrial espionage or price fixing;

- Con men may defraud a company with schemes involving products, services, or investment opportunities that never materialize; and

- Customers can commit fraud through false credits posted to their accounts or through rebate coupon frauds.

The various internal and external sources of fraud are depicted in Figure 1.2.

Figure 1.2

How a Company Can Be Victimized - Internal

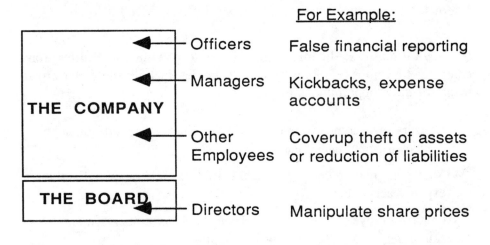

For Example:

Officers	False financial reporting
Managers	Kickbacks, expense accounts
Other Employees	Coverup theft of assets or reduction of liabilities
Directors	Manipulate share prices

How a Company Can Be Victimized - External

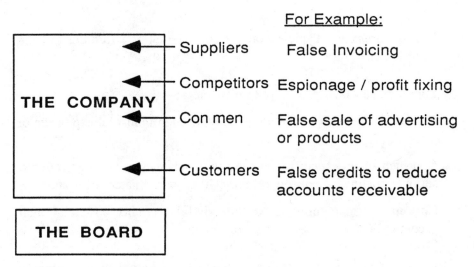

For Example:

Suppliers	False Invoicing
Competitors	Espionage / profit fixing
Con men	False sale of advertising or products
Customers	False credits to reduce accounts receivable

§1.2   About This Handbook

The objective of *The Accountant's Handbook of Fraud and Commercial Crime* is to provide accountants with a practical resource on fraud and commercial crime, with an emphasis on prevention. A brief overview of the Handbook's organization is set out below.

(a)   Prevention: General Techniques

Chapters 2 through 5 of the Handbook cover general fraud prevention techniques.

(i) Managing the Risk of Fraud.   Chapter 2, *Managing the Risk of Fraud*, describes the concept of fraud risk: understanding it and guarding against the threat posed by it. The specific factors that impact fraud risk are dealt with, including the key internal controls—basic, supervisory and audit—which help prevent fraud. A comprehensive and practical checklist is included with the chapter.

(ii) Promoting an Ethical Environment.   Chapter 3, *Promoting an Ethical Environment*, describes the various steps that can be taken to promote an ethical environment within an organization, and thereby reduce the risk of fraud. A sample code of ethics and business conduct is included along with a practical checklist.

(iii) Risk Financing and Fidelity Insurance.   Chapter 4, *Risk Financing and Fidelity Insurance*, deals with the concept of risk financing, describes the types of fidelity insurance policies that are available—including some of the more typical policy clauses and insured's responsibilities—and describes the factors that enter into the fidelity insurance purchase decision. A practical checklist is included with this chapter.

(iv) Computer Security and System Recovery.   Adequate computer security is an indispensable fraud prevention tool. Chapter 5, *Computer Security and System Recovery*, provides a comprehensive overview of computer security, including physical security, logical security, and system recovery. A checklist is also included with this chapter.

9

(b) Prevention: Specific Types of Fraud

Chapters 6 through 9 of this Handbook deal with specific types of fraud under the following group headings.

(i) Asset Misappropriation from Within. Chapter 6, *Asset Misappropriation from Within*, deals with the various ways fraud is committed against an organization by a perpetrator from within that organization—the most common form of fraud. Frauds are classified according to the various accounting cycles to which they relate: sales and collection, acquisition and payment, payroll and personnel, inventory and warehousing, and capital acquisition and repayment. A separate section deals with cash misappropriation.

(ii) Frauds Perpetrated by Outsiders. Frauds can also be committed against organizations by suppliers, professional con artists and other outside perpetrators. Chapter 7, *Frauds Perpetrated by Outsiders*, deals with the various ways such frauds are committed against small businesses and individuals, the government, and financial institutions such as banks and insurance companies.

(iii) Computer Crime and Computer Criminals. Although it has resulted in very few genuinely new frauds, the computer has dramatically changed the environment in which fraud is committed. Chapter 8, *Computer Crime and Computer Criminals*, describes the nature of computer-related crime and computer criminals, deals with the control considerations that affect the risk of fraud in a computer environment, and provides some selected computer crime case studies.

(iv) Commercial Crime. In addition to being victimized by fraud, organizations can also perpetrate it. Chapter 9, *Commercial Crime*, provides an overview of the topic, describes the various forms commercial crime can take—false advertising, industrial espionage and trade secret theft, insider trading, securities fraud, organizational bribegiving, etc.—and offers preventive solutions.

(c)   Crisis Management—Dealing With a Known or Suspected Fraud

Despite the best prevention strategies, an actual crisis may sometimes strike. Chapter 10, *Dealing With a Known or Suspected Fraud*, deals with this topic and, more particularly, forensic accounting.

(d)   Back Matter

Finally, the back matter contains a listing of selected books dealing with the subject of fraud and commercial crime, definitions, and explanations for a number of fraud-related terms. The appendix contains reprints and/or excerpts from relevant professional studies and pronouncements such as the Treadway report and SAS 53 and 54 from the AICPA.

PART II

Prevention: General Techniques

CHAPTER TWO

Managing the Risk of Fraud

§2.1 Introduction
    (a) Understanding the Risk
        (i) Fraud Versus Theft
        (ii) Generic Versus Individual Risk Factors
    (b) Guarding Against the Threat
        (i) Choosing Acceptable Risk Levels
        (ii) Internal Controls
        (iii) Promoting an Ethical Environment
        (iv) Risk Financing
        (v) Computer Security

§2.2 Fraud Risk Factors
    (a) Generic Risk Factors
        (i) Opportunity to Commit Fraud
        (ii) Likelihood of Discovery
        (iii) Nature and Extent of Punishment
    (b) Individual Risk Factors
        (i) Moral Character (Greed Factor)
        (ii) Motivation (Need Factor)
        (iii) Profiles of Fraud Perpetrators
    (c) High Fraud/Low Fraud Environments

§2.3 Internal Controls and "Fraudproofing"
    (a) Defining Internal Control Objectives
    (b) Basic Controls
        (i) Physical Access
        (ii) Job Descriptions
        (iii) Accounting Reconciliations and Analyses

 (c) Supervision
   (i) Fraud Awareness
   (ii) Approval, Review and Reperformance
 (d) Audit
   (i) Internal Audit
   (ii) External Audit

§2.4 The Risk Management Checklist

Of the two available ways to combat fraud—prevention and detection—a prevention strategy is obviously the preferred approach. Such a strategy can be either general or specific in its objective. This and the next three chapters deal with general prevention techniques.

In this chapter:

- The first section (2.1) provides a general introduction to the concept of fraud risk: understanding it and guarding against the threat posed by it;

- The second section (2.2) describes in greater detail the specific factors that determine fraud risk;

- The third section (2.3) deals with internal control, a key fraud prevention tool; and

- Finally, the last section (2.4) presents a practical checklist that reflects the key points in this chapter.

§2.1 Introduction

Managing the risk of fraud involves many steps. The purpose of this section is to provide a general introduction to the topic and describe how this and the next three chapters fit into the risk management process.

Risk management can be divided into two main elements: understanding the risk and guarding against it.

(a) Understanding the Risk

(i) Fraud Versus Theft

"Resolved: fraud is not the same as theft."

§2.1 Introduction

In a debate, most people would choose to defend the above statement. They would win—for example, by arguing that:

- "Theft is like robbing a bank, fraud is like stealing petty cash";
- "People committing theft do so at night and wear masks, people who commit fraud wear suits and do so during the day";
- "Theft is direct, fraud is indirect"; or
- "Theft is what lower-class criminals commit, fraud is what upper-class criminals commit."

However, few if any people will point out what is perhaps the most important difference between fraud and theft: the risk of fraud is much greater, as described below.

With the increasingly high media profile given to the crime issue—particularly in large cities—most people are acutely aware of the need to protect themselves against the more overt forms of crime. In a bad neighborhood, for example, one would not wish to leave the keys in the car or the doors unlocked. In fact, one might not wish to be there at all. In this case the risk of theft—a relatively more overt and direct form of criminal act than is fraud—is easy to assess and deal with.

Now consider a different scenario: if you were to briefly leave your wallet on your desk at work, you would also be exposing yourself to a risk. However, assuming access to your workplace is restricted to other employees, you would probably consider this risk to be a very small one. The people you work with probably aren't criminals and would never pick up your wallet in a direct form of theft. The risk of being seen or detected—as perceived by a perpetrator—would be relatively high. At the very least, you would certainly know that your wallet had been stolen and a thorough investigation would ensue, implicating a coworker.

Herein lies the first of two pillars on which the greater threat of fraud is built: most people believe that those who are relatively close to them—their friends and coworkers—are basically honest. *"They would never steal. As long as we lock the doors at night to keep out the 'real crooks', we'll be safe."*

The other pillar is based on the perception that fraud is, in some sense, an indirect form of theft. Although it is a criminal act, people who perpetrate it will in many cases rationalize their behavior, believing that because it's indirect, it's victimless. Alternatively, the perpetrator may rationalize that the victim deserves it or, where the amount involved in the fraud is low in relation to the total assets available, that the victim can afford it and/or won't even miss it. And so the second pillar is formed from the rationalizations of most fraudsters—the denial that the fraud is morally wrong: *"No one will be hurt by this. The company won't even miss it. Besides, they deserve it for the lousy way they treat me."*

These two pillars—lower respect for the threat of fraud on the part of potential victims and a higher degree of rationalization by potential perpetrators—combine to make fraud a much more insidious threat than ordinary theft. A further illustration of this greater risk: by the early 1980s losses suffered by U.S. banks from computer fraud alone were about 10 times the amount lost to bank robberies, according to FBI statistics; by 1985, fraud losses were 26 times that of robberies.

(ii) Generic Versus Individual Risk Factors. There are obviously a large number of factors that can have an impact on the risk of fraud in any given situation. The challenge in a Handbook such as this is to develop an approach—a system of categorization—which facilitates the understanding of fraud risk and the development of an appropriate strategy to manage it.

The literature is filled with many different systems of categorizing fraud risk. The one developed for purposes of this Handbook splits the risk factors into two groups: generic and individual.

Generic risk factors are those that remain relatively constant in their impact on any subject individual or group of individuals. They are largely within the control of the organization or entity that is protecting itself and largely outside the control of potential perpetrators. Because they apply in the same way to any employee in a given circumstance, they can be set and manipulated by an organization without regard to individual differences among employees. It also follows that employee turnover has virtually no effect on these risk factors.

On the other hand, individual risk factors are those that change from person to person or even for the same person over time. They are only partially within the control of the organization or entity that is protecting itself, and this control is more difficult to exercise because it is applied to each individual separately. Whenever turnover takes place, the individual risk factors change and must be managed. Even worse, whenever an individual's personality, state of mind, circumstances, or motivations change—which, after all, is a constant process—the associated risk factors may also change.

Generic and individual risk factors are dealt with in greater detail later in this chapter.

(b) Guarding Against the Threat

Once the risk of fraud is understood in a particular environment, an appropriate strategy must be developed and policies implemented to guard against the threat. The main elements of this process are:

- Choosing acceptable risk levels;
- Developing and implementing internal controls;
- Promoting an ethical environment;
- Putting in place appropriate risk financing (insurance); and
- Ensuring adequate computer security (a subset of internal controls, but important enough to warrant separate attention).

Each of these elements is briefly described in the following sections.

(i) Choosing Acceptable Risk Levels. The risk of fraud can never be completely eliminated. Even if this were possible, it would probably not be desirable because (1) the cost would be prohibitive and (2) controls would be so tight that creativity would be stifled and employee morale would suffer. The first step in a fraud prevention strategy is to decide what level of risk is acceptable.

The process of choosing acceptable risk levels is intertwined with the process of assessing the various risk factors in a given environment. For example, one of the generic risk factors in a given situation is the opportunity risk that is provided to potential perpetrators [section 2.2(a)(i)]. The process of assessing this opportunity risk will assist in decision making—i.e., Do we need to lower this risk and if so by how much?

(ii) Internal Controls. Internal controls—consisting of basic controls, supervisory controls, and audit—represent the cornerstone of any fraud prevention strategy.

The design and implementation of an internal control system is something that must be undertaken *regardless* of the risk of fraud—for example, to ensure complete and accurate reporting. However, this does not mean that such a system should *disregard* the risk of fraud; indeed, such disregard would amount to a virtual invitation to potential perpetrators.

Internal controls are dealt with in greater detail in section 2.3 of this chapter.

(iii) Promoting an Ethical Environment. Promoting an ethical environment is another key element in a prevention strategy. In particular, a formal code of ethics and business conduct helps to set the tone for all employees within an organization.

This topic is dealt with in greater detail in Chapter 3.

(iv) Risk Financing. Recognizing, as previously noted, that there will always be some risk of fraud, organizations must finance this risk either externally and explicitly (fidelity insurance) or internally and implicitly (self-insurance).

This topic is dealt with in greater detail in Chapter 4.

(v) Computer Security. Finally, computers and information technology are playing an increasingly important role in business and society generally. The pervasive nature of these technologies demands that adequate computer security be made an integral part of any prevention strategy.

Although computer security may be considered a subset of internal control, it is important enough in its own right to warrant separate coverage and is therefore dealt with in greater detail in Chapter 5.

§2.2 Fraud Risk Factors

Several factors contribute to the risk of fraud in a given environment. Different systems of categorizing these factors have been used; however, under most systems the elements that combine to determine fraud risk are largely the same.

For example, one classification system is known as the GONE theory, an acronym for Greed, Opportunity, Need, and Exposure. Under this system, the Greed and Need factors relate largely to the individual (i.e., the potential perpetrator), while the Opportunity and Exposure factors relate largely to the organization (i.e., the potential victim). The four elements of the GONE theory all interact together to determine the level of fraud risk, and no one factor can be said to be universally more important than any other. Each of the factors is unfavorable to some extent in virtually all situations. It is when the combination of all four factors is allowed to be sufficiently unfavorable in a given environment that, as one fraud investigator put it, "You can consider your money GONE."

A slightly different system is used for purposes of this Handbook, grouping the risk factors into generic or individual, as previously defined. However, as described below, many of the same elements of the GONE theory apply under this system as well.

(a) Generic Risk Factors

Generic risk factors—those largely under the control of the organization or entity that is protecting itself—include:

- The opportunity given to potential perpetrators;

- The likelihood that a fraud will be uncovered, if it is committed; and

- The nature and extent of the punishment which a perpetrator will receive, once the fraud is uncovered and the perpetrator is caught.

Note that the first factor corresponds to the O in the GONE theory. The second and third factors together correspond to the E or Exposure risk element of the GONE theory—in other words, the Exposure risk under the GONE theory is a product of two generic factors: the likelihood of getting caught and the consequences of getting caught. Both must be positive for there to be any risk. For example, if the likelihood of getting caught is 0 percent, then the Exposure risk is zero. Similarly, if the consequences of getting caught are insignificant, then the Exposure risk would be negligible.

Each of the generic risk factors is briefly described in the following sections.

(i) Opportunity to Commit Fraud. The opportunity to commit fraud refers primarily to the positioning of a potential perpetrator with respect to the assets or object of the fraud. Opportunity cannot be completely eliminated; to attempt to do so would be uneconomical and counterproductive.

As long as organizations have assets of value and these assets flow, are traded, or come under the control of others—such as employees, customers, and suppliers—the opportunity to commit fraud will always exist.

21

The challenge in fraud prevention is to ensure that the opportunity level is reasonable in the circumstances:

- Either explicitly or implicitly, each employee should be assigned an appropriate maximum opportunity level. For example, a junior clerk's opportunity level might be limited to certain smaller fixed assets not bolted down in the office. A more senior clerk's maximum opportunity level might be an additional $500 petty cash fund or the day's cash receipts, while a senior executive might be limited to an additional $5,000 check signing limit; and

- "Catastrophic" opportunity levels should not be permitted. What a catastrophic level is will depend on the circumstances, in particular the size of the organization. For example, a small business with $50,000 in cash should probably not allow anyone but its owner(s) access to the full amount.

(ii) Likelihood of Discovery. To the extent that an opportunity to commit fraud exists, the risk can be reduced by making the chances of discovery high. In fact, even the *perception* that the chances of discovery are high can act as a deterrent. And of course, if a fraud does occur, discovery of it may result in recovery of some of the lost assets.

The likelihood of discovery is determined primarily by the system of internal controls, which are dealt with in greater detail later in this chapter. While these controls can never be so tight as to preclude any fraud from taking place, they should, ideally, be sufficient to prevent most material frauds from going undetected for any length of time.

(iii) Nature and Extent of Punishment. Discovery of a fraud is in itself insufficient to act as a deterrent against future fraud. There must be some adverse consequences from the point of view of potential perpetrators. Most importantly, there must be a perception of adverse consequences.

Although research has not provided proof, conventional wisdom holds that the nature and extent of punishment have a deterrent impact. The occurrence of theft in countries governed by Islamic law is extremely low compared to Western countries. Presumably this is at least partly due to the punishment being so severe (amputation of one or both of the hands). Can anyone doubt that the occurrence of theft in North America would diminish if perpetrators knew they would face the same punishment? Of course, the reality is that the punishment must fit the crime and be consistent with a society's justice system.

Organizations or entities wishing to protect themselves from fraud should have clear policies with respect to the nature and extent of the consequences of getting caught, for example:

- Anyone who commits a fraud will be dismissed; and

- All frauds will be reported to the authorities and charges pressed.

(b)   Individual Risk Factors

Individual risk factors—those that vary from employee to employee and are largely outside the control of the organization or entity that is protecting itself—fall into two categories:

- Moral character; and

- Motivation.

Moral character corresponds to the G or Greed factor in the GONE theory, while motivation is equivalent to the N or Need factor. Each of these categories is described below.

(i) Moral Character (Greed Factor).   Greed, like Opportunity, conveniently fits the GONE acronym. In fact, however, the word *greed* is intended to represent somewhat broader concepts, i.e., ethics and moral character or the lack thereof.

Greed and *ethics* are words that essentially relate to the internal or personality attributes of an individual, as do the words *character, integrity, honesty,* and the like. It is difficult to know whether an individual possesses these attributes, without being able to read that individual's mind. Even if this were possible, personal interpretation would still come into play.

Social values also have an impact. Many sociologists lamented a trend in Western societies during the 1980s, namely the pursuit of wealth as an overriding objective. The *'Me' Generation* and the *Decade Of Greed* were phrases coined in connection with this trend, which was perhaps best epitomized by the memorable speech of Michael Douglas' Gordon Geco character in the 1987 movie *Wall Street:* "Greed is right. Greed is good. . . ."

In fact there may be some element of truth in Gordon Geco's philosophy. A certain amount of greed, tough-mindedness, and competitive instinct may greatly enhance the chances of success of an organization—or indeed an individual—in a free enterprise society. In any case, regardless of one's own value judgement in this regard, there is no doubt that these attributes do exist in society. This poses a problem, however, because while greed may not necessarily preclude the existence of ethics and good moral character, if left unchecked or promoted to too great an extent, it can have an adverse impact vis-a-vis the risk of fraud. All of which leads to the essential question at issue here: What can or should an organization do to minimize the risk of fraud posed by greed and other 'negative' human attributes. A number of areas need to be considered.

- *Corporate Mission Statement:* The goals of an organization should be set out in a corporate mission statement, which should be communicated to all managers and employees. The primary goal of most businesses is to maximize profits, presumably over the long-term if the business is to survive. Other objectives could include maintaining a high market share or leadership in an industry. However, it should also be stated that these goals are to be pursued in a manner consistent with good corporate citizenship and standing in the community. Such an emphasis on corporate responsibility sets the tone for management and employees and thereby encourages personal responsibility on their part. Conversely, irresponsible actions—and by extension, fraud—are discouraged;

- *Written Codes of Business Conduct:* "Good moral character" means different things to different people; it is a term that must be defined and related to particular types of behavior. For example, does an organization consider it moral and ethical for its employees to accept gifts from its customers and, if so, up to what value? A written code of ethics and business conduct—dealt with in the next chapter—can help translate the relative concepts of greed, ethics, and morality into more specific behaviors that are either acceptable or unacceptable;

- *Management Style and Role Models:* Management has to set the right example for employees by itself acting responsibly and living up to the spirit of the corporate mission statement and code of business conduct. Moreover, it must clearly and visibly appear to be doing so in its dealings and communications with employees. Policy statements mean nothing if they are undermined by management actions. In fact, such a situation may be worse than having no policy at all, because it promotes a kind of cynicism and 'rules are made to be broken' philosophy, which can actually encourage fraud and commercial crime; and

- *Hiring Practices:* Regardless of corporate mission statements, codes of business conduct, and good role models, moral character ultimately depends on the individual employee. It is therefore desirable to have hiring practices that, to the extent possible, weed out those of low moral character. Chapter 3 deals with this issue in greater detail.

(ii) Motivation (Need Factor). Why do people commit fraud? There is obviously no single, specific answer. People commit fraud for a variety of reasons.

Probably the most common group of fraud motivations relates to economic need. For example, the perpetrator may be experiencing an actual or perceived cash emergency: a mortgage that has to be paid, drugs that have to be purchased to satisfy an addiction, or gambling losses that have to be won back. Alternatively, there may be no emergency but simply an unchecked desire for the good life: expensive restaurants, clothes, furs, jewelry, vacations, cars, homes, and summer cottages.

Less frequently, there may be other reasons such as disenchantment, revenge, or simply the fact that everyone else around seems to be doing it. Even more rarely, the motivations may be eccentric: a sense of challenge or thrill. Finally, the cause may be some form of psychological illness: compulsion, anxiety, paranoia, or outright psychosis.

What to do about all these complex motivations, seemingly locked up in the "black box" of an employee's mind? Admittedly, the options are limited but they include:

- *Creating a Favorable Environment:* Creating the right environment can reduce the motivation among employees to commit fraud. In an unfavorable environment, morale will suffer and feelings of disenchantment—even hate and the desire for revenge—may take hold. The right environment can be promoted by treating employees fairly, keeping communication lines open and providing mechanisms where grievances can be discussed and resolved;

- *Performance Appraisal and Reward Systems:* In addition to creating an environment that is favorable in a general sense, each employee should feel that they are being treated fairly by the performance appraisal and reward system;

- *Employee Assistance Programs:* Many enlightened employers provide free counseling and other assistance to employees who are facing personal problems, for example alcohol and drug abuse. From the point of view of fraud prevention, this approach is preferable to keeping these problems "bottled up";

- *Employee Testing and Screening:* As part of their hiring practices and sometimes on a regular basis thereafter, some employers use testing and screening procedures that may identify and weed out high risk individuals, and/or form the basis for remedial action. Psychological testing, drug testing, and even honesty testing in the form of lie detector tests—where not prohibited by law—are all possible. Obviously, these tests can be highly controversial and in some instances may cause more harm than good (e.g., to employee morale, the organization's reputation among prospective employees, etc.). Nevertheless, in especially sensitive occupations or circumstances, such testing may be appropriate and even necessary; and

- *Common Sense and a Watchful Eye:* While motivations are not observable, the product of those motivations often is. An employee with a drug addiction or gambling problem may not be able to keep it a secret, or may not even try. And beware the $25,000-a-year bookkeeper who starts showing up for work in a Mercedes or, in a more subtle way, never takes a vacation.

(iii) Profiles of Fraud Perpetrators. While external pressures do play a major role in whether or not an individual commits fraud, some generalizations about the characteristics of fraud perpetrators have emerged. Gwynn Nettler in his book *Lying, Cheating and Stealing* makes the following observations:

1. People who have experienced failure are more likely to cheat.
2. People who are disliked and who dislike themselves tend to be more deceitful.
3. People who are impulsive, distractible, and unable to postpone gratification are more likely to engage in deceitful crimes.
4. People who have a conscience (fear, apprehension, and punishment) are more resistant to the temptation to deceive.

5. Intelligent people tend to be more honest than do ignorant people.

6. Middle- and upper-class people tend to be more honest than lower-class people.

7. The easier it is to cheat and steal, the more people will do so.

8. Individuals have different needs and therefore different levels at which they will be moved to lie, cheat, or steal.

9. Lying, cheating, and stealing increase when people have great pressure to achieve important objectives.

10. The struggle to survive generates deceit.

While the highly publicized cases of computer hackers in recent years have led to a public perception that individuals who are highly knowledgeable about computers are more likely to commit fraud, there is no real evidence of this.

(c) High Fraud/Low Fraud Environments

[NOTE: *The material in section 2.2(c) is reprinted and/or adapted from* Fraud Auditing and Forensic Accounting *by G. Jack Bologna and Robert J. Lindquist (Wiley, 1987, pp. 46–49)*].

Employee fraud, theft, and embezzlement are more likely to occur in some organizations than in others. Organizations that are most vulnerable are usually hampered by weak management and inadequate accounting and security controls. Solutions often proposed are:

- Tight accounting and audit controls;
- Thorough screening of applicants for employment;
- Close supervision and monitoring of employee performance and behavior; and
- Explicit rules against theft, fraud, embezzlement, sabotage, and information piracy, and strict sanctions for their breach.

While these solutions are obvious, other considerations also affect the likelihood of employee crime. Organizations that are most vulnerable to employee misbehavior can also be distinguished from those that are less vulnerable by the environmental and cultural contrasts set out in the following table.

High Fraud/Low Fraud Environment

Variable	High Fraud Potential	Low Fraud Potential
1. Management style	a. Autocratic	a. Participative
2. Management orientation	a. Low trust b. Power driven	a. High trust b. Achievement driven
3. Distribution of authority	a. Centralized, reserved by top management	a. Decentralized, dispersed to all levels, delegated
4. Planning	a. Centralized b. Short-range	a. Decentralized b. Long-range
5. Performance	a. Measured quantitatively and on a short-term basis	a. Measured both quantitatively and qualitatively and on a long-term basis
6. Business focus	a. Profit focused	a. Customer focused
7. Management strategy	a. Management by crisis	a. Management by objectives
8. Reporting	a. Reporting by routine	a. Reporting by exception
9. Policies and rules	a. Rigid and inflexible, strongly policed	a. Reasonable, fairly enforced
10. Primary management concern	a. Capital assets	a. Human, then capital and technological assets
11. Reward system	a. Punitive b. Penurious c. Politically administered	a. Generous b. Reinforcing c. Fairly administered
12. Feedback on performance	a. Critical b. Negative	a. Positive b. Stroking

High Fraud/Low Fraud Environment *(continued)*

Variable	High Fraud Potential	Low Fraud Potential
13. Interaction mode	a. Issues and personal differences are skirted or repressed	a. Issues and personal differences are confronted and addressed openly
14. Payoffs for good behavior	a. Mainly monetary	a. Recognition, promotion, added responsibility, choice assignments, plus money
15. Business ethics	a. Ambivalent, rides the tide	a. Clearly defined and regularly followed
16. Internal relationships	a. Highly competitive, hostile	a. Friendly, competitive, supportive
17. Values and beliefs	a. Economic, political, self-centered	a. Social, spiritual, group centered
18. Success formula	a. Works harder	a. Works smarter
19. Human resources	a. Burnout	a. Not enough promotional opportunities for all the talent
	b. High turnover	b. Low turnover
	c. Grievances	c. Job satisfaction
20. Company loyalty	a. Low	a. High
21. Major financial concern	a. Cash flow shortage	a. Opportunities for new investment
22. Growth pattern	a. Sporadic	a. Consistent
23. Relationship with competitors	a. Hostile	a. Professional
24. Innovativeness	a. Copy cat, reactive	a. Leader, proactive

High Fraud/Low Fraud Environment *(continued)*

Variable	*High Fraud Potential*	*Low Fraud Potential*
25. CEO characteristics	a. Swinger, braggart, self-interested, driver, insensitive to people, feared, insecure, gambler, impulsive, tightfisted, numbers and things oriented, profit seeker, vain, bombastic, highly emotional, partial, pretend to be more than they are	a. Professional; decisive; fast-paced; respected by peers; secure risk taker; thoughtful; generous with personal time and money; people, products, and market oriented; builder-helper; self-confident; composed; calm; deliberate; even disposition; fair; know who they are, what they are, and where they are going
26. Management structure, systems and controls	a. Bureaucratic b. Regimented c. Inflexible d. Imposed controls e. Many-tiered structure, vertical f. Everything documented, a rule for everything	a. Collegial b. Systematic c. Open to change d. Self-controlled e. Flat structure, horizontal f. Documentation is adequate but not burdensome, some discretion is afforded

High Fraud/Low Fraud Environment *(continued)*

Variable	*High Fraud Potential*	*Low Fraud Potential*
27. Internal communication	a. Formal, written, stiff, pompous, ambiguous	a. Informal, oral, clear, friendly, open, candid
28. Peer relationships	a. Hostile, aggressive, rivalrous	a. Cooperative, friendly, trusting

§2.3 Internal Controls and "Fraudproofing"

Developing an understanding of the various factors that contribute to the risk of fraud is only the first step in a fraud prevention strategy. It is then necessary to implement policies that will help to reduce that threat.

Some of the measures that can guard against the threat of fraud were set out previously in this chapter; still others appear in Chapters 3, 4, and 5. This section, however, deals with what is perhaps the main—and certainly the most common—prevention tool: a good system of internal controls.

(a) Defining Internal Control Objectives

In recent years, the term *fraudproofing* has appeared in the literature and some seminars. The term is somewhat misleading, however, because no internal control system can completely eliminate the risk of fraud. What it should do in theory is reduce the risk of fraud to an acceptable level.

The risk of fraud will not be the only factor in defining internal control objectives; for example, management information and reporting requirements will be important considerations. However, the acceptable risk and opportunity levels, as dealt with previously in this chapter, should also be one of the considerations. This means ensuring that the basic, supervisory, and audit controls act together to limit the risk of fraud to those acceptable levels.

The three levels of internal control (basic, supervisory, and audit) are described in the following sections.

(b) Basic Controls

A variety of basic controls exist in a typical system of internal controls. Those that are most relevant for purposes of fraud prevention can be grouped into three categories: physical access, job descriptions, and accounting reconciliations and analyses.

(i) Physical Access. The need to control physical access to valuable assets—including intangible assets such as information—is something that most people are aware of. Measures to control physical access include the obvious practice of locking doors, desks, and file cabinets, so that unauthorized personnel—either within or outside the organization—cannot gain access. Other measures include employee IDs and passwords, computerized security systems (e.g., using access cards that record time of entry and exit), and electronic surveillance systems.

As a general rule, physical access should be restricted to those who require it to perform their job function. Of course, controlling physical access in this way will not completely reduce the risk of fraud. However, it will help to reduce the risk in the following ways:

- Many frauds require the perpetrator to come into physical contact with either (1) the asset being misappropriated, or (2) the related asset records, in order to cover up the fraud. Reducing physical access reduces opportunity;

- Physical access controls are often the most visible to potential perpetrators. As such, strong controls in this area send a powerful deterrent message vis-a-vis the other controls in the system. Conversely, loose physical controls invite challenge; and

- Even if the fraud is not prevented through access controls, these controls often assist in the fraud investigation process (e.g., the determination of what actually happened and the narrowing of suspects).

(ii) Job Descriptions. Formal, specific job descriptions can also be a very effective fraud prevention tool. These documents should spell out exactly what each employee is expected to do. As a general rule, employees should not perform duties outside their job description. This is a significant red flag.

Job descriptions should reflect the important principle of division of duties. For example, employees with physical control over an asset should not also keep the records relating to that asset (this will only make it easier for them to cover up the fraud). Other especially sensitive duties—for example purchasing and check signing—should also be segregated.

The need for job descriptions goes beyond the widely recognized concept of segregation of duties, although that is certainly one of the important consequences of job descriptions. In some cases, a duplication of duties may result—entirely appropriate, for example, in the case of the double signing of checks. The job description should also specify that annual vacations *must* be taken (another well-known fraud prevention tool, because perpetrators running an ongoing fraud scheme are more likely to be found out when they're removed from the scene).

Based on the foregoing, it should be apparent that the process of formulating job descriptions for the employees of an organization must be approached in an integrated fashion. From an internal control and fraud prevention point of view, different tasks performed by different individuals may be interrelated; therefore, an appropriate job description for one employee will often depend on the job descriptions of others, and vice versa.

The need for formal job descriptions is very often ignored or underestimated—written off as "more useless paper." At other times, job descriptions may exist but are ignored. This attitude invites trouble. As one leading fraud investigator put it: "When people begin to do things outside their job description, you have reason to be concerned. If it goes unrewarded, they begin to develop a justification to steal. It's very important that job descriptions be clear, agreed upon, and adhered to."

(iii) Accounting Reconciliations and Analyses. After access controls and the existence of job descriptions, accounting reconciliations and analyses represent the third most important grouping of basic controls that prevent fraud. One of the essential ingredients of a successful fraud is successful concealment. Regular, appropriately performed accounting reconciliations and analyses often make such concealment difficult or impossible.

Accounting reconciliations that should be performed on a regular (e.g., monthly basis) include:

- Bank reconciliations, for all accounts;
- Accounts receivable reconciliations (both month to month and general ledger to subledger); and

- Accounts payable reconciliations (again, both month to month and general ledger to subledger).

The exact nature of the accounting analyses that are performed will depend on the nature of the organization's operations. Analyses that will be relevant for most organizations include:

- Variance analysis of general ledger accounts (budget to actual, current year versus prior year, etc.);

- Vertical analysis of profit and loss accounts—i.e., calculation of expenses as a percentage of sales, and comparison of these percentages with historical standards and/or budgets; and

- Detailed sales and major expense analyses, for example, by product line or territory.

Of course, accounting reconciliations and analyses are often undertaken with other purposes in mind—e.g., management decision making and/or to ensure the accuracy of the accounting records. Nevertheless, this process can also highlight discrepancies that point to fraud.

(c) Supervision

Supervision represents the second level of internal control. From a fraud prevention point of view—especially in small businesses where segregation of duties may be difficult to achieve—strong supervision is vital.

It should be noted that active supervision is definitely *not* the same as supervisory or management override, whereby a manager or supervisor actually takes charge of or alters the work of a subordinate. In fact, such override is itself a red flag—i.e., it suggests that the manager or supervisor may be engaged in fraud or the covering up of one. Basic controls should be allowed to operate as they were intended to and not be circumvented by those at higher levels.

As a fraud prevention mechanism, good supervision consists of (1) fraud awareness, and (2) approval, review, and reperformance.

(i) Fraud Awareness. Fraud prevention specialists constantly emphasize the need for fraud awareness, to the point that the term has almost become a cliche. However, such awareness is perhaps the key prerequisite in build-

ing any effective fraud prevention strategy, and is especially important at the supervisory level.

Specifically, supervisors must be alert to the *possibility* of fraud whenever an unusual or exceptional situation occurs, such as complaints from suppliers or customers, discrepancies that don't make sense, or accounting reconciliations that don't balance. If the manager's mind is closed to the possibility of fraud when an unusual or exceptional situation occurs, then the risk of the fraud continuing unabated is greatly increased.

(ii) Approval, Review, and Reperformance. In addition to being aware, fraud prevention demands that supervisors actually supervise. This means going beyond the approval function—such as initialing invoices—that most supervisors and managers are conscious of. A more thorough review, and even reperformance in some instances, may be necessary and should be approached diligently. For example, supervisors should consider reperforming important procedures such as monthly bank reconciliation— e.g., comparing the numbers shown on it to the those on the bank statement and in the general ledger, making sure it adds, at least test-checking outstanding items, and so on. To simply initial the bank reconciliation in a habitual or reflex-like manner—without really reviewing and reperforming it—invites fraud.

For example, the owner of a busy downtown restaurant had the following system of internal control for sales: all prenumbered customer bills were rung up on the cash register, and at least once each day the hostess/ bookkeeper would batch the customer bills, list them on a deposit sheet, and make the related bank deposit. The owner would match up the totals on the deposit sheet with the amounts shown in the stamped deposit book, considering this adequate supervision.

As it turned out, the supervision of the bookkeeper was inadequate, especially since she was responsible for both the handling of cash (the bank deposit) and related records (customer bills, cash register tapes, deposit sheets). Over a 3-month period, the bookkeeper was skimming a portion of the day's cash receipts off the top by omitting some of the cash sales bills and pocketing the corresponding amount. The fraud could have been uncovered by:

- Segregation of duties; however, the owner trusted the bookkeeper and did not want to incur the cost of an additional person;

35

- Accounting for all prenumbered bills; however, the owner never considered this because it was too time-consuming (purposely by the bookkeeper, the bills were not listed in numbered order on the deposit sheet, and prenumbered books would be issued out of sequence to waiters and waitresses); or

- Simply and most appropriately, matching daily cash register tapes to the daily cash deposit. The owner never did this because the tapes were a messy "dog's breakfast" kept in a shoe box by the bookkeeper—also entirely by design, of course, to cover up the fraud. The fraud was eventually uncovered when the bookkeeper became greedy and withheld a bit too much from what the owner knew was an especially good cash sales day, raising suspicions and leading to an investigation.

This example illustrates why supervision is vital: it is often the primary defense against ongoing frauds such as the skimming of cash described above, or the lapping of accounts receivable. The maximum opportunity level for the bookkeeper in the previous example should have been the outright theft of the day's receipts—typically about $10,000 in total, less than half of which were cash sales. However, inadequate supervision allowed a smaller amount of cash—about $700 a day—to be stolen over a 3-month-period, for a total of over $60,000.

(d) Audit

From a fraud prevention point of view, audit represents the third level of an organization's internal control system. The auditor's role in dealing with fraud is discussed in greater detail in the Appendix (Professional Studies and Pronouncements), and is therefore given only brief treatment here.

(i) Internal Audit. Internal auditors work for the organization and perform the kinds of work defined by senior management. In that sense, internal auditors are an extension of senior management—they have the same concerns and deal with the same issues described throughout this chapter. Thus, their work may include fraud detection and/or developing fraud prevention mechanisms.

The training and literature of internal auditors—such as that provided by the Institute of Internal Auditors (IIA)—pays specific attention to the issue of fraud prevention and detection. This differs from what has historically been the case for external auditors, as described below.

(ii) External Audit. External auditors are independent of the organization. They report on financial statements and perform other independent reviews. This work does not include fraud detection and/or developing fraud prevention mechanisms.

This more restricted role of the external auditor has evolved over time. During the late 1800s and into the early 1900s auditors were expected to actively look for fraud—to be a kind of "bloodhound." Through court cases, this role was then redefined to that of a "watchdog": auditors should be expected to bark if they see something suspicious, but they should not be expected to sniff around for suspicious things.

The watchdog metaphor has persisted throughout most of this century. In particular, the concept of materiality has played an important part in the accounting profession's view of fraud. Specifically, the profession's view is that an auditor's procedures cannot be expected to detect immaterial frauds. Indeed, no audit can be expected to give absolute assurances in this area, and even limited assurances would require procedures so extensive as to make the audit uneconomical. On the other hand, if a fraud is material enough to affect the financial statements of an organization—and an auditor's opinion on those financial statements—then the auditor's procedures may uncover it. However, there is certainly no guarantee of detection. For example, even when the auditor's procedures are sound, the perpetrator(s) may go to extensive lengths to deceive the auditor and hide the defalcation.

In recent years, the bloodhound/watchdog debate has been reopened to some extent, primarily in response to the public's expectation that the auditor should be responsible for detecting significant frauds, even if these are not material to the total worth of an organization.

§2.4 The Risk Management Checklist

A Risk Management Checklist, summarizing many of the issues raised in this chapter, appears on the following pages.

The Risk Management Checklist

This checklist is designed to assist accountants in assessing and managing the risk of fraud in their organizations and that of their clients. Generally, all 'No' answers require investigation and follow-up, the results of which should be documented. Where there is such additional documentation, the purpose of the "Ref" column is to cross-reference the checklist to the appropriate working paper (or to the notes on the reverse).

The checklist is intended for general use only. Use of the checklist does not guarantee the prevention or detection of fraud, and it is not intended as a substitute for audit or similar procedures. If fraud prevention is an especially vital concern or if fraud is suspected, the advice of a specialist should be sought.

Risk Management Checklist	*Yes*	*No*	*N/a*	*Ref*

1. Does the organization have an adequate level of fraud awareness and are appropriate policies in place to minimize fraud risk, specifically:

   a. Generic Risk Factors:

   - Has each employee been assigned a maximum "opportunity level" to commit fraud—i.e., for each employee, has management asked itself the question, "What is the maximum amount that this employee could defraud the organization of, and does this represent an acceptable risk?" ☐ ☐ ☐ ___

   - Has a "catastrophic" opportunity level been set, i.e., has management asked itself the question, "Have we ensured that no single employee—*or group of employees in collusion*—can commit a fraud that would place the organization in imminent risk of survival?" ☐ ☐ ☐ ___

§2.4   The Risk Management Checklist

	Yes	No	N/a	Ref
• Does the organization have a policy of immediately dismissing any employee who is found to have committed fraud?	☐	☐	☐	___
• Does the organization have a policy of reporting all frauds to the authorities and pressing charges?	☐	☐	☐	___
• For any and all frauds that the company has experienced in the past, have the reasons that led to the fraud been evaluated and corrective action taken?	☐	☐	☐	___

b. To manage individual risk factors (i.e., to promote moral behavior and minimize the motivation to commit fraud):

	Yes	No	N/a	Ref
• Does the organization have a corporate mission statement, which includes as an objective good corporate citizenship (i.e., the maintenance of good standing in the community)?	☐	☐	☐	___
• Does the organization have a written code of ethics and business conduct (see separate checklist in Chapter 3 for details)?	☐	☐	☐	___
• Does the organization conduct ethical and security training for new employees, with periodic updates for existing employees?	☐	☐	☐	___
• Does management set the right example, e.g., does it follow the corporate mission statement, code of ethics and business conduct, and other policies of the organization, and is it clearly seen to be doing so in the eyes of employees?	☐	☐	☐	___

	Yes	No	N/a	Ref

- Does the corporate culture avoid characteristics that promote unethical behavior, e.g., high or even hostile competitiveness within the organization, pushing employees to the point of burnout, rigid and/or petty policies with no apparent purpose, and over-centralization of authority? ☐ ☐ ☐ ____

- Do the organization's hiring policies, to the extent possible, seek out individuals of high moral character and weed out those of low moral character (see also separate checklist in Chapter 3)? ☐ ☐ ☐ ____

- For especially sensitive positions, are screening and/or testing procedures used (e.g., psychological testing, drug testing, lie detector tests) where these are permitted by law? ☐ ☐ ☐ ____

- Does the organization provide and/or encourage counselling for employees with personal problems, (e.g., alcohol and drug abuse)? ☐ ☐ ☐ ____

- Does the organization have fair policies in the area of employee relations and compensation (e.g., salaries, fringe benefits, performance appraisal, promotions, severance pay)—i.e., do these policies compare favorably with competitors and promote an environment that minimizes disenchantment and similar motivations to commit fraud? ☐ ☐ ☐ ____

- Are fair mechanisms in place for dealing with employee grievances? ☐ ☐ ☐ ____

- As a feedback mechanism on its policies with respect to employee

	Yes	No	N/a	Ref
relations, does the organization conduct exit interviews of departing employees?	☐	☐	☐	___

c. Overall, does management exhibit an awareness of fraud and its possible manifestations—e.g., signs of employee problems such as drug addictions and the low-paid employee who suddenly appears with the trappings of wealth? ☐ ☐ ☐ ___

2. Does the organization have an adequate system of internal controls, specifically:

a. Has the need for fraud prevention been explicitly considered in the design and maintenance of the system of internal controls? ☐ ☐ ☐ ___

b. Control over physical and logical access:

- Policy of locking doors, desks, and cabinets after hours and when unattended, especially for areas with valuable assets including files and records, e.g., personnel and payroll, customer and vendor lists, corporate strategies, marketing plans, and research? ☐ ☐ ☐ ___

- Use of IDs and passwords, e.g., for computer files? ☐ ☐ ☐ ___

- Stated and enforced policy that access is restricted to those requiring it to perform their job function, including strict policy against employees allowing access to unauthorized personnel, e.g., by loaning keys, sharing passwords? ☐ ☐ ☐ ___

41

	Yes	No	N/a	Ref
• For especially sensitive areas, computerized security and/or electronic surveillance systems?	☐	☐	☐	___
• To an impartial observer, does the workplace *appear* to have adequate access controls?	☐	☐	☐	___

c. Job descriptions:

	Yes	No	N/a	Ref
• Does the organization have written, specific job descriptions?	☐	☐	☐	___
• Are job descriptions adhered to?	☐	☐	☐	___
• Does the company have an organization chart that reflects and is consistent with the job descriptions of its employees?	☐	☐	☐	___
• Are incompatible duties segregated (e.g., handling of valuable assets— especially cash—and related records)?	☐	☐	☐	___
• Is the purchasing function properly segregated, e.g., to ensure that one individual cannot requisition goods or services, approve and make the related payment, and access accounts payable records?	☐	☐	☐	___
• Are especially sensitive duties duplicated (e.g., the double-signing of checks over a specified amount)?	☐	☐	☐	___
• Do job descriptions specify that annual vacations *must* be taken?	☐	☐	☐	___
• Overall, has the process of formulating job descriptions been an integrated one, giving adequate consideration to the importance of fraud prevention?	☐	☐	☐	___

d. Regular accounting reconciliations and analyses:

§2.4 The Risk Management Checklist

	Yes	No	N/a	Ref
• Bank reconciliations, for all accounts?	☐	☐	☐	___
• Accounts receivable reconciliations (month to month, general ledger to subledger)?	☐	☐	☐	___
• Accounts payable reconciliations (month to month, general ledger to subledger)?	☐	☐	☐	___
• Variance analysis of general ledger accounts (budget to actual, current year versus prior year)?	☐	☐	☐	___
• Vertical analysis of profit and loss accounts (i.e., as a percentage of sales, against historical and/or budget standards)?	☐	☐	☐	___
• Detailed sales and major expense analysis (e.g., by product line or geographic territory)?	☐	☐	☐	___

e. Supervision:

	Yes	No	N/a	Ref
• Do supervisors and managers have adequate fraud awareness (i.e., are they alert to the possibility of fraud whenever an unusual or exceptional situation occurs, such as supplier or customer complaints about their accounts)?	☐	☐	☐	___
• Do supervisors and managers diligently review the work of their subordinates, (e.g., accounting reconciliations), and where appropriate, even reperform the work?	☐	☐	☐	___
• For smaller businesses or where division of duties is not possible, is close supervision in place so as to compensate?	☐	☐	☐	___

	Yes	No	N/a	Ref
• Is supervisory or management override (i.e., a manager or supervisor taking charge of, altering or otherwise interfering in the work of a subordinate) prohibited, and are others in the hierarchy alert to this situation as a fraud "red flag?"	☐	☐	☐	___

f. Audit:

	Yes	No	N/a	Ref
• Is there an internal audit function?	☐	☐	☐	___
• Does the internal audit function perform regular checks to ensure that fraud prevention mechanisms are in place and operating as intended?	☐	☐	☐	___
• Are external audits performed on a regular basis (e.g., quarterly for larger businesses)?	☐	☐	☐	___
• Do external auditors receive full cooperation from management with respect to their work in general and fraud matters in particular (e.g., through the audit committee)?	☐	☐	☐	___

3. Has the organization addressed the following fraud prevention issues:

	Yes	No	N/a	Ref
a. Promoting an Ethical Environment (see separate checklist in Chapter 3)?	☐	☐	☐	___
b. Risk Financing (see separate checklist in Chapter 4)?	☐	☐	☐	___
c. Computer Security (see separate checklist in Chapter 5)?	☐	☐	☐	___

CHAPTER THREE

Promoting an Ethical Environment

§3.1   Introduction
   (a)   Setting the Tone
   (b)   Enforcement
   (c)   Employee Hiring and Employee Relations
§3.2   Sample Code of Business Conduct
   (a)   Purpose
   (b)   Compliance with Laws and Regulations
   (c)   Conflict of Interest
      (i)   Outside Activities, Employment and Directorships
      (ii)   Relationships with Clients and Suppliers
      (iii)   Personal Investments
      (iv)   Gifts, Entertainment and Favors
      (v)   Internal Company Activities
   (d)   Political Activity
   (e)   Company Funds
   (f)   Company Records
   (g)   Dealing with Outside Persons and Organizations
   (h)   Prompt Communications
   (i)   Privacy and Confidentiality
§3.3   Ethical Environment Checklist

§3.1 Introduction

An ethical environment is an especially important element in a prevention strategy. In this chapter:

- This section (3.1) provides a general introduction to the topic;

- The second section (3.2) sets out a sample code of business conduct; and

- The third section (3.3) presents a practical checklist which reflects the key points in this chapter.

(a) Setting the Tone

Chapter 2 of this Handbook describes the generic and individual risk factors that contribute to the risk of fraud. These factors do not exist in a vacuum; rather, they impact in different ways on different environments. In fact, the relationship works both ways—the environment itself can have a major impact on fraud risk factors.

The most important requirement in promoting an ethical environment is having a written code of ethics and business conduct, such as the one set out in section 3.2 of this chapter. A written code helps set the right ethical tone within an organization—provided that management itself sets the right example by following the stated policies. Even minor "fudging" of expense accounts by management, or unauthorized use of company assets, can send the wrong signal and undermine an organization's stated policies.

(b) Enforcement

As was also noted in Chapter 2, an effective prevention strategy demands that there be some adverse consequences when an employee is caught committing fraud (for example, dismissal of the employee and the pressing of charges). Similarly, there must also be some adverse consequences—commensurate with the severity of the breach—when an employee contravenes an organization's stated policies, and in particular its code of ethics and business conduct. For especially severe breaches—or for repeat offenders—dismissal may be an appropriate consequence and the organization's policies should so state.

To ensure that all employees are aware of their responsibilities, organizations should require that they sign an annual declaration stating that they are aware of the company's code of ethics and business conduct and that they have complied and will comply with it.

(c)   Employee Hiring and Employee Relations

Ultimately, the existence of a good ethical climate is determined not by an organization's policies but rather by its employees. Employee hiring practices and employee relations are therefore important fraud prevention variables. The checklist at the end of this chapter provides a fairly comprehensive list of the factors to be considered.

Generally, it should be noted that organizations face a balancing act: on the one hand, the need to minimize the risk of fraud and to be cost-effective in employee remuneration; and on the other hand, the need to promote an open environment in which employee morale and creativity can flourish, and in which employees feel rewarded for their efforts. Tipping the scale too far to one side or the other can lead to problems and/or reduce the competitiveness of an organization. Success is achieved at a point somewhere in between—a point which can only be found through the good judgment of management.

§3.2 Sample Code of Business Conduct

(NOTE: *Set out below is the Code of Business Conduct of Sun Life Assurance Company of Canada.*)

(a) Purpose

The Company is committed to a policy of fair dealing and integrity in the conduct of all aspects of its business. This commitment is based on a fundamental belief in law, honesty, and fairness. The Company expects its employees to share its commitment to high legal, ethical, and moral standards.

This handbook summarizes the Code of Business Conduct to be followed by the Company and all of its employees. Careful study of this material will provide you with an understanding of the Company's expectations and your own obligations.

Anyone in doubt about the application of the Code should discuss the matter with their superior. Anyone who is aware of, or suspects, a contravention of the Code must also promptly advise their superior or report the matter directly to Human Resources, Internal Audit or the Law Department.

This Code of Business Conduct is mandatory and full compliance is expected under all circumstances by all employees of the Company and its subsidiaries. The Company will monitor compliance, and any violation of the Code may result in disciplinary action, which could include termination of employment.

(b) Compliance with Laws and Regulations

The Company and its employees must at all times comply with all applicable laws and regulations. The Company will not condone the activities of any employee who achieves results through violation of the law or unethical business dealings. This includes any payments for an illegal act, indirect contributions, rebates, and bribery. No activity is to be carried on that will not stand the closest possible public scrutiny.

All business conduct should typically be well above the minimum required by the law. Accordingly, employees must ensure that their conduct cannot be interpreted as being in any way in contravention of the laws and regulations governing the Company's worldwide operations. Whenever any employee is in doubt about the application or interpretation of any legal requirement, the individual should refer the matter to their superior who, if necessary, should seek the advice of the Law Department.

(c) Conflict of Interest

The Company expects that employees will perform their duties conscientiously, honestly and in accordance with the best interests of the Company.

Employees must not use their position or the knowledge gained through it, for private or personal advantage, or in such a manner that a conflict or an appearance of conflict arises between the Company's interest and their personal interest.

Whatever the circumstances may be in a given situation, if an employee feels that a course that they have pursued, are pursuing, or are contemplating pursuing may involve them in a conflict of interest, they should immediately make all the facts known to their superior.

(i) Outside Activities, Employment, and Directorships. All employees share a very real responsibility for good Company public relations, especially on the community level. Their readiness to help with religious, charitable, educational, and civic activities has brought great credit to the Company and is encouraged. Employees must, however, avoid acquiring any business interest or participating in any other activity outside the Company, which would, or would appear:

1. To create an excessive demand upon their time and attention, thus depriving the Company of their best efforts on the job; or

2. To create a conflict of interest—that is, an obligation, interest, or distraction that would interfere with the independent exercise of judgement in the Company's best interest.

(ii) Relationships with Clients and Suppliers. Employees should avoid investing in or acquiring a financial interest for their own accounts in any business organizations having a contractual relationship with the Company or providing goods and/or services to the Company if such investment or interest might influence or create the impression of influencing their decisions in the performance of their duties on behalf of the Company.

(iii) Personal Investments. An employee must not purchase or sell any security for their own account or for the account of anyone else when such person is aware that the same security is currently being purchased or sold, or is being considered for purchase or sale by the Company unless prior approval is obtained from a general manager, an assistant general manager, or the head of the local law department. In addition, when a security is currently held by the Company, no employee shall purchase or sell the same security for their own account, if such purchase or sale could reasonably be expected to adversely influence their judgement or decisions in the performance of their duties on behalf of the Company or is made or might reasonably be considered to have been made on the basis of material nonpublic information acquired by reason of their connection with the Company.

(iv) Gifts, Entertainment, and Favors. An employee must not accept entertainment, gifts, or favors that could in any way influence, or appear to influence, business decisions in favor of any person or organization with whom or that the Company has or is likely to have business dealings. In addition, no personal favors or other preferential treatment should be accepted by any employee when they are given because of their position with the Company, and, therefore, might tend to place the recipient under obligation.

(v) Internal Company Activities. An employee must not, with respect to insurance products issued by the Company, participate in any decision concerning the issuance of any insurance or the payment or defense of any claim where the employee is:

1. affiliated with the applicant or claimant when it is an organization; or

2. related to an individual applicant or claimant by blood or marriage.

Employees, except salaried field representatives, must not receive commissions or other compensation on any policy or contract, or on any extension or conversion thereof, unless such policy, contract, extension, or conversion was written and effective prior to their election or appointment as an employee, or unless otherwise specifically permitted by Company policy.

An employee must not receive any money or thing of value (other than fixed salary, fringe benefits, or other regular compensation paid by the Company), either directly or indirectly, for negotiating, procuring, recommending, or aiding in any loan, deposit, purchase, sale, payment, or exchange made by or on behalf of the Company, nor have any direct or indirect financial interest in any such transaction, except that an employee who is a policyholder shall be entitled to all benefits under the contract.

An employee who has knowledge of any material nonpublic information obtained in the course of the performance of their duties on behalf of the Company concerning a corporation or other business entity must not utilize such information for their own benefit in connection with the purchase and sale of securities issued by the particular corporations or other business entity, nor should such information be passed on to others for their use.

In addition, information with respect to any confidential product, plan, or program of the Company, or personal information regarding employees and contained in employment files, must not be disclosed to any outside person by any employee unless and until proper authorization for such disclosure has been obtained from the vice-president primarily responsible for such information.

(d) Political Activity

The Company encourages the personal participation of its employees in the political process, respects the employee's right to absolute privacy with regard to personal political activity, and will not attempt to influence any such activity.

Company funds, goods, or services, however, must not be used as contributions to political parties, and Company facilities must not be made available to candidates or campaigns unless authorized by the board of directors.

(e) Company Funds

An employee who has access to Company funds in any form must follow the prescribed procedures for recording, handling, and protecting money as detailed in the Company's instructional manuals and/or other explanatory materials. The Company imposes strict standards to prevent fraud and dishonesty and where an individual is aware of any evidence that this may have occurred they should immediately advise their superior or the law department, so that further investigation can be promptly initiated.

Where any employee's position requires spending of Company funds or incurring any personal expenses to be later reimbursed by the Company, it is the individual's responsibility to use good judgement on the Company's behalf and to ensure that good value is received for every expenditure. Company funds should only be used for Company purposes and must not be used for personal benefit.

(f) Company Records

Accurate and reliable records of many kinds are necessary to meet the Company's legal and financial obligations and to manage the affairs of the Company. The Company's books and records must reflect in an accurate and timely manner all business transactions. Undisclosed or unrecorded funds or assets or liabilities are not permissible, and the employees responsible for accounting and record-keeping functions are expected to be diligent in enforcing these requirements.

(g) Dealing with Outside Persons and Organizations

Employees must take care to separate their personal roles from their Company positions when communicating on matters not involving Company business. Company identification, stationery, supplies, and equipment must not be used for personal or political matters.

When communicating publicly on matters that do involve Company business, individuals must not presume to speak for the Company on any matter, unless they are certain that the views they express are those of the Company, and that it is the Company's desire that such views be publicly disseminated.

An employee, when dealing with anyone outside the Company, including public officials, must take care not to compromise the integrity of or damage the reputation of any outside individual, business, or government body, or that of the Company.

(h) Prompt Communications

Every effort must be made to achieve complete, accurate, and timely communications with applicants, policyholders, claimants, government authorities, the public, and others in the Company in all matters relevant to them. A prompt and courteous response must be made to all proper requests for information and to all complaints.

(i) Privacy and Confidentiality

When handling financial and personal information about policyholders and other clients, the following principles are to be observed.

- Only such personal information as is necessary to the Company's business should be collected, used, and retained. When information is needed, as much as possible it should be obtained directly from the person concerned. Only reputable and reliable sources should be used to supplement this information.

- Information should only be retained as long as it is needed or as required by law, and the physical security of such information should be protected.

- Internal access to personal information should be limited to those with a legitimate business reason to seek the information. Personal information should only be used for the purposes for which it was originally obtained. The consent of the person concerned should be obtained before there is external disclosure of personal information, unless legal process or contractual obligation provides otherwise.

- The Company recognizes the right of a person to review their personal record retained by the Company. This right is subject to a corresponding right to privacy of the source of such information. Some information is not disclosable due to legal and ethical prohibition or privilege. Personal health or medical information will usually be made available to a person through their attending physician, although where required by law such information may be given directly to the person.

- A person may correct or clarify erroneous personal information retained by the Company. If the Company does not agree with the requested corrections, the person concerned will be given the opportunity to file their written opinion in the Company's records.

If there is any question as to the application of these principles, employees should refer the matter to their superior.

§3.3   Ethical Environment Checklist

[NOTE: *This checklist is reprinted and/or adapted from Chapter 5 of the* Computer Security Handbook, *a chapter entitled* Computer Crime and Computer Criminals *by G. Jack Bologna (Edited by Arthur E. Hutt, Seymour Bosworth, and Douglas B. Hoyt, Macmillan, 1988, pp. 76-79)*].

An Ethical Environment Checklist, summarizing many of the issues raised in this chapter, appears on the following pages. The checklist is comprehensive and some sections may not be considered applicable or appropriate in certain instances. For example, most organizations will not conduct the extensive employee screening described in section 3 of the checklist.

Ethical Environment Checklist

This checklist is designed to assist accountants in promoting an ethical environment in their organizations and that of their clients. 'No' answers may require investigation and follow-up, the results of which should be documented. Where there is such additional documentation, the purpose of the "Ref" column is to cross-reference the checklist to the appropriate working paper (or to the notes on the reverse).

The checklist is intended for general use only. Use of the checklist does not guarantee the prevention of fraud. If fraud prevention is an especially vital concern or if fraud is suspected, the advice of a specialist should be sought.

Ethical Environment Checklist	*Yes*	*No*	*N/a*	*Ref*
1. Does your company have *written* policies which restrict or prohibit the following:				
a. Outside employment (moonlighting)?	☐	☐	☐	___
b. Conflicts of interest?	☐	☐	☐	___
c. Accepting gratuities, expensive gifts or lavish entertainments from vendors, contractors, and suppliers?	☐	☐	☐	___
d. Compromising or bribing customers?	☐	☐	☐	___
e. Disclosing company trade secrets to unauthorized persons?	☐	☐	☐	___
f. Fixing prices with competitors?	☐	☐	☐	___
g. Gambling on-the-job?	☐	☐	☐	___
h. Drug and alcohol abuse?	☐	☐	☐	___
i. Fighting on-the-job?	☐	☐	☐	___
j. Stealing company property?	☐	☐	☐	___
k. Destroying company property?	☐	☐	☐	___
l. Falsifying time and attendance reports?	☐	☐	☐	___

§3.3 Ethical Environment Checklist

	Yes	No	N/a	Ref
m. Falsifying production reports?	☐	☐	☐	___
n. Falsifying personal data on job applications?	☐	☐	☐	___
o. Falsifying or forging accounting records?	☐	☐	☐	___
p. Destroying accounting records?	☐	☐	☐	___
q. Falsifying expense accounts?	☐	☐	☐	___
r. Allowing nonauthorized persons to gain access to confidential records, i.e., payroll and personnel records, customer and vendor lists, research results, product and marketing plans?	☐	☐	☐	___
s. Allowing nonauthorized persons to gain access to company buildings or critical work areas?	☐	☐	☐	___
t. Loaning company building access identification cards, badges or door keys to nonauthorized persons?	☐	☐	☐	___
u. Disclosing computer log-on codes or passwords to nonauthorized persons?	☐	☐	☐	___
v. Allowing nonauthorized persons to use computer terminals?	☐	☐	☐	___
2. Does your company conduct background inquiries to confirm:				
a. Identity of applicants?	☐	☐	☐	___
b. Educational achievements?	☐	☐	☐	___
c. Credit standing?	☐	☐	☐	___
d. Satisfactory past employments?	☐	☐	☐	___
e. Freedom from criminal convictions (name and/or fingerprint checks)?	☐	☐	☐	___
f. Reputation?	☐	☐	☐	___
g. Character?	☐	☐	☐	___

Promoting an Ethical Environment

	Yes	No	N/a	Ref
3. Does your company administer any of the following to new hires or applicants:				
a. Polygraph?	☐	☐	☐	___
b. Paper and pencil honesty tests?	☐	☐	☐	___
c. Voice stress analysis?	☐	☐	☐	___
d. Handwriting analysis?	☐	☐	☐	___
e. Intelligence tests?	☐	☐	☐	___
f. Psychological diagnostic tests like the MMPI, PF 16, etc.?	☐	☐	☐	___
4. Does your company conduct and/or provide:				
a. Security orientation training for new hires?	☐	☐	☐	___
b. Ongoing security awareness training programs for all employees?	☐	☐	☐	___
c. Written rules of employee conduct?	☐	☐	☐	___
d. Annual, signed employee declaration acknowledging that they are aware of the company's code of conduct, and that they have adhered and will adhere to it?	☐	☐	☐	___
e. Hearings for employees charged with punishable offenses?	☐	☐	☐	___
f. Employee representation at such hearings?	☐	☐	☐	___
5. Does your company utilize or provide:				
a. Job descriptions?	☐	☐	☐	___
b. Organization charts?	☐	☐	☐	___
c. Standards of performance?	☐	☐	☐	___
d. Performance appraisals?	☐	☐	☐	___
e. Coaching and counselling of employees whose work is unsatisfactory?	☐	☐	☐	___

§3.3 Ethical Environment Checklist

	Yes	No	N/a	Ref
f. Counselling of employees with substance abuse problems?	☐	☐	☐	____
g. Technical training programs?	☐	☐	☐	____
h. Human resource development programs?	☐	☐	☐	____
i. Quality of work-life programs?	☐	☐	☐	____
j. Quality circles programs?	☐	☐	☐	____
k. Tuition reimbursement?	☐	☐	☐	____
l. Time off for study?	☐	☐	☐	____
m. Time off for family emergencies?	☐	☐	☐	____
n. Employee involvement programs?	☐	☐	☐	____
o. Job enlargement/enrichment/rotation programs?	☐	☐	☐	____
p. Exit interviews of departing employees?	☐	☐	☐	____
6. Does your company compare favorably or at least equally with other firms in your industry and/or areas of operations with respect to:				
a. Salaries?	☐	☐	☐	____
b. Fringe benefits?	☐	☐	☐	____
c. Blue collar turnover?	☐	☐	☐	____
d. White collar turnover?	☐	☐	☐	____
e. Absenteeism?	☐	☐	☐	____
f. Employee firings?	☐	☐	☐	____
g. Promotions from within the company?	☐	☐	☐	____
h. Ability to recruit new employees?	☐	☐	☐	____
i. Skills of its employees?	☐	☐	☐	____
j. Educational level of employees?	☐	☐	☐	____
k. Employee attitudes toward their work?	☐	☐	☐	____
l. Employee loyalty?	☐	☐	☐	____

	Yes	No	N/a	Ref
7. Does your company, as a matter of written policy, refer incidents of employee crimes on-the-job to police or prosecutorial authorities?	☐	☐	☐	___
8. Does your company have:				
a. Internal auditors?	☐	☐	☐	___
b. EDP auditors?	☐	☐	☐	___
c. At least one Data Security Officer or Administrator?	☐	☐	☐	___
d. A Corporate Security or Loss Prevention Unit?	☐	☐	☐	___
e. An investigative staff?	☐	☐	☐	___
9. If your company has experienced any of the following incidents in the past five years, have the causes been established and remedial action taken:				
a. A substantial inventory shortage corporate-wide?	☐	☐	☐	___
b. A substantial inventory shortage in a major operating division?	☐	☐	☐	___
c. A major embezzlement, involving a loss of more than $10,000?	☐	☐	☐	___
d. A successful penetration of your main office computers by outsiders?	☐	☐	☐	___
e. An accounts payable, accounts receivable, payroll, or benefit claim fraud of any amount?	☐	☐	☐	___
f. Commercial bribery of purchasing or other personnel?	☐	☐	☐	___

CHAPTER FOUR

Risk Financing and Fidelity Insurance

§4.1 **Introduction**
    (a)   The Concept of Risk Financing
    (b)   Historical Background
§4.2 **Types of Fidelity Insurance Policies**
    (a)   General Comments
    (b)   Dishonesty, Destruction, and Disappearance Bonds (3-D)
        (i)   Employee Dishonesty (Insuring Agreement I)
        (ii)   Loss Inside the Premises (Insuring Agreement II)
        (iii)   Loss Outside the Premises (Insuring Agreement III)
        (iv)   Counterfeit Paper Currency (Insuring Agreement IV)
        (v)   Depositors Forgery (Insuring Agreement V)
    (c)   Bankers Blanket Bond
        (i)   Fidelity
        (ii)   On Premises
        (iii)   In Transit
        (iv)   Forgery or Alteration
        (v)   Securities
        (vi)   Counterfeit Currency
    (d)   Brokers Blanket Bond
        (i)   Fidelity
        (ii)   On Premises
        (iii)   In Transit
        (iv)   Forgery or Alteration
        (v)   Securities

      (vi)   Counterfeit Currency
   (e) Other Bonds
§4.3 Important Clauses in Fidelity Policies
   (a) Definitions
      (i)   Money
      (ii)   Securities
      (iii)   Employee
      (iv)   Premises
      (v)   Banking Premises
      (vi)   Messenger
      (vii) Custodian
      (viii) Robbery
      (ix)   Safe Burglary
      (x)   Loss
   (b) Exclusions
   (c) Loss Under Prior Bond or Policy
   (d) Bond Period; Territory Discovery
   (e) Loss Caused by Unidentifiable Employees
   (f) Ownership of Property; Interests Covered
   (g) Books and Records
   (h) Prior Fraud, Dishonesty, or Cancellation
   (i) Loss-Notice-Proof-Action Against Underwriter
   (j) Valuation-Payment-Replacement
   (k) Recoveries
   (l) Limits of Liability
   (m) Limit of Liability Under Current Bond and Prior Insurance
   (n) Other Insurance
   (o) Subrogation
   (p) Cancellation as to any Employee
   (q) Cancellation of Bond or Insuring Agreement
   (r) No Benefit to Bailee
   (s) Assignment
§4.4 Insured's Responsibilities
   (a) Insured's Ongoing Responsibilities
   (b) Insured's Responsibilities in the Event of a Loss
§4.5 The Purchase Decision
   (a) General Comments
   (b) Factors Affecting Cost
   (c) Summary

§4.6   Risk Financing Checklist

Since the risk of fraud can never be completely eliminated, organizations must finance this risk either externally and explicitly (fidelity insurance) or internally and implicitly (self-insurance). Where the risk is significant, the first option should be seriously considered; however, the reality is that many organizations choose the second option by default, because they fail to address the issue entirely or are simply unfamiliar with fidelity insurance.

This chapter covers the subject of risk financing and fidelity insurance as follows:

- The first section (4.1) provides a general introduction to the concept of risk financing, along with some historical background;

- The second section (4.2) describes the types of fidelity insurance policies that are available;

- The third section (4.3) deals in greater detail with some of the more typical clauses found in fidelity insurance policies;

- The fourth section (4.4) describes the insured's responsibilities under a fidelity insurance policy;

- The fifth section (4.5) deals with the fidelity insurance purchase decision; and

- Finally, the last section (4.6) presents a practical checklist that reflects the key points in this chapter.

§4.1   Introduction

(a)   The Concept of Risk Financing

All risks are financed in one form or another, either explicitly or implicitly. A lack of insurance, or an explicit decision not to buy insurance, does not eliminate the risk. It merely results in a situation where the risk is self-financed, i.e., paid out of one's own pocket if and when losses are incurred.

Most individuals and businesses would never—or at least should never—consider self-insurance as a viable option in the case of potentially catastrophic risk. Life and disability insurance for the breadwinner supporting a family, fire insurance for the homeowner, and liability insurance for doctors and automobile owners are all examples of insuring against potentially catastrophic risk. In some cases such insurance may be mandated by statute or by contractual agreement, e.g., fire insurance may be required as part of a mortgage agreement.

The risk of loss from fraud, e.g., employee dishonesty, can be financed through fidelity insurance. Some types of businesses—e.g., banks, brokerage houses, and armored car companies—may be required by statute to carry such coverage because of the potentially catastrophic losses that could result. For other types of businesses, the coverage is optional and often overlooked (self-financed), even though the potential losses may still be quite significant.

(b) Historical Background

The custom of one person standing guarantee for another dates back beyond recorded history, perhaps to the first tribal life. Suretyship was a familiar commercial and social factor many centuries before Christ. The Bible mentions several cases and in the old Roman empire certain types of this form of insurance were governed by law; but surprisingly, it was not until 1840 in London, England that corporate suretyship or guarantee insurance was founded with the formation of the Guarantee Society of London.

In a sense, corporate suretyship came to North America on a train. Following the formation of the Grand Trunk Railway, Sir Alexander Galt realized the need for some kind of fidelity insurance for the railway's money-handling employees.

The product being provided at that time was based upon a strategy wherein a set of rules and guidelines were prepared regarding the sort of person acceptable for bonding, which included the applicant's occupation, history, and habits on a per-individual basis.

Procedures were also developed to help insureds minimize losses, such as suggestions as to how bank officials could best prevent defalcations and embezzlements. The techniques for investigating prospective fidelity risks became so highly refined that a willingness to bond a person soon came to be taken as important evidence of good character.

In the 1920s, with the expansion of business and commerce, employees became more transient. To facilitate the underwriting of various "positions" within a company, a "blanket fidelity bond," which covered all the employees an insured might have at any given time, was introduced.

Since that time the product offered by bonding companies has been further refined to provide coverage for most of a company's assets through a broadform policy entitled "Comprehensive Dishonesty, Destruction, and Disappearance."

In an effort to address the unique generic needs of certain business ventures, the Comprehensive Dishonesty, Destruction, and Disappearance bond has been expanded to include specialty inherent risks for certain types of insureds. These specialty bonds have been named to address the specific business for which they afford the unique coverage, (e.g., Financial Institution Bond, Bankers Blanket Bond, Brokers Blanket Bond, Insurance Companies Blanket Bond, Mail Policies, and Charge Card Issuers Bond).

The following precis has been prepared in order to provide a broad overview of the various types of coverage afforded by fidelity policies, and to assist prospective insureds in determining what is covered by these policies and what is not.

CAVEAT: THE FOLLOWING IS INTENDED TO BE INFORMATIVE ONLY. THE TERMS AND PROVISIONS OF THE BOND AND RIDERS WILL GOVERN ANY QUESTION ARISING IN CONNECTION THEREWITH.

§4.2 Types of Fidelity Insurance Policies

(a) General Comments

As previously noted, fidelity insurance policies can be either generic or specific. The most generic policy is referred to as Comprehensive Dishonesty, Destruction, and Disappearance. Specific industry policies include Bankers Blanket Bond, Brokers Blanket Bond, General and Life Insurance Companies Blanket Bond, and Financial Institution Bond.

Each of these various policies are described in the material that follows. This material, in particular the excerpts of policy wording and definitions, has been supplied by The Guarantee Company of North America, a fidelity insurer. However, the information and terminology is fairly standard across the industry.

It should be noted that fidelity insurance policies provide coverage for *actual sustained losses*, which the Insured has suffered as a result of a specified covered activity only. Accordingly, *consequential or indirect losses, i.e., loss of interest, potential income, damages, and work ethic are not covered.*

In addition, in the case of employee dishonesty policies, the underwriter will only provide coverage based upon the assumption that all the employees so covered are honest and the Insured does not anticipate dishonesty.

(b)   Dishonesty, Destruction, and Disappearance Bonds (3-D)

Comprehensive Dishonesty, Destruction, and Disappearance bonds, commonly referred to in the industry as *3-D bonds*, set out general business coverage provided on a "broad base" to all types of companies that are not engaged in specialty bond activity.

3-D bonds typically contain several insuring agreements that specify the types of losses that are covered, such as those described in the following sections.

(i) Employee Dishonesty (Insuring Agreement I). The main part of the 3-D policy deals with employee dishonesty, also referred to as fidelity. This coverage can take two main forms:

- Form A: Loss resulting from dishonest activity on the part of *one or more employees*. One aggregate amount applies with one deductible for the loss or occurrence as claimed;

    —OR—

- Form B: Loss resulting from dishonest activity on the part of *one employee only*. One amount applies to all activity of that employee with one deductible. (If several employees are involved, then corresponding bond limits and deductibles may apply.)

Dishonesty is defined as "manifest intent . . . to cause *such loss* to the employer and a gain to the employee or someone to whom he directs the gain . . . excluding salaries, commissions, bonuses (etc.) . . . earned in the normal course of employment."

(ii) Loss Inside the Premises (Insuring Agreement II). "Loss of money and securities by the actual destruction, disappearance or wrongful abstraction . . . within the premises . . . or banking premises . . . including loss resulting from safe burglary or robbery within the premises . . . locked cash drawer (force required to open) . . . only property of the Insured."

(iii) Loss Outside the Premises (Insuring Agreement III). "Loss of money and securities and other property (as defined) . . . while being conveyed by messenger (or while within his home) or armored car company."

(iv) Counterfeit Paper Currency (Insuring Agreement IV). "Loss due to the acceptance in good faith, in exchange for merchandise, money [etc.] . . . in the normal course of business of counterfeit currency, money orders, etc."

(v) Depositors Forgery (Insuring Agreement V). "Loss as a result of the Insured having someone process forged cheques, money orders, (etc.) through the Insured's bank account (excluding employees)."

(c) Bankers Blanket Bond

This coverage is provided to banks and trust companies, and indemnifies the named insured from a loss sustained if discovered during the bond period. The breakdown into specific coverages is normally slightly different than with the 3-D policy, as described in the following sections.

(i) Fidelity. Employee dishonesty having manifest intent to cause the employer a loss and a gain for himself (or a directed party), excluding salaries, bonuses, etc. earned in the normal course of employment. Includes loss resulting from loan activity that is covered only if the employee acts in collusion with another party to the transaction and has personally received a financial benefit of at least $2,500. (Note: this number may vary).

(ii) On Premises. "Loss of property . . . through robbery, burglary . . . theft, holdup, misplacement, mysterious unexplained disappearance . . . except . . . in the mail or with a carrier for hire, other than an armored motor vehicle company, for the purpose of transportation." False pretences and larceny *must* be committed by a person on the bank/trust

company premises, although the property may be located "within offices or premises located anywhere."

(iii) In Transit. "Loss of property (specified instruments) . . . through robbery, larceny, theft, holdup, misplacement, mysterious unexplained disappearance . . . while the property is in the custody of a messenger (a defined term) . . . except while in the mail or with a carrier for hire other than an armored motor vehicle company."

(iv) Forgery or Alteration. "Loss to the Insured by forgery or alteration, through payment of false instrument (as specified), etc."

(v) Securities. "Loss through any securities, documents or other written instruments which prove to have been either counterfeited or forged as to the signature of any maker, drawer, issuer, surety or guarantor, or raised or otherwise altered, lost or stolen."
However, there are exclusions to third party activity.

(vi) Counterfeit Currency. "Loss through the receipt, by the Named Insured, of any counterfeit currency, coin, etc."

(d)   Brokers Blanket Bond

This coverage is provided to stock brokerage houses by indemnifying the named insured from a loss sustained at any time, but discovered during the bond period. The breakdown into specific coverages is virtually identical to the Bankers Blanket Bond and is set out in the following sections.

(i) Fidelity. Similar to Bankers Blanket Bond coverage, however, financial benefit must flow to the employee.

(ii) On Premises. Similar to Bankers Blanket Bond coverage, but does not provide coverage to customers on premises.

(iii) In Transit. Similar to Bankers Blanket Bond coverage.

(iv) Forgery or Alteration. Generally similar to Bankers Blanket Bond coverage.

(v) Securities. Generally similar to Bankers Blanket Bond coverage, but takes into consideration a brokerage operation with expanded exclusion to third party activities.

(vi) Counterfeit Currency. Similar to Bankers Blanket Bond coverage.

(e)   Other Bonds

Other major types of bonds include General and Life Insurance Companies Blanket Bond and Financial Institution Bond. These coverages are similar to the aforementioned bonds in that they address several areas of risk. However, under the agreement of fidelity, special distinction is given to the various "agents" employed by the named insured, with varying degrees of coverage afforded.

CAVEAT: THE FOREGOING AND FOLLOWING MATERIAL IS INTENDED TO BE INFORMATIVE ONLY. THE TERMS AND PROVISIONS OF THE BOND AND RIDERS WILL GOVERN ANY QUESTION ARISING IN CONNECTION THEREWITH.

§4.3 Important Clauses in Fidelity Policies

The previous section described in broad terms the kinds of fidelity insurance policies available on the market and the types of losses they are intended to cover. As with any insurance policy, however, it is important to be aware of the "fine print" and how it impacts your coverage. The following sections set out typical wording for some of the more important clauses, which insureds should be aware of.

(a)   Definitions

(i) Money. "*Money* means currency, coins, bank notes, traveller's checks, and money orders held for sale to the public."

(ii) Securities. "*Securities* means all negotiable and non-negotiable instruments or contracts representing either money or other property, and includes revenue and other stamps in current use, tokens and tickets, but does not include money."

(iii) Employee. "*Employee* means any person (*except a director* or trustee of the Insured who is not also an officer or employee thereof in some other capacity) while in the regular service of the Insured in the ordinary course of the Insured's business during the bond period and whom the Insured compensates by salary, wages or commissions and has the right to govern and direct in the performance of such service, *but does not mean any broker, factor, commission merchant, consignee, contractor or other agent or representative of the same general character.*"

(iv) Premises. "*Premises* means the interior of that portion of any building which is occupied by the Insured in conducting its business."

(v) Banking Premises. "*Banking Premises* means the interior of that portion of any building which is occupied by a banking institution in conducting its business."

(vi) Messenger. "*Messenger* means the Insured or a partner of the Insured or any employee who is duly authorized by the Insured to have the care and custody of the insured property outside the premises."

(vii) Custodian. "*Custodian* means the Insured or a partner of the Insured or any employee who is duly authorized by the Insured to have the care and custody of the insured property within the premises, excluding any person while acting as a watchman, porter or janitor."

(viii) Robbery. "*Robbery* means the taking of insured property . . . by violence inflicted upon a messenger or custodian . . . by putting him in fear of violence . . . by any other overt felonious act committed in his presence and of which he was actually cognizant, provided such other act is not committed by a partner or employee of the Insured. Under Insuring Agreement II (loss inside premises) . . . from within the premises by means of compelling a messenger or custodian by violence or threat of violence while outside the premises to admit a person into the premises, or from a showcase or show window within the premises while regularly open for business by a person who has broken the glass thereof from outside the premises."

(ix) Safe Burglary. "*Safe Burglary* means the felonious abstraction of insured property from within a vault or safe, the door of which is equipped with a combination lock, located within the premises by a person making

felonious entry into such vault or safe when all doors thereof are duly closed and locked by all combination locks thereon, provided such entry shall be made by actual force and violence (with visible marks made by tools, explosives, etc.)."

(x) Loss. "*Loss* includes damage, except under Insuring Agreement I (fidelity) and V (depositor's forgery coverage)."

(b) Exclusions

Contained in all of the foregoing bonds are several areas where the bond prohibits coverage. Some of these exclusions are outlined below; however, for a detailed review of the exclusions applicable to the bond, the actual policy should in all cases be referred to.

- To the defence of any legal proceeding brought against the Insured (see specific "Court Costs and Attorney's Fees" riders accompanying most Brokers and Bankers Blanket Bonds).

- To potential income, etc. . . .;

- To damages of any type . . .;

- To costs incurred in the preparation of the Proof of Loss (unless waived in a rider);

- To loss as a result of activity of any Insured or partner therein . . . acting alone or in collusion with others;

- To a loss (factual existence or to its amount) that is dependent upon calculation and/or determination by a profit and loss calculation or by an inventory computation;

- To the defence of any legal proceeding . . . or to fees, costs, or expenses incurred . . . in prosecuting or defending any legal proceeding whether or not such proceeding results . . . in a loss to the Insured covered by this bond; and

- To damages of any type for which the Insured is legally liable, except direct compensatory damages arising from a loss covered under this bond.

(c)   Loss Under Prior Bond or Policy

"If the coverage . . . of this bond (other than Insuring Agreement V, depositor's forgery coverage) is substituted for any prior bond or policy of insurance which is terminated, cancelled or allowed to expire . . . it is agreed that coverage afforded by this bond applies to loss which is discovered within this bond's term and which would have been recoverable by the Insured under a prior bond or policy except for the fact that the time within which to discover this loss had expired, provided that the insurance shall be part of and not in addition to the amount of insurance afforded by this bond and such loss would have been covered under such prior bond had such prior bond been in force when the acts or events causing such loss were committed or occurred, and recovery under such prior bond on account of such loss shall in no event exceed the amount which would have been recoverable under such prior bond had such bond continued in force until the discovery of such loss if the latter amount be smaller." (Coverage is afforded only to the least of the amount of insurance afforded at the time or the amount covered under the current policy).

(d)   Bond Period; Territory Discovery

"Loss is covered under this bond only if discovered not later than 120 days from the end of the bond period." (The "tailing" effect of the bond varies with each policy. In some instances the period after termination is nonexistent or can be as lengthy as one year. Refer to actual policy for confirmation as to time period if any allowable for discovery of a loss which occurred during the bond period after termination.)

"This bond (except under Insuring Agreement I - fidelity, and V - depositor's forgery) applies only to loss which occurs during the bond period in Canada or any of the states of the United States of America.

"Insuring Agreement I (fidelity) applies only to loss sustained by the Insured through fraudulent or dishonest acts committed during the bond period . . . by an employee engaged in the regular service of the Insured within the territory designated (Canada and the United States), or while such employees are elsewhere for a limited period.

"Insuring Agreement V (depositor's forgery) applies only to loss sustained during the bond period."

(e)   Loss Caused by Unidentifiable Employees

"If a loss is alleged to have been caused by the fraud or dishonesty of any one or more of the employees and the Insured shall be unable to designate the specific employee or employees causing such loss, the Insured shall nevertheless have the benefit of coverage provided that the evidence submitted reasonably proves that the loss was in fact due to the fraud or dishonesty of an employee, and provided that the aggregate liability of this bond for any such loss shall not exceed the amount of coverage afforded to Insuring Agreement I (fidelity)."

(f)   Ownership of Property; Interests Covered

"The property insured by the bond may be owned by the Insured or held by the Insured in any capacity whether or not the Insured is liable for the loss thereof."

(g)   Books and Records

"The Insured shall keep records of all the insured property in such manner that the underwriter can accurately determine therefrom the amount of the loss."

(h)   Prior Fraud, Dishonesty, or Cancellation

"The coverage under Insuring Agreement I (fidelity) shall not apply to an employee from and after the time that the Insured or any partner or officer not in collusion with such employee shall have knowledge or information that such employee has committed *any fraudulent or dishonest act in the service of the Insured or otherwise,* whether such act be committed before or after the date of employment by the Insured." (It should be noted that the bond in its entirety does not cease with respect to other employees, but would cease to provide coverage to the employee once *any dishonesty* is known to the Insured, partner or officer of the company.)

(i) Loss-Notice-Proof-Action Against Underwriter

"*Upon discovery* of a loss or of an occurrence which may give rise to a claim for loss, *the Insured shall:*

(a) *Give notice as soon as practicable* to the underwriter, and under certain circumstances to the police if the loss is due to a violation of law; and

(b) *File detailed proof of loss,* duly sworn to, with the underwriter *within four months after the discovery of loss.*

"Upon the underwriter's request, the Insured shall submit to examination, subscribe the same, under oath if required, and produce all pertinent records, and shall cooperate in all matters pertaining to the loss.

"No action shall lie against the underwriter unless, *as a condition precedent thereto,* there shall have been full compliance with all the terms of the bond, *nor until ninety days after the required proofs of loss have been filed, nor at all unless commenced within two years from the date when the Insured discovers the loss.*"

(j) Valuation-Payment-Replacement

"In no event shall the underwriter be liable as respects securities for more than the actual cash value thereof at the close of business on the business day next preceding the day on which the loss was discovered, nor as respects other property, for more than the actual cash value thereof at the time of loss; provided, however, the actual cash value of such other property held by the Insured as a pledge, or as collateral for an advance or a loan, shall be deemed not to exceed the value of the property as determined and recorded by the Insured when making the advance or loan plus accrued interest thereon at legal rates.

"The underwriter may, with the consent of the Insured, settle any claim for loss of property with the owner thereof. Any property for which the underwriter has made indemnification shall become the property of the underwriter.

"In case of damage of the premises or loss of property other than securities, the underwriter shall not be liable for more than the actual cash value of such property, or for more than the actual cost of repairing such premises or property or of replacing same with property or material of like quality and value. The underwriter may, at its election, pay such actual cash value, or make such repairs or replacements.''

(k) Recoveries

''If the Insured shall sustain any loss covered by this bond to which a deductible amount applies and such loss exceeds the applicable amount of insurance (plus the deductible), the Insured shall be entitled to all recoveries made after payment by the underwriter of loss covered by this bond (except from other insurance), less the actual cost of effecting such recoveries, until reimbursed for such excess loss; however, if there be no such excess loss, any such recoveries shall be applied first in reimbursement to the underwriter and thereafter in reimbursement of the Insured for the deductible.'' (If a loss does not exceed the bond limit and recoveries are made, the ''right of first recovery'' is to the underwriter and then to the Insured to satisfy the deductible. However, if loss exceeds the bond amount the ''right of first recovery'' is to the Insured for the amount of loss in excess of the bond coverage only, then the aforementioned rule would apply.)

(l) Limits of Liability

''The applicable limit of liability stated in the ''Table of Limits of Liability'' (the Declarations page of the policy) is the total limit of the underwriter's liability with respect to *all loss of property of one or more persons or organizations arising out of any one occurrence. All loss incidental to an actual or attempted fraudulent, dishonest or criminal act or series of related acts at the premises, whether committed by one or more persons, shall be deemed to arise out of one occurrence.*

''Regardless of the number of years this bond shall continue in force and the number of premiums which shall be payable or paid, the limit of liability *shall not be cumulative from year to year or period to period.*

''The deductible amount shall be carried by the Insured as self-insurance.

''The Insured shall, in the time and in the manner prescribed in this bond, give notice to the underwriter of any loss of the kind covered by the terms of this bond, whether or not the underwriter is liable therefor, and upon the request of the underwriter shall file with it a brief statement giving the particulars concerning such loss.''

(m) Limit of Liability Under Current Bond and Prior Insurance

"This section shall apply only to Insuring Agreements I (fidelity) and V (depositor's forgery).

"With respect to loss caused by any person (whether a known employee or an ''unidentifiable employee'') and which occurs partly during this bond period and partly during the period of other bonds or policies issued by this underwriter which has been terminated or cancelled or allowed to expire and in which the period for discovery has not expired at the time any such loss thereunder is discovered, the total liability under this bond and under such other bonds shall not exceed, in the aggregate, the amount carried under the applicable Insuring Agreement of this bond for such loss or the amount available to the Insured under such prior bonds.'' (Only one bond amount shall apply, whichever is the least.)

(n) Other Insurance

"If there is available to the Insured any other insurance or indemnity covering any loss covered by Insuring Agreement I (fidelity) or V (depositor's forgery), the underwriter shall be liable only for that part of such loss which is in excess of the amount recoverable or recovered from such other insurance.''

(o) Subrogation

"In the event of any payment under this bond, the underwriter shall be subrogated to all the Insured's rights of recovery therefor against any person or organization and the Insured shall execute and deliver instruments and papers and do whatever else is necessary to secure such rights. The Insured shall do nothing after loss to prejudice such rights.''

(p)   Cancellation as to any Employee

"Insuring Agreement I (fidelity) shall be deemed cancelled as to any employee:

(a) Immediately upon discovery by the Insured, or by any partner or officer thereof not in collusion with such employee, of any fraudulent or dishonest act on the part of such employee; or

(b) At 12:01 a.m., standard time, upon the effective date specified in a written notice mailed to the Insured. Such date shall be not less than fifteen days after the date of mailing. Delivery of such written notice by the underwriter shall be equivalent to mailing."

(q)   Cancellation of Bond or Insuring Agreement

"This bond or any Insuring Agreement may be cancelled by the Insured by mailing to the underwriter written notice stating when thereafter the cancellation shall be effective.

"If the Insured cancels, earned premium shall be computed in accordance with the customary short rate table and procedure. If the underwriter cancels, earned premium shall be computed pro rata."

(r)   No Benefit to Bailee

"This section applies only to Insuring Agreements II and III (loss inside/outside premises coverage). The insurance afforded by this bond shall not inure directly or indirectly to the benefit of any carrier or other bailee for hire."

(s)   Assignment

"Assignment of interest under this bond shall not bind the underwriter until its consent is endorsed thereon."

CAVEAT: THE FOREGOING IS INTENDED TO BE INFORMATIVE ONLY. THE TERMS AND PROVISIONS OF THE BOND AND RIDERS WILL GOVERN ANY QUESTION ARISING IN CONNECTION THEREWITH.

§4.4 Insured's Responsibilities

(a) Insured's Ongoing Responsibilities

A contract of insurance is made on the basis of good faith in that each party shall not prejudice the other and will abide by the terms of the contract. In this regard an underwriter will review the application for insurance based upon the facts as provided by the insured generally in answer to several questions.

If the conditions of the Insured's operation or the nature of the risk being covered has changed, there is a strict onus on the part of the Insured to inform the underwriter of such changes. Failure on the part of the Insured to inform the underwriter *MAY RESULT IN THE POLICY OF INSURANCE BEING CANCELLED AND CONSIDERED NULL AND VOID NOTWITHSTANDING THE OCCURRENCE OF A LOSS.*

The courts have held that the Insured should conduct themselves in a manner consistent with the Insured acting as if there was no insurance coverage. Therefore, the Insured shall act in the best interests of the insurer taking into consideration the generally accepted "best business rule."

(b) Insured's Responsibilities in the Event of a Loss

The following precis has been prepared as a form of checklist in assisting the reader in the event that there has been a loss for which insurance coverage may be afforded. However, it is recommended that the actual policy be reviewed in detail for clarification.

Immediately upon discovery of a loss, the following steps should be undertaken:

1. Take action to limit the loss, i.e. remove the employee and secure the premises, etc.;

2. Notify your insurance carrier and/or broker advising of all details as known at the time;

3. Remember that it is *YOUR PROPERTY* and you should conduct yourself as if no insurance existed. Attempt to minimize further loss. Take steps to assist in recoveries, i.e., identify what has been taken, where it may have gone, and appoint counsel to initiate recoveries;

4. If a loss has been detected but the employee/perpetrator has not been identified, tighten procedures and controls to minimize the loss. Initiate an investigation in an effort to identify the party responsible; and

5. Cooperate with your insurance company and/or its representative in the gathering of facts. Failure to do so may prejudice your claim and cast a shadow on the loss.

§4.5   The Purchase Decision

(a)   General Comments

The decision to purchase fidelity coverage will be based on an assessment of the risk versus the cost of coverage. As a general rule, however, if the insured's operation is of the type that either handles cash or securities, or manufactures/supplies easily disposable high-value products, then a comprehensive insurance program should be in place as a means of *deferring part of the identifiable risk.*

Fidelity coverage is underwritten by a relatively small number of companies. These include The Guarantee Company of North America, Chubb, Lloyds of London, and US F&G. It is highly recommended that the prospective insured contact a reputable insurance broker to discuss in detail the type, size, and extent of their operations, in order that a proposal for adequate coverage may be assembled.

(b)   Factors Affecting Cost

The availability and cost of fidelity coverage varies widely depending on a number of factors, and it would therefore be inappropriate to generalize as to cost. However the factors that will influence cost include:

- The nature of the business, i.e., the inherent risk;
- The limit of the coverage;
- The amount of the deductible;
- The number of employees;
- The number of branches;
- The location of the branches;

- The perceived effectiveness of internal controls and other preventive mechanisms;

- The loss experience; and

- Market competition.

Fidelity insurance is a loss-rated product, therefore prior history of losses has an impact on today's price. This is one more reason why, even when fidelity insurance is in place, it is in the best interests of insureds to have adequate controls and to establish an environment that minimizes the risk of loss.

(c) Summary

The policies that have been reviewed in this chapter are provided by the insurance industry as a means of assisting business in minimizing its exposure to a defined loss. The coverages as afforded *do not* provide coverage nor anticipate a claim for issues of liability, consequential losses (loss of income, interest, etc.), or damages (other than real), however sustained.

In addition, prospective insureds should be aware that an underwriter will only provide coverage with the view that the employees covered are honest, the premises are secure, and the risk has been properly stated.

Fidelity insurance should not be viewed as a supplement to good controls and procedures. Nevertheless, losses do occur, notwithstanding the best efforts put forth by competent management. The decision to purchase insurance should be made assessing the values of deferring such risk versus the premium charged.

§4.6 Risk Financing Checklist

A Risk Financing Checklist, summarizing many of the issues raised in this chapter, appears on the following pages. Buyers of this book are authorized to reproduce and/or adapt the checklist for use in their own organization or practice.

The Risk Financing Checklist

This checklist is designed to assist accountants in addressing risk financing issues in their organizations and that of their clients. Generally, all 'No' answers require investigation and follow-up, the results of which should be documented. Where there is such additional documentation, the purpose of the "Ref" column is to cross-reference the checklist to the appropriate working paper (or to the notes on the reverse).

The checklist is intended for general use only. Use of the checklist does not guarantee the adequacy of risk financing or of procedures followed to comply with fidelity insurance policies. If risk financing is an especially vital concern, the advice of a specialist should be sought.

Risk Financing Checklist	*Yes*	*No*	*N/a*	*Ref*
1. Initial Purchase of Fidelity Coverage				
a. Has management reviewed operations with a view to determining the nature and extent of potential losses from fraud and commercial crime?	☐	☐	☐	___
b. Has management considered the extent to which the the organization is capable of self-financing such risk, i.e., an appropriate deductible level, and conversely the extent to which fidelity insurance is desirable?	☐	☐	☐	___
c. Has contact been established with a reputable broker capable of placing the required fidelity coverage?	☐	☐	☐	___
d. Has an appropriate person been assigned the task of liaising with the broker to determine alternative types, levels, and costs of coverage, and to report back to management on these alternatives and appropriate recommendations?	☐	☐	☐	___
e. Prior to finalizing the recommended fidelity coverage, has the wording of the policy been carefully reviewed, if				

	Yes	No	N/a	Ref

necessary by legal counsel, to ensure that:

i) definitions, exclusions, and other clauses are acceptable and consistent with the nature of the business? ☐ ☐ ☐ ____

ii) where possible, duplication with other insurance (e.g. fire and theft policies) have been avoided? ☐ ☐ ☐ ____

f. Prior to signing, has the wording of the policy been reviewed to determine what changes, if any, will need or ought to be made in the conduct of the business, e.g.:

i) hiring/screening of new employees? ☐ ☐ ☐ ____

ii) use of contract employees, who may not be covered? ☐ ☐ ☐ ____

iii) bookkeeping and reporting practices? ☐ ☐ ☐ ____

iv) internal controls? ☐ ☐ ☐ ____

2. Maintenance of Fidelity Coverage

a. Is a mechanism in place to ensure that important terms in the policy are met, in order to keep the policy in good standing, e.g.:

i) payment of premiums when due? ☐ ☐ ☐ ____

ii) reporting of any loss incidents to the underwriter, even those below the deductible where no loss claim is filed? ☐ ☐ ☐ ____

iii) maintenance of adequate internal controls and good security practices, e.g., locking of safes? ☐ ☐ ☐ ____

iv) reporting of changes in the accounting system? ☐ ☐ ☐ ____

v) reporting of changes in the nature and scope of operations, which may affect risk? ☐ ☐ ☐ ____

§4.6 Risk Financing Checklist

	Yes	No	N/a	Ref
b. Is fidelity coverage reviewed on at least an annual basis, to ensure that the coverage remains adequate and continues to meet acceptable cost/benefit criteria?	☐	☐	☐	___

3. Fidelity Insurance Claims

	Yes	No	N/a	Ref
a. Upon first suspicion or discovery of a loss incident, have the following steps been taken immediately:				
i) protection of assets from further loss?	☐	☐	☐	___
ii) preservation of evidence?	☐	☐	☐	___
iii) notification of the underwriter, by hand delivery or registered mail?	☐	☐	☐	___
b. Internally and/or in cooperation with the underwriter, are adequate personnel and policies in place to permit a thorough investigation to be undertaken?	☐	☐	☐	___
c. Once reasonable suspicion of a criminal act has been established, have the police been called in?	☐	☐	☐	___
d. Are policies in place to ensure that no actions are taken to prejudice the insurance claim and/or the underwriter's ability to make recoveries, e.g., underwriter permission before settlement with third parties or suspected perpetrators?	☐	☐	☐	___
e. Are adequate personnel and procedures in place to:				
i) document the insurance claim, i.e., the Proof of Loss?	☐	☐	☐	___
ii) follow-up with the underwriter as required, until the claim is settled?	☐	☐	☐	___

81

CHAPTER FIVE

Computer Security and System Recovery

§5.1 Computer Security—A Vital Concern
  (a) The Computer in Today's Business Environment
  (b) The Concerns
    (i) Theft of Confidential Information
    (ii) Information Integrity
    (iii) System Availability
  (c) Securing Computer Systems
    (i) Accidental Versus Deliberate Events
    (ii) Prevention, Detection, and Recovery Controls
    (iii) Security in the Micro and Office Automation Era
  (d) Computer Security Checklist

§5.2 Physical Security
  (a) Introduction
  (b) Computer Room Construction
  (c) Fire Detection and Suppression
  (d) Water Protection
  (e) Electrical Power Reliability
  (f) Environmental Control
  (g) Computer Room Access
  (h) Physical Security for Microcomputers

§5.3 Logical Security
  (a) Introduction
  (b) Communications Security
    (i) Passwords and Administration

       (ii) Network Security Features

       (iii) Dial-up Security

   (c) Data Security

       (i)   "On-line" Data Files

       (ii) "Off-line" Data Files

       (iii) Reports and Documents

   (d) Software Integrity

       (i)   "On-line" Software Libraries

       (ii) "Off-line" Software

       (iii) Migration of Programs to Production

   (e) Computer Operations Security

   (f) Logical Security for Microcomputers

§5.4 System Recovery

   (a) Introduction

   (b) Recovery from Operational Failures

       (i)   Data File and Software Back-up

       (ii) Recovery Procedures

   (c) Disaster Recovery Plans

       (i)   Definition

       (ii) Elements of Effective Disaster Recovery Plans

   (d) Insurance

   (e) System Recovery for Microcomputers

§5.5 Summary

   (a) Management's Responsibility

   (b) Policy, Standards, Guidelines, and Procedures

   (c) The Security Function

   (d) Policing

When it comes to fraud and commercial crime, prevention is the best medicine. Establishing and maintaining adequate computer security is a vital part of any prevention strategy.

In this chapter:

- The first section (5.1) provides a general introduction to computer security, along with a checklist that summarizes the key points in this chapter;

- The second through the fourth sections deal in greater detail with physical security (5.2), logical security (5.3) and system recovery (5.4); and

- The last section (5.5) presents some final thoughts on the computer security issue.

This chapter deals with computer security issues in a comprehensive way, including, for example, system recovery after a disaster. While some issues may not appear at first glance to relate to the topic of fraud and commercial crime—for example, water protection, environmental controls, and system recovery after a disaster—in fact they can be relevant. For example, in order to cover up their crimes, fraudsters may attempt to destroy or sabotage computer records and facilities.

§5.1 Computer Security—A Vital Concern

[NOTE: *Much of the material in the remainder of this chapter [excluding section 5.1(c)(iii)) has been adapted from Chapter 15 of* The Handbook of Information Technology, *a chapter entitled* Computer Security *by David A. Griffiths (Thomson Professional Publishing Canada, 1991, pp. 15-1– 15-35)*].

(a)   The Computer in Today's Business Environment

In today's business environment, the computer is no longer regarded as simply a "number cruncher" used to process accounting transactions such as receivables and payables. It has become an integral part of business and of numerous business processes. For example, the computer is being increasingly used to:

- Store sensitive and confidential information on products, employees, or customers in a central location, to which access needs to be controlled and expanded for corporate benefit;

- Provide timely information to assist in the business decision-making process—for example, revised projections of performance against marketing plans and budgets;

- Improve the personal productivity of employees—for example, analysis of data, preparation of correspondence and reports, and electronic mail; and

- Gain a competitive advantage by reducing order turnaround time and improved customer service.

Obviously, as more and more organizations implement applications of this nature, the reliance that they place on computer processing increases. This in turn increases the need for an effective computer security program, because criminals also use computers—both their own and those of others—in the commission of fraud and commercial crime.

In addition, information itself is being increasingly recognized as an asset of value. Individuals, companies, and even governments covet the information held by others as a source of financial gain, power, or other advantage. Given that computers have become the primary depositories of information, this change in perception has also served to highlight the requirements for effective security over automated systems. Security is no longer viewed as an option; it is seen as a necessary element of business survival.

(b)   The Concerns

Management in business and government has recognized the growing importance of computer processing to their organizations and, over the last few years, have expressed their concerns both verbally and in a wide variety of publications. These concerns have been expressed in many forms, but generally they fall into one of the following three categories.

(i) Theft of Confidential Information. Recognizing that more and more information is being stored in computer systems, management is seeking assurance that this information is well protected and that only appropriately authorized persons have access to it.

For example, theft of proposed pay scales prior to labor negotiations could be detrimental to the process and result in increased production costs. Theft of marketing or pricing plans might result in a loss of competitive advantage. Similarly, theft of personal or financial customer information could result not only in embarrassment, but also a direct loss of business and possible litigation.

(ii) Information Integrity. Since the volume of information processed often makes it infeasible to confirm the validity or accuracy of processing results, management is seeking assurance that they can rely on the integrity of computer-generated information—that it is protected against unauthorized tampering by employees, computer viruses, "hackers," or other forms of sabotage.

For example, tampering that results in inaccurate reporting of sales figures could in turn cause inappropriate production, excessive inventory levels, and lost product sales. Unauthorized altering of the accounts payable records could result in altered mailing labels or shipping amounts, and direct financial loss.

(iii) System Availability. Recognizing the organization's dependence on the data processing service, management is seeking assurance that not only has everything been done to reduce the likelihood of disruption, but also that there are plans in place for the resumption of data processing in the unlikely event of a major catastrophe. The total or partial loss of data processing services would make it difficult, if not impossible, for most organizations to perform routine business operations.

(c)   Securing Computer Systems

An effective computer security program can help alleviate the above concerns. The design of an effective computer security program must take into account the nature of the risk and the nature and cost of the controls required to reduce exposure. This in turn requires that the following areas be addressed.

(i) Accidental Versus Deliberate Events. The events that create confidentiality, integrity, or availability problems may be accidental or deliberate in nature and the direct result of actions internal or external to the organization.

Clearly, the most likely event to occur is an internal accident such as an employee deleting an essential data file. It has been claimed that 25–35 percent of an organization's information systems budget is wasted through errors, accidents, and omissions.

The occurrence of deliberate events—theft of information, malicious damage, viruses, etc.—is much less likely than simple accidents. However, for purposes of this Handbook, the accidental versus deliberate distinction has little relevance. "Accidents" can be arranged by would-be perpetrators of fraud, and a well-designed computer security program will consider all possible events, both accidental and deliberate. The concentration of effort should be on minimizing the possibility of the most likely events occurring, while also considering less likely events, which may result in greater financial loss. To achieve the most cost-effective level of security in any organization, a combination of controls are required.

(ii) Prevention, Detection, and Recovery Controls. Obviously, the best and most appealing way to minimize the impact of an unwanted event, which will affect information confidentiality, integrity, or availability, is to prevent the event from occurring. In the case of deliberate acts, preventive controls will reduce opportunity and thereby remove temptation.

Preventive controls, however, cannot provide a 100 percent guarantee that a problem will not occur. As a result, it is usual to find complementary detective controls, which will highlight any actual or attempted security violation. As an example, software features may exist that prevent unauthorized users from gaining access to data. In such a situation it is also usual for a report to be produced that documents all attempts by users to gain access to information to which they had no right—the detective control.

In addition to preventive and detective controls, it is necessary to provide for recovery from events that can occur. Using the example of the deletion of a data file, the existence of a backup copy will constitute such a recovery control.

A well-designed security program will include elements of all three types of control: preventive, detective, and recovery. The mix of controls used will depend on the nature of the information stored on the computer, the reliance placed on the computer, and management's willingness to accept the associated risks.

(iii) Security in the Micro and Office Automation Era

[NOTE: *This section is reprinted and/or adapted from part of Chapter 5 of the* Computer Security Handbook, *a chapter entitled* Computer Crime and Computer Criminals *by G. Jack Bologna (Edited by Arthur E. Hutt, Seymour Bosworth, and Douglas B. Hoyt, Macmillan, 1988, pp. 74–75)*].

Office information today is much more than correspondence between the headquarter's sales staff and distant customers and field representatives. The automation of offices permits access to sensitive information by way of local data base, word processing equipment, on-line computer terminals, and networking services, i.e., financial, research, technological, economic, and competitive data bases.

The sensitivity of information flowing through modern office machines can be evidenced by a number of recent cases. At one Wall Street law firm, an office manager accessed information about proposed mergers and acquisitions by way of browsing on his word processing unit. He, in turn, sold such inside information to a few friends and relatives who made several million dollars trading in the securities of the about-to-be-acquired firms.

In another New York City law firm, a proofreader and a word processing operator jointly deciphered the internal office encryption code contained in the word processing system and thereby gained access to data about the firm's clients who were about to make tender offers. They passed the information to several outsiders in exchange for a share of the profits—$60,000 on one series of transactions alone.

A Michigan labor union was shocked to receive a monthly phone bill showing a balance due of $320,000, as its average phone bill was $600. "Hackers" had gotten the union's telephone credit card number from an injudicious remark and had posted the number on electronic bulletin boards all over the country.

Office employees have been apprehended while leaving the premises with all manner of confidential and proprietary data in disk, diskette, and tape form (e.g., listings of customers, clients, vendors, and employees; research and development studies; and software application packages for micros).

There was a time when a clean-desk policy offered some immunity to theft. Today, information security takes far more time than placing the contents of your in/out box in a locked file cabinet at night. Now program and file disks and backup media must be secured, that is, stored in tamper-proof, fireproof, and climatically controlled cabinets or vaults. Microcomputers, electronic typewriters, and word processors may need to be secured by time locks after working hours to protect them from unauthorized persons. Even paper waste and carbons of confidential and sensitive documents may need to be destroyed (burned or shredded) to ensure against late-night viewing by outsiders and daytime viewing by unauthorized insiders. And terminals and word processors need to be anchored in place, or they may not be available in the morning. So securing the office workplace is no longer a matter of locking doors and placing documents in file cabinets at night. Clean terminal policies are far more important than clean desk policies today. Employees must be educated and trained in security principles, policies, plans, and procedures.

The fundamental purpose of security is to minimize the risk of loss from (1) physical damage or destruction, (2) human errors and omissions, and (3) theft or unauthorized disclosure. That purpose is best fulfilled by effective loss-prevention efforts. Loss-prevention efforts involve the identification and assessment of risks to capital, human, informational, and technological assets, and the development of suitable and cost-feasible countermeasures.

(d)   Computer Security Checklist

A Computer Security Checklist, summarizing many of the issues raised in this chapter, appears on the following pages.

Buyers of this Handbook are authorized to reproduce and/or adapt the checklist for use in their own organization or practice.

The Computer Security Checklist

This checklist is designed to assist accountants in dealing with computer security in their organizations and that of their clients. Generally, all 'No' answers require investigation and follow-up, the results of which should be documented. Where there is such additional documentation, the purpose of the "Ref" column is to cross-reference the checklist to the appropriate working paper (or to the notes on the reverse).

The checklist is intended for general use only. Use of the checklist does not guarantee the adequacy of computer security, and it is not intended as a substitute for audit or similar procedures. If computer security is an especially vital concern or if computer fraud is suspected, the advice of a specialist should be sought.

Computer Security Checklist	*Yes*	*No*	*N/a*	*Ref*

1. Physical Security

   a. Are adequate fire detection and
      suppression systems in place (e.g.,
      computer room construction to a

§5.1 Computer Security—A Vital Concern

		Yes	*No*	*N/a*	*Ref*
	minimum one-hour fire resistance rating, smoke detectors, fire alarms, sprinklers)?	☐	☐	☐	—
b.	Are adequate systems in place to protect against water damage (e.g., underfloor water detectors, floor drains, waterproof equipment covers)?	☐	☐	☐	—
c.	Where power supplies are unreliable or the nature of processing is critical, are suitable precautions in place (e.g., batteries or backup generators, surge protectors)?	☐	☐	☐	—
d.	Are appropriate environmental controls in place with respect to temperature, humidity, and dust particles?	☐	☐	☐	—
e.	Is access to especially sensitive computer installations restricted, e.g., through key locks, combination or cypher locks, or card access systems?	☐	☐	☐	—
f.	Is overall computer security on the premises adequate?	☐	☐	☐	—

2. Communications Security

a.	Is a user ID and password system in place?	☐	☐	☐	—
b.	Is the ID and password system properly administered, e.g., is the distribution of new ID's controlled and are terminated users promptly deleted from the system?	☐	☐	☐	—
c.	Are users aware of the responsibility associated with their password, e.g., are they instructed to maintain password secrecy and not to choose simplistic or easily guessed passwords?	☐	☐	☐	—
d.	Are passwords changed regularly, e.g., every 30 days?	☐	☐	☐	—

	Yes	No	N/a	Ref

e. Does the system monitor and control use, e.g., by restricting users to specific terminals or specific times, automatically logging-out inactive users, limiting the number of log-on attempts, and recording all usage for later follow-up and investigation if required? ☐ ☐ ☐ ___

f. For especially sensitive systems, is security to control remote access in place, e.g., callback devices? ☐ ☐ ☐ ___

3. Data Security

a. Is access to on-line data limited to authorized persons only, through built-in software restrictions or screening? ☐ ☐ ☐ ___

b. For extremely sensitive data, has data encryption been considered as a security measure? ☐ ☐ ☐ ___

c. Are data files stored on magnetic media (including all backups) kept in a physically secure location to which only authorized persons are allowed access? ☐ ☐ ☐ ___

d. Are all printed reports subject to appropriate control, and appropriate destruction (e.g., shredding) when no longer required? ☐ ☐ ☐ ___

4. Software Integrity

a. Is access to production versions of all software tightly controlled by a production librarian or similar authorized person? ☐ ☐ ☐ ___

b. Is access to all software programming code controlled, so that tested and approved software cannot be

§5.1 Computer Security—A Vital Concern

	Yes	No	N/a	Ref
subsequently altered by programmers or others?	☐	☐	☐	___
c. Are appropriate policies in place to guard against computer viruses, such as prohibiting the installation of any copied or borrowed software, and the screening of all software with virus detection programs?	☐	☐	☐	___

5. Operations Security

	Yes	No	N/a	Ref
a. Do detailed operator instructions (e.g., manuals) exist?	☐	☐	☐	___
b. Are computer operations personnel prohibited from altering program code and the Job Control Language, which matches the program and data files to be run?	☐	☐	☐	___
c. Are all software and data storage media clearly and correctly labelled, including dates, to avoid errors?	☐	☐	☐	___
d. Are data files reconciled from run to run?	☐	☐	☐	___
e. Are all data storage media erased (wiped clean) before being disposed of?	☐	☐	☐	___
f. Is computer activity logged and any unusual operator activity investigated?	☐	☐	☐	___

6. System Recovery

	Yes	No	N/a	Ref
a. Are copies of all data files and software made on a regular basis (e.g., weekly, with daily backups of transaction files)?	☐	☐	☐	___
b. Is at least one backup copy of all data files and software stored off-site?	☐	☐	☐	___

	Yes	No	N/a	Ref
c. Has training been provided and do written instructions exist with respect to disaster recovery procedures?	☐	☐	☐	___
d. In the case of catastrophic failure, do alternative processing arrangements exist?	☐	☐	☐	___
e. Is adequate insurance in place covering computer equipment, software, recovery expenses, and business interruption?	☐	☐	☐	___

§5.2 Physical Security

Chapter 2 of this Handbook discussed the need for physical access controls, noting that they help to reduce the risk of fraud because:

- Many frauds require the perpetrator to come into physical contact with either (1) the asset being misappropriated, or (2) the related asset records, in order to cover up the fraud. Reducing physical access reduces opportunity;

- Physical access controls are often the most visible to potential perpetrators. As such, strong controls in this area send a powerful deterrent message vis-a-vis the other controls in the system. Conversely, loose physical controls invite challenge; and

- Even if the fraud is not prevented through access controls, these controls often assist in the fraud investigation process (e.g., the determination of what actually happened and the narrowing of suspects).

For the same reasons, physical security over computer installations is important in fraud prevention. It should also be noted that white-collar criminals and irate employees can resort to so-called blue-collar crimes like arson and destruction of property. When they do, even blue-collar crimes may be classified as commercial or economic in nature.

§5.2 Physical Security

(a) Introduction

Physical security is the generic term used to describe the protection of the computing facility. The controls exercised under the heading of "physical security" are typically preventive and detective in nature.

Physical security primarily addresses the availability concern and attempts to minimize the potential for system loss as a result of equipment damage. To achieve this objective, consideration must be given to each of the areas dealt with as follows.

(b) Computer Room Construction

The most concise definition of recommended computer room construction is found in the National Fire Prevention Association (NFPA) standards. In summary, to provide an appropriate level of protection, computer room perimeter walls should be constructed to a minimum of a 1-hour fire resistance rating. These walls should extend from concrete ceiling to concrete floor (slab to slab).

The purpose of this construction is to minimize the possibility of fires originating in general office areas and migrating to the computer room before they can be extinguished. The use of glass partitions to segregate the computer room from the general office environment will not usually provide sufficient protection against such a migration fire.

(c) Fire Detection and Suppression

Fire detection and suppression systems are essential in the computer room if the investment in computer equipment, and the information stored thereon, is to be protected. They are designed to detect and suppress fire before it advances to a serious state. Automated detection and suppression systems are recommended since they will reduce the dependence on manual fire-fighting techniques, which may prove unsatisfactory or late in arriving.

The most common fire suppression systems are water sprinklers and Halon 1301 gas. Water sprinkler systems may be "wet" or "dry". Wet systems contain water in the pipes at all times, while a dry pipe system does not contain water until an alarm situation occurs, at which point a valve is automatically opened to charge the system.

Fire detection systems can also provide a direct linkage to other significant support functions, such as opening fire exits, shutting off equipment and fans, and immediate notification of an alarm company or the fire department via a communications link.

(d) Water Protection

Water and electrical systems do not mix, but both are generally found in computer rooms to operate the equipment and to cool the equipment or environment. It is, therefore, important to ensure that precautions are taken to detect and remove water leakage before it contacts the electrical supply. Water protection usually involves the provision of:

- Underfloor water detectors, normally in the vicinity of the air conditioning units. Water-detection systems are usually monitored in the same manner as fire alarms;

- Floor drains to remove any water buildup. Unless specified during construction, floor drains are not usually provided in modern office towers; and

- Waterproof equipment covers. Where sprinkler systems or other above-floor water sources are present, equipment covers or rolls of plastic, which may be pulled over the equipment in the event of a problem, should be available.

(e) Electrical Power Reliability

A disruption to the electrical power supply will, unless suitable precautions are taken, result in the loss of computer service. The provision of backup power sources can be expensive, and it may not be cost justified if the computer center is located in an area where the electric power supply is reliable. If the electric power supply is unreliable, or the nature of processing critical, consideration should be given to the provision of:

- Uninterruptible power supply (UPS), which provides battery backup in the event of power failures or brownouts. The regular power supply is monitored at all times, and battery power automatically provided when required; and

- Backup generators, since UPS can only provide battery backup power for a limited time. In computer centers that provide critical processing services or in areas where electric power is unreliable, UPS systems are often supported by diesel generators that can produce electric power for an indefinite period.

Finally, regardless of the local power supply outage record, it is likely that power conditioners will be used in larger computer installations. Power conditioners monitor the electric power supply and remove voltage sags and surges.

(f) Environmental Control

Environmental control is an issue that has primarily been a concern for the larger mainframe computer environments. But even smaller machines that manufacturers claim can operate in a general office environment cannot totally ignore the environmental issues set out below.

- *Temperature control*: Computers cannot operate in extreme temperatures. It is true that the range of operating temperatures is increasing; for example the DEC VAX specifications indicate that the machine will operate in temperature ranges of 15–32 degrees Celsius (59–90 degrees Fahrenheit). However, it is not advisable to operate near either the lower or upper limits, and air conditioning is usually installed to reduce the likelihood of system outage or damage as a result of overheating;

- *Humidity control*: The computer manufacturers normally indicate a range of humidity that is acceptable for their machines. Using the DEC VAX example, the specifications indicate a 20–80 percent humidity tolerance. Humidity control is normally provided by the air conditioning unit; and

- *Environment contamination*: Dust can cause major problems in a computer environment. If dust gets into a disk pack it may cause a head crash, and result in the information on that disk being inaccessible. In addition accumulations of paper dust from printers represent a potential fire hazard. To minimize the potential for dust contamination, it is advisable that the areas where dust normally accumulates be vacuumed on a regular basis.

(g) Computer Room Access

The only employees who should require access to computer equipment are those responsible for its operation. Any third-party engineers performing maintenance should be accompanied by operations staff at all times. To provide more liberal access increases the potential for vandalism, mischief, and accidental error, any of which can result in processing disruptions.

Limiting access to the computer room involves securing the doors and keeping them closed at all times. There are a variety of devices available for achieving this, the most common being:

- *Key locks*: These are the cheapest to install, but are usually the least secure since duplicate keys can be made and distributed without control;

- *Cypher locks*: Push button combination devices. These are generally more secure, provided the combination is changed on a regular basis; and

- *Card access devices*: Probably the most secure mechanisms, in that cards cannot be readily duplicated and card distribution can be controlled.

(h) Physical Security for Microcomputers

Most of the preceding discussion relates to large computer systems. Although many of the same principles apply, some especially important measures necessary to physically secure micros are as follows.

- *Restrict physical access*: lock doors during off hours or when an office is vacant;

- Use the locks provided on some microcomputers, which prevent their use by anyone without a key; and

- Ensure that the receptionist and others watch for unauthorized personnel in areas where micros are located.

§5.3 Logical Security

(a)   Introduction

Logical security is the term used to describe the protection of information stored on a computer system. The controls involved are usually a blend of preventive and detective controls. Logical security addresses confidentiality and integrity concerns and helps to reduce the potential for inappropriate information disclosure, modification, or deletion.

Achieving an appropriate level of logical security requires consideration as to how the user gains access to information. Diagrams and flowcharts can assist in this regard. For example, Figure 5.1 depicts computer access in an IBM mainframe environment. As can be seen, in addition to the security controls for the data itself, it is necessary to consider the controls over the software that provides access to the data and to the system. To achieve this, the following issues need to be addressed.

(b)   Communications Security

Communications security focuses on controlling the various methods of access to the computer system. Of course, the primary purpose of communications security is to ensure that valid transmissions between computer systems are complete and accurate; however, such security also presents an obstacle to criminal activity.

(i) Passwords and Administration. The provision of a valid user identification (ID) and password is the first line of access control on most computer systems. The validation of the ID and password by a computer program represents the preventive part of the control, and the rejection and recording of an invalid ID or password represents the detection control. To be effective the detective aspect of password control requires the investigation of all reported access failures.

For passwords to be an effective control, procedures must also be in place to ensure that:

- Passwords are not simplistic in nature, e.g., initials, wife/husband's name or other similar personal passwords, since simplistic passwords can be readily guessed and the system compromised;

Figure 5.1

LOGICAL SECURITY

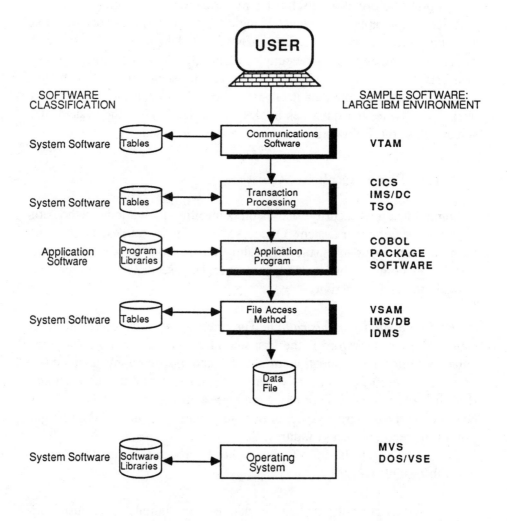

- Passwords are changed on a regular basis, say every 30–90 days, depending on the nature of the information accessed;

- New user IDs and passwords are distributed to users in a controlled manner; and

- Users who have left the organization have their IDs and passwords revoked on a timely basis.

(ii) Network Security Features. The programmed network security features that are available vary from system to system. Some of the common features include:

- Providing a maximum number of log-on attempts. If the user has not successfully logged on in the specified number of attempts, the session is terminated, and the incident recorded on a log for investigation. On some systems the user's account is locked to prohibit further attempts until action is taken by the operators or security officer function. This feature is intended to prevent unauthorized users from repeatedly attempting to gain access;

- Automatic log-out of inactive terminals. If an employee leaves a terminal logged on, anyone who gains access to that terminal has the access rights of the previous user. Password security is effectively breached. In recognition of this, many systems now provide for users to be logged out automatically if the terminal has been inactive for a defined period of time;

- Restrictions of users to specific terminals and/or specific times of the day; and

- Echo checking of transmitted information to ensure that the information is complete and accurate. This is achieved by a retransmission of the message to the source terminal for validation.

(iii) Dial-up Security. "Hackers" have received considerable publicity in recent years, having successfully gained access to numerous computer systems. In response to the problems created by hackers, several companies have developed and marketed security devices to control dial-up access. The purpose of these devices is to limit dial-up access to authorized employees.

One common device available to help control dial-up access is the callback device. When an employee dials in, the call is intercepted by the device, a special code is entered by the employee, and the device then calls back to the phone number associated with the code entered. The communication link is then established, and the user ID and password are entered in the normal way.

(c) Data Security

The provision of inappropriate access to information can result in disclosure, modification, or deletion. To achieve appropriate data security, it is important to implement a system to evaluate the sensitivity of the data, so as to provide a level of protection commensurate with the nature and perceived value of the information. Data security addresses the issue of protecting information stored on computer files, magnetic media, and hardcopy reports.

(i) "On-line" Data Files. On-line data files are the files stored on disk, which can be directly accessed by the users of a computer system. Two effective techniques are available to secure on-line data files.

- *Software restrictions*: A program, or series of programs, is used to reference established security tables to determine whether the requesting user is allowed the requested access, e.g., read or write, to the requested data file. If the request is valid, the user will be permitted access; if not, access is denied and the access violation reported on a log file for subsequent investigation. This process is illustrated by the flowchart in Figure 5.2.

  On some computer systems, the software restriction facility is an integral part of the operating system, while on others, a separate security software product which interfaces with the operating system must be used.

- *Data encryption*: This is a technique that can be used to scramble information using a predefined algorithm or key, so that it is not meaningful to anyone who gains access to the disk file. A Data Encryption Standard (DES) has been approved for use by the US National Bureau of Standards.

The use of data encryption remains relatively limited at present outside of the defense sector. Data encryption and decryption adds an additional

Figure 5.2

SECURITY SOFTWARE

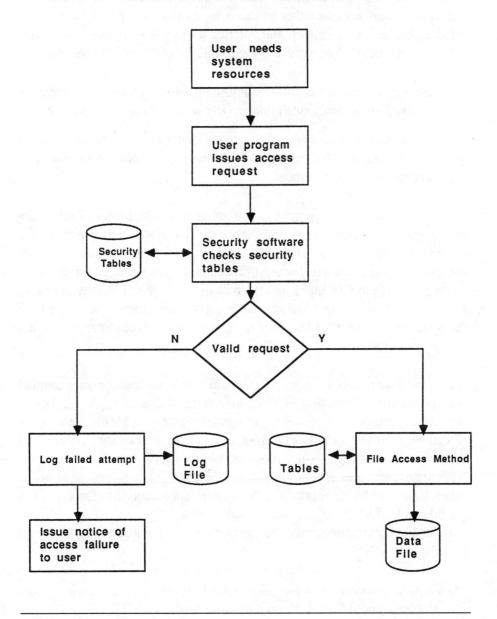

system overhead, which most users find unwarranted given the nature of their data.

(ii) "Off-line" Data Files. Off-line data files represent the information stored in libraries on magnetic tape, exchangeable disks, and diskettes. The information stored on this media is as readily susceptible to inappropriate disclosure, amendment, and deletion as on-line data files, unless it is properly controlled. The preventive controls usually applied include:

- Keeping the media library in a physically secure room where the door is locked at all times when authorized staff are not present; and

- Media library procedures that require that the files are only issued from the library for approved purposes, e.g., production use and transport to off-site storage.

The detective controls normally consist of an investigation of all media issued but not returned in a reasonable time, and the performance of a periodic inventory check. However, many smaller organizations consider the use of comprehensive library procedures impractical, given the relatively small number of tapes in use and limited staff availability. In these situations and in microenvironments, computer information (e.g. on hard disks and diskettes) should be backed up on a regular basis and stored in a secure location.

(iii) Reports and Documents. It is not difficult to become preoccupied with protecting information on computer systems and to neglect information on input forms and printed on computer reports. Generally, reliance is placed on internal controls exercised by user departments to ensure that data approved for input is not modified before it is entered into the computer. However, less concern appears to be given to securing input documents before and after input. Yet these input documents contain all of the confidential information ultimately stored on disk.

In addition, attention must be given to printed output, which should include:

- *Printing Control*: Any partially printed reports resulting from printer problems should be appropriately destroyed;

- *Distribution Control*: Ensuring that computer printed reports are distributed only to authorized recipients, particularly reports containing sensitive or confidential information;

- *Secure Storage*: Computer reports should be appropriately secured in the user department outside of regular office hours; and

- *Controlled Destruction*: All reports should be appropriately destroyed when no longer required (this applies to all offices, not just computer areas). Even when information is out-of-date, inappropriate disclosure may still prove embarrassing.

(d)   Software Integrity

The integrity of information is dependent on the integrity of the programs that produce and use it. In addition, dependence is also placed on the integrity of the communications software, transaction processors, file access software, security software, and operating system (known collectively as the system software, which controls the operation of-and may be used by-application programs). Software integrity refers to the protection of all such software, stored on magnetic media, and the migration of programs to production.

(i) "On-line" Software Libraries. Computer programs are stored on disk files in libraries or software directories. The most effective means of restricting user access to those libraries is through the use of security software restrictions, as described earlier for on-line data files (section 5.3(c)(i)), although library control software may also assist.

Programming staff require access to copies of the programs to perform their job function. They do not, however, require access to the production version. Providing programmers with direct access to the production version compromises software control and increases the possibility that unauthorized changes may be made. In general, only a deemed "production librarian" should require access to the production programs and only that person should copy new versions of programs into production, as required.

(ii) "Off-line" Software. Off-line software refers to the backup copies of program libraries or directories stored on magnetic tape, exchangeable disks, and diskettes. The controls required to secure these versions of the

software are identical to those discussed for off-line data files earlier in this chapter.

(iii) Migration of Programs to Production. If a programmer can gain access to a program and make changes between the program tests being performed by the user and the program being put into production, the version used in production may not be that which was tested and approved. Changes may be introduced, which could impact information integrity and expose the organization to financial loss. This problem can be addressed in a variety of ways including:

- Restricting access to the test version of the program to the users who are running the test and the librarian function responsible for the transfer to production; and

- Monitoring the time when the last change was made, if that information is retained by the system or library control software. The date of the last change should not be after the date when the tests were run and the software approved for use.

(e)   Computer Operations Security

The proper operation of computer programs and, therefore, the integrity of information, can also be impacted by improper operator intervention. In particular, computer operators can create problems by:

- Running the incorrect version of a program against the correct data files. This may introduce errors through the use of untested program code, or the possibility of fraud through the use of unauthorized code; and

- Running the correct version of the program against incorrect versions of data files. Obviously the results produced by this action would be incorrect and could have serious implications.

To effectively control operator activity, a number of measures can be taken. These include:

- Restricting the operator's ability to change the Job Control Language. Job Control Language directs the processing of a program, identifying the program to be run and the data files to be used;

- The use of internal tape label checking, to ensure the correct tape file has been mounted;

- The provision of detailed operations instructions, to reduce the possibility of accidental error;

- Monitoring operator intervention by reviewing the computer activity/ console logs and investigating unusual activity; and

- Reconciling data file totals from run to run, to ensure that the correct version of the file was used.

(f) Logical Security for Microcomputers

Some of the important points to note with respect to logical security for microcomputers include:

- Be wary of leaving sensitive information on hard disks. Consider using removable cartridge devices such as the Bernoulli Box;

- Use cryptic passwords, and don't leave passwords lying around next to the micro;

- Regularly back up hard disks to micro diskettes or tape; and

- When erasing a hard disk, remember that the normal Erase procedures of some operating systems may leave the file on the disk (i.e., it may only remove the file from the directory). To prevent any possible recovery of sensitive files, use the disk-wiping functions provided by special utilities programs (e.g., Norton Utilities for IBM and compatibles).

§5.4 System Recovery

(a) Introduction

The preventive and detective controls provided by physical and logical security will, if properly applied, minimize the possibility of problems occurring. However, problems do occur—either accidentally or deliberately. System recovery procedures are intended to assist in an orderly and controlled return to normal operations, should a problem occur.

Recovery controls address the availability concern. They are necessary in order to address problems expected to be short-term in nature, as well as to address more catastrophic long-term events.

(b) Recovery from Operational Failures

Operational failures are those problems which occur during the performance of day-to-day processing. Examples include:

- The use of incorrect files;
- The deletion of disk files;
- The destruction of disk files;
- Job processing failures; and
- Computer equipment failure.

Overcoming problems of this nature requires an appropriate combination of backup and written recovery procedures.

(i) Data File and Software Back-up. To protect against accidental or deliberate destruction (for example, by hackers), it is essential that copies of all data files and software libraries/directories be made on a regular basis. How often is regular? This will vary from installation to installation. In determining an appropriate backup cycle the following factors are typically considered:

- How often the file, library or directory is updated. For example, if system software libraries are rarely changed, it may be more appropriate to make backup copies only after a change has been made;
- How many transactions are processed each time the file is updated. This determines the amount of effort required to reprocess all transactions entered since the time the last available backup was taken; and
- The amount of processing time available for backup.

In the past, a backup cycle tended to be determined on an application-by-application basis. Today it is more usual to find organizations taking a weekly copy of all files and libraries and supplementing this with daily incremental backup. Incremental backup takes copies of only those files and libraries that have been updated during the day.

To assist in recovery from day-to-day operational failures, a backup copy of the data files and software should be kept on-site. A copy should also be sent off-site for use in the event of more catastrophic problems where all on-site material is either unavailable or destroyed. This area will be dealt with later in this chapter.

(ii) Recovery Procedures. In addition to the backup copies of the files and libraries, detailed written instructions are required for the operators to ensure that recovery can be efficiently and effectively achieved. These procedures, which usually form part of the computer operations manual, should address such matters as:

- Application failure recovery, procedures normally documented for each application and for each job step within the application. These describe how the operators can restore processing at an earlier point and reprocess transactions. In some cases this may not be possible, and direction should be provided on obtaining programming or technical support to resolve the problem;

- The use of utilities to recover from backup copies. The involvement of operators in recovery varies from organization to organization. In some installations the operators copy the files and libraries to a predefined recovery area on disk, and it is a user or support group's responsibility to copy them from the recovery area to the production area. Other organizations will recover directly to the production areas; and

- Obtaining vendor support for equipment failures or head crashes. All equipment failures should be documented together with details of the request for vendor assistance and the vendor's response.

(c) Disaster Recovery Plans

Disaster recovery plans are intended to aid recovery from a more catastrophic event. They are not intended to deal with day-to-day operational failures. The term *disaster* is used in the broadest sense—it need not be an act of God. As previously noted, white-collar criminals can also arrange disasters to cover up their crimes.

(i) Definition. A disaster recovery plan is a documented description of the action to be taken, the resources to be used, and the procedures to be followed before, during, and after the data processing capability is disrupted.

Given the reliance now being placed on computers in the business environment, many executives would probably find the loss of the computer center for a lengthy period inconceivable. However, the same executive's organization has likely taken no action on developing a contingency plan. A survey in the 1980s suggested that less than 50 percent of the Fortune 1,000 companies had disaster recovery plans, and of those that did only half were workable.

(ii) Elements of Effective Disaster Recovery Plans. The actions that should be taken before the disaster occurs include ensuring that off-site backup is capable of supporting recovery operations. Off-site backup copies of data files and software should be kept at a distance from the principal site, such that access to it will not be denied in the event of a disaster affecting the local geographic area. (Although it doesn't relate to fraud, the 1979 train derailment in Mississauga, Ontario provides a good example. In this case the authorities closed access to a sizeable city area for five days because of a dangerous chemical spill. Any organization whose data center and off-site storage was in that geographical area would have had difficulty invoking its recovery plan).

In addition to keeping off-site backup copies of data files and software, consideration should be given to keeping off-site supplies of other materials required for processing. Examples will include check stock, special invoice forms, forms overlays for laser printers, operations documentation, and a copy of the recovery plan.

Perhaps the most important actions to be taken before a disaster occurs are the documentation of detailed recovery procedures and regular testing. Disaster recovery operations require that information be channeled to management in order to assist in decision making during the chaos of a disaster. If the reporting channels and decision points are not clearly identified in advance, inappropriate action may be taken.

Similarly, detailed procedures should be prepared for system recovery, since operations staff may not perform standard procedures as expected when under the stress created by a disaster. Testing on a regular basis ensures that the plan is workable and helps to keep the plan up to date.

During the disaster, the staff with recovery responsibility should follow documented procedures to:

- Notify all necessary parties that a problem has occurred;
- Assess the extent of the damage and the expected period of system outage for communication to the recovery team; and
- Report to a predetermined emergency control center.

After the disaster recovery plan has been invoked, the recovery staff should follow the documented procedures for:

- Recovering the critical systems at the identified alternative processing location;
- Operating at the alternative site;
- Refurbishing or replacing the damaged site; and
- Returning to normal operations once the damaged site has been refurbished.

It should be noted that only critical systems are normally recovered at the alternative processing site. These are the application systems that must be run to ensure continued business operations. If sufficient resources exist at the alternative site to run other systems, they should not be recovered until the critical systems are running.

A schematic of an approach to developing a disaster recovery plan that will address all of these elements is set out in Figure 5.3.

(d) Insurance

For most businesses that rely heavily on computer processing, an effective disaster recovery plan is likely the only effective means of ensuring continued business survival following a major computer system disruption. However, it is possible to mitigate some of the financial loss through insurance coverage. Fidelity insurance was discussed in detail in Chapter 4 of this Handbook. For the sake of completeness, some examples of the other types of insurance coverage available are set out below:

- *Data processing equipment coverage:* To assist in defraying the cost of replacement computer hardware and air conditioning equipment. Some policies also cover the cost of removing the debris from covered equipment.

111

Figure 5.3

The Disaster Recovery Planning Process

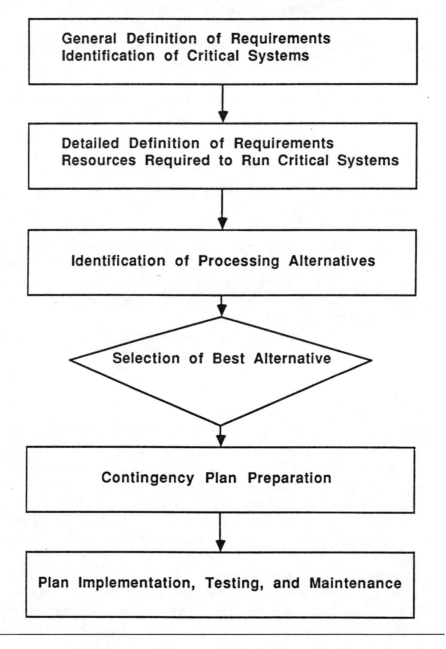

- Data, computer programs, and media coverage:

- These policies only cover data and programs in computer format, not hard copy. Insurance can be taken out to cover the estimated potential loss if data and programs are destroyed.

- Extra expense coverage:

- Covers the extra expenses involved in continuing data processing operations if the equipment, air conditioning, or building housing the equipment is damaged.

- Business interruption:

- Covers the business losses incurred following a disaster in the computer department, subject to limits on the amount to be paid per day, and a total amount payable.

(e) System Recovery for Microcomputers

Equipment failure for microcomputers is generally not as great a concern as it is for larger systems. Normally another machine is available or can be obtained with relative ease. The biggest concern is the potential loss of data that is stored on hard disk or diskettes.

A regular policy of backing up hard disks is advisable. Norton Utilities and similar programs should also be considered, because under certain conditions they enable the recovery of files that may have been accidentally erased.

§5.5 Summary

(a) Management's Responsibility

Management is responsible for providing protection for the organization's assets, including protection against dishonest employees and outside criminal acts. The information asset, administered in most organizations by the information systems or computer department, is as vital and vulnerable as any other asset. However, while many organizations have invested heavily in developing computerized systems to support their business operations, they have not yet put the appropriate effort into establishing a security program to protect that investment. Computer security is often neglected because of the pressures to deal with day-to-day operating needs first; yet security can be fundamental to business survival.

The implementation of effective security can be achieved through the identification of the:

- Information in your organization that requires protection;

- Current level of protection provided for that information; and

- Risks and exposures to which that information is currently vulnerable.

Using this approach, it is possible to achieve a level of security that is appropriate to the organization's requirements. Once the above steps have been taken, a security program can be implemented to address the exposures. This program should incorporate the development of policy, standards, guidelines, and procedures, the assignment of security responsibility, and the monitoring of progress.

(b) Policy, Standards, Guidelines, and Procedures

It is generally unwise to assume that employees will act in a security conscious manner if the organization's expectations in this regard have never been communicated to them. This can be achieved through the development and implementation of corporate policy statements on computer security. Emphasis should be placed on security and fraud awareness. To be effective, the policies must be short and succinct. If they are too detailed and lengthy, it is unlikely that they will have the desired effect (especially with junior-level employees). To achieve brevity it is usually preferable to simply cross-reference more detailed standards rather than attempt to include this material in the policy statement itself. The policy, standards, guidelines, and procedures provide a framework for effective security in any organization.

(c) The Security Function

Having recognized the importance of computer security to the organization, management must assign responsibility for this function. The person identified to take on the security function will usually be responsible for:

- Assisting in the development of policies, standards, guidelines, and procedures;
- Developing a formal security program to improve the level of security in accordance with management's expectations;
- Raising security and fraud awareness;
- Reporting on progress to senior management; and
- Liaising with specialists in case of a crisis (e.g., police, forensic accountants, specialists in computer viruses).

Depending on the size of the organization, this may be a full-time or part-time responsibility. Even in the latter case, it will probably be a full-time job to initially set up the program.

(d) Policing

Once the security program is underway and the policy, standards, guidelines, and procedures are in place, it is necessary to ensure compliance with expectations on an ongoing basis. This is a policing function.

Most organizations have an internal audit department that performs the policing function for controls that operate in other areas of the business. As such, internal audit may be an ideal candidate to become involved in testing compliance with corporate security expectations. Alternatively, external auditors or consultants can fill this role.

PART III

Prevention: Specific Types of Fraud

CHAPTER SIX

Asset Misappropriation from Within

§6.1 Introduction
    (a) Classification of Frauds
        (i)   On-Book Frauds
        (ii) Off-Book Frauds
    (b) Cycles
§6.2 Sales and Collection Cycle
    (a) Perpetration
        (i)   Theft of Cash
        (ii) Theft of Other Assets
        (iii) Kickbacks to Customers
    (b) Detection
        (i)   Theft of Cash
        (ii) Theft of Other Assets
        (iii) Kickbacks to Customers
    (c) Prevention
        (i)   Honesty Testing
        (ii) Separation of Duties
        (iii) Physical Safeguards over Assets
        (iv) Proper Documentation
        (v) Proper Approvals
        (vi) Independent Checks on Performance
§6.3 Acquisition and Payment Cycle
    (a) Operation of Cycle
    (b) Functions

(c) Financial Statement Accounts
    (i) Balance Sheet
    (ii) Income Statement
(d) Perpetration
    (i) Buyer Acting Alone
    (ii) Buyer and Vendor in Collusion
    (iii) Vendor Acting Alone
(e) Detection
(f) Prevention—Key Controls
(g) Prevention—Policies
    (i) Accepting Gifts
    (ii) Providing Gifts
    (iii) Hotlines
    (iv) Disposals
    (v) Job Rotation
    (vi) Competitive Bidding
    (vii) Compensation

§6.4 Payroll and Personnel Cycle
(a) Operation of Cycle
(b) Functions
(c) Financial Statement Accounts
    (i) Balance Sheet
    (ii) Income Statement
(d) Perpetration
(e) Detection
(f) Prevention
    (i) Proper Documentation
    (ii) Proper Approval
    (iii) Separation of Duties
    (iv) Independent Verification

§6.5 Inventory and Warehousing Cycle
(a) Operation of Cycle
(b) Functions
(c) Financial Statement Accounts
(d) Perpetration
(e) Detection
(f) Prevention

§6.6 Capital Acquisition and Repayment Cycle
(a) Operation and Functions of Cycle

    (b) Financial Statement Accounts
    (c) Perpetration
    (d) Detection
    (e) Prevention
§6.7 **Cash Misappropriation**
    (a) Perpetration
        (i)   Theft of Petty Cash
        (ii)   Theft of Bank Deposits—Common Schemes
    (b) Detection and Prevention

Fraud committed against an organization by a perpetrator from within that organization is probably the most common form of fraud. Certainly it is the most widely recognized. In this chapter:

- The first section (6.1) provides a general introduction to this topic;

- The second through sixth sections (6.2 through 6.6) describe frauds that are related to the various accounting cycles found within an organization: sales and collection, acquisition and payment, payroll and personnel, inventory and warehousing, and capital acquisition and repayment; and

- The last section (6.7) deals with cash misappropriation.

§6.1 Introduction

As difficult as it is to believe, many experts are convinced that the worst threat to business is from the people who work there. In the United States and Canada, it is estimated that at least one-third of all employees steal in some quantity. In retail organizations, only thirty percent of retail losses are from shoplifters; the remainder is stolen by employees. And in the infamous savings and loan scandal, it would take robbers 4,000 years to match what has been taken by trusted insiders and owners.

(a) Classification of Frauds

Regardless of the type of industry, internal frauds can be classified in several different ways. One way is by the type of concealment.

(i) On-Book Frauds. An on-book fraud is one that principally occurs within the business, and where an audit trail (sometimes obscure) exists that will aid in the detection. Examples include phony vendors and ghost employees. On-book frauds are normally detected at the point of payment.

(ii) Off-Book Frauds. Off-book frauds are those that occur outside the accounting environment, and where no audit trail is likely to exist. Examples include bribery and kickbacks. If an employee received a bribe for selecting a certain vendor, that payment would be made by the vendor and therefore would not be reflected in the books of the affected company. These frauds are detected in an indirect manner (other vendor complaints, lifestyle of the person receiving the bribes, etc.). If it is suspected that an employee is receiving illicit payments, this would ideally be proven by examining the employee's personal finances.

(b) Cycles

Fraud occurring within the business environment can also be classified by one of the six cycles in the accounting system. These cycles include the sales and collection cycle, the acquisition and payment cycle, the payroll and personnel cycle, the inventory and warehousing cycle, the capital acquisition and repayment cycle, and cash. Following are common frauds occurring within each cycle.

§6.2 Sales and Collection Cycle

(a) Perpetration

Frauds in the sales and collection cycle most commonly involve the theft of cash, the theft of other assets, and kickbacks to customers.

(i) Theft of Cash. By far, the most common sales cycle fraud is the theft of cash. The main schemes include not recording sales, underringing sales, lapping, theft of funds from voids and returns, overbilling and keeping the difference, simple theft of cash, writing off receivables as uncollectible, and issuing bogus credit memoranda.

For example, in one lapping fraud a cashier was able to misappropriate cash receipts totalling over $35,000 and cover the shortage by subsequent receipts. The prelisted receipts were not compared to the deposits by an independent person, allowing the fraud to go undetected over time. This scheme was eventually discovered as a result of a staff accountant following up on the clearing of deposits in transit listed on the year-end bank reconciliation.

(ii) Theft of Other Assets. These schemes include ordering and shipping company goods to the residence of the employee and ordering goods for personal use.

(iii) Kickbacks to Customers. The most common schemes for kickbacks to customers include underbilling for merchandise and splitting the difference and writing off receivables owed to the company for a fee.

(b) Detection

Generally, the detection of frauds in the sales and collection cycle can best be accomplished through the analysis of cash and/or inventory.

(i) Theft of Cash. Following are some detection methods involving the theft of cash:

- Investigate customer complaints;
- Insist that customers examine receipts;
- Use statistical sampling of sales invoices;
- Compare receipts with deposits;
- Follow up on deposits in transit at the end of each period;
- Account for consecutive sales orders and cash register transactions;
- Compare volume of credit memos by period;
- Independently verify customers who don't pay ;
- Examine gross margin by product; and
- Use computer to
    —identify missing invoices by number;
    —match shipping documents, sales invoices, and customer orders;
    —verify numerical sequence of documents;
    —analyze sales volume by employee; and
    —match daily deposits with customer credits.

For example, in one fraud case an accountant for a retail client noted a skip in the perpetual transaction count for one of the cash registers. During a 1-year period, an employee had destroyed sections of cash register tapes totalling $17,000. The irregularity was directly related to the company's failure to institute and maintain adequate internal controls and procedures over cash register tapes.

(ii) Theft of Other Assets. Detecting theft of other assets can be accomplished by the following methods:

- Resolve customer disputes;
- Conduct periodic surprise inventory counts;
- Use statistical sampling of sales invoices, examining the shipping address; and
- Use computer to:
  —match sales invoices with customer orders;
  —compare customer names and addresses with employee names and addresses; and
  —verify delivery addresses against addresses of customers.

(iii) Kickbacks to Customers. The common schemes in kickbacks to customers can usually be detected by one or a combination of the following:

- Follow up on customer disputes;
- Conduct statistical sampling of sales invoices by customer regarding prices and terms; and
- Conduct computer analysis of:
  —prices charged by product by customer;
  —credit granting approval versus actual sales to customers;
  —customer balances versus sales;
  —customer balances versus length of time doing business with the customer;
  —receivable write-offs;
  —credit memos by customers;
  —time between order and delivery; and
  —discounts by customer in descending volume of purchase.

(c) Prevention

Prevention of sales and collection frauds can be generally accomplished by adequate internal controls. More specifically, the following methods typically form part of an overall prevention strategy.

(i) Honesty Testing. The legality of using certain types of honesty testing as part of the hiring process varies from jurisdiction to jurisdiction. For example, with the advent of the U.S. Polygraph Protection Act of 1988, it is generally unlawful in the United States to require preemployment polygraphs of prospective employees. A number of companies have turned to pencil and paper honesty tests, which are touted by their designers to be accurate.

(ii) Separation of Duties. Most frauds can be prevented with proper segregation of the custody, authorization, and record keeping functions. In the case of sales and collections, it is important that the function of credit granting and sales be separated. In addition, the functions of sales, record keeping, and cash handling should be separate.

(iii) Physical Safeguards over Assets. If assets and records have physical safeguards, misappropriation is much more difficult. In the area of computers, physical safeguards such as restricted access, locks, and similar controls are especially important.

(iv) Proper Documentation. Proper documentation requires adequate records, including prenumbered checks and invoices to make fictitious entries more difficult. Documentation in sales and collections should include the following prenumbered documents:

- Sales orders;

- Shipping documents;

- Sales invoices;

- Credit memos; and

- Remittance advices.

(v) Proper Approvals. Approval should be sought and evidenced before each of the following:

- Credit granting;
- Write-offs; and
- Shipment of goods.

(vi) Independent Checks on Performance. It is not only necessary to have an independent review of employee adherence to internal controls, it is also necessary that potential perpetrators be aware that their performance is being monitored. Independent verification steps include the reconciliation of bank accounts, audits, and supervision.

§6.3 Acquisition and Payment Cycle

(a) Operation of Cycle

The acquisition and payment cycle deals with the procurement and payment of all goods and services except for payroll and capital acquisitions. Because funds flow out of the entity in this cycle, it is especially vulnerable to fraudulent transactions.

(b) Functions

The functions of the acquisition and payment cycle include:

- Processing purchase orders and dealing with vendors;
- Receiving and recording goods and services;
- Accounting for the liability of items or services purchased; and
- Processing and recording cash disbursements.

(c) Financial Statement Accounts

(i) Balance Sheet. The following balance sheet accounts are affected by the acquisition and payment cycle:

- Cash;
- Inventories;
- Prepaid expenses;
- Land;
- Buildings;
- Equipment;
- Accumulated depreciation;
- Accounts payable;
- Deferred taxes; and
- Other payables.

(ii) Income Statement. The following income statement accounts are affected by the acquisition and payment cycle:

- Cost of goods sold;
- Advertising expense;
- Travel and entertainment expense;
- Miscellaneous expenses;
- Income tax expense;
- Professional fees;
- All expense accounts; and
- Gains and losses on sales of assets.

(d) Perpetration

By far the most common fraud in the acquisition and payment cycle involves the purchasing agent (buyer), who is especially vulnerable to the temptation of accepting kickbacks and gifts in connection with outside vendors.

In one study, companies who caught employees accepting small gifts were hesitant to discharge them. Only 2 percent suspended the employee, while 12 percent fired them. Two-thirds reprimanded the employee and made them return the gift.

Acquisition and payment cycle frauds can be classified as three general types. The first is that in which the buyer/employee is acting alone, and without outside assistance. The second is where the buyer acts in collusion with the vendor, and the third is where the vendor acts alone. As is the case with other methods of prevention and detection, the collusion between both parties is the most difficult to prevent and detect.

(i) Buyer Acting Alone. Noncollusive purchasing frauds usually involve the use of a nominee entity, i.e., an apparent third party that is owned by the buyer. Examples include the use of a nominee entity to submit fictitious invoices (the most common fraud), or to order goods for personal use.

In one case, a sixty-one-year-old employee of a major department store was indicted for allegedly stealing $2 million from the company. His responsibilities included the leasing of buildings to house the retailer's stores. On 22 leases between 1972 and 1984, he, through a nominee company, altered leases to receive overpayments and forged invoices billing the company for fictitious legal and buildings services.

In another example, an executive was indicted for defrauding a large cosmetics company of $1.1 million over 4 years. During the 4 years, he allegedly approved more than 150 vendor invoices for services that were never rendered in connection with a newsletter that the company was going to publish. The executive (salary $124,000 per year) helped set up two nominee printing companies, which bilked his employer with these fraudulent invoices.

Finally, in one case the director of customer service technology was able to defraud his company of over $2 million in one year by taking advantage of defects in internal control. The fraudster set up a legitimate agreement with a legitimate vendor to provide certain equipment. Then he set up a fake distributorship and told the vendor the company would purchase only from this one distributor. The vendor was content to have the business and proceeded to invoice the distributor. The fraudster, through his nominee distributorship, then inflated the invoices and billed them to his employer. The fraud was possible because the employee had the authority to set up the agreement and to approve invoices for payment. The fraud was discovered by a manager who thought it was strange that the employee was hand-walking invoices to accounts payable.

(ii) Buyer and Vendor in Collusion. Nearly all collusion between buyer and vendor involves some form of secret commission or kickback from the vendor to the buyer. Such secret benefits are given by a vendor in order to

buy business, or are requested by the buyer for direct financial benefit. The question arises as to who took the initiative. Collusion fraud often involves more than one type of scheme perpetrated over time.

For example, one case started out involving inferior goods and later graduated to inflated invoices. A purchasing agent of a midsized municipality was responsible for acquiring a long list of janitorial supplies, including mops, pails, soap, plywood, rakes, and paper goods. Area paper jobbers—experienced connivers—approached the civil servant with a deal. "Without changing our invoice price," they told him, "if you agree, we can deliver a cheaper brand of paper towels. Half the extra is for us; the other half is for you." Once the purchasing agent accepted a lesser brand, the vendor raised the price on the invoice and billed for five times the amount of merchandise actually shipped.

In another case involving the ordering of unneeded items, three people were involved in the collusion: (1) a company's purchasing agent, who was also the receiving department supervisor; (2) the company's accounts payable clerk (who was having an affair with the purchasing agent); and (3) a process materials salesman with one of the company's vendors. The salesman proposed a fraud following a discussion regarding the volume used by the company. The purchasing agent knew that the material usage was significantly short of the standard that had been established when the plan was in a start-up mode. The salesman established an out-of-state phone number and post office box, but used a legitimate company name. He provided invoices, bills of lading, copies of freight bills, and so forth. The purchasing agent prepared receiving reports and told the receiving clerk (whom he supervised) that he received goods after hours or when the clerk was on break. The false invoices cost the company $40,000. The purchasing agent, who had been with the company 2 years, was terminated and prosecuted.

Monetary payments are not the only benefit that can be offered. Other common ways of corrupting a buyer include products or services; gifts, trips, or sex; promises of subsequent employment; reduced prices for personal items; and employment of friends or relatives.

(iii) Vendor Acting Alone. Common schemes by vendors include product substitutions, billing for work not performed or services not provided, undershipping, padding overhead charges, and courtesy billings.

(e) Detection

Because of the difficulty of detection, the practice of fraud awareness and prevention is the best policy—i.e., know your vendors, and have an effective tendering process for all contracts. Fraud in procurement contracts always poses special problems, and detection is difficult. Common red flags include sole source contracts, unhappy purchasing agents, significant price changes or changed orders (especially after a contract is awarded), and vendor complaints.

In one case detected through vendor complaints, a buyer with 6-years' seniority obtained purchase requisitions from various departments at his plant. He then created a nominee company and placed orders with it. The nominee company would then place real orders with a legitimate vendor and have them ship the merchandise to his employer. The merchandise would be billed through his company at 150 percent of the real amount. The scheme was unraveled when the buyer failed to pay one of the vendors, who then complained to his employer.

Sometimes schemes can also be detected through a computer analysis of the following:

- Timing of bids;
- Patterns of bids;
- Amount of work performed by vendors;
- Patterns of hiring new vendors; and
- Vendors with post office box addresses.

In an example involving post office box addresses, a junior buyer who had been with his company for two years created five nominee companies, and then placed these companies on the approved vendor list. Thereafter, he did business with these phony companies, placing various orders with them. The scheme was unraveled when the auditors noticed that these particular vendors all had post office boxes for addresses and were not listed in the telephone book. The amount of money lost was in excess of $250,000, over a period of more than a year.

If it is suspected that the buyer and vendor are in collusion, the following items should be considered: assessment of tender process if any, patterns of business and bids, noncompetitive pricing, inferior products, buying unnecessary goods or services, and lack of competitive bidding.

(f)   Prevention—Key Controls

As previously noted, prevention of procurement fraud can best be achieved through fraud awareness, effective tendering and budgeting, and knowledge of your vendors. Other prevention controls include proper documentation, approvals, and segregation of duties.

Proper documentation includes prenumbered purchase requisitions, purchase orders, receiving reports, and checks. Proper approvals should include detailed background information on the vendor; ideally, purchase contracts should include a right of audit access clause to the vendor's books. In addition, irregularly scheduled audits should be conducted of the purchasing function, as well as an assessment of the performance and happiness of the purchasing agent.

(g)   Prevention—Policies

(i) Accepting Gifts. Written policies should cover the acceptance of gifts and gratuities. The following is a sample statement.

"Employees, and members of their immediate families, should not accept gifts, favors or entertainment which might create or appear to create a favored position for someone doing business with the company. Advertising novelties or trinkets are not considered as gifts and are excluded from these restrictions.

Gifts that are received by an employee should be returned to the donor and may be accompanied with a copy of this policy. Perishable gifts that are received should be donated to a charitable organization and the donor notified of the action taken.

It is not the intent of this policy to preclude the acceptance by employees of the company of an occasional meal or refreshments that are provided in the normal course of business/work relationships, with other persons. Discretion must be used, however, in the limited acceptance of meals, refreshments or incidental hospitality to avoid situations which could create a conflict of interest or appear to do so."

(ii) Providing Gifts. *"Occasionally, it may be appropriate for employees, acting for the company, to provide people outside the company with promotional items, meals, refreshments, transportation, lodgings or incidental hospitality. Expenditures for such purposes should be moderate and should only be done within the framework of good taste. All such expendi-*

tures are subject to the overall company policy that an employee shall avoid constituting improper influence of others.''

Following are some additional prevention and detection suggestions.

(iii) Hotlines. Entities should study the feasibility of installing hotlines to monitor complaints by employees and other vendors.

(iv) Disposals. The purchasing department should normally not be in charge of disposing of obsolete inventory, scrap, or fixed assets.

(v) Job Rotation. Frequently rotate buyers within a department to keep them from getting too close to vendors. In addition, enforce mandatory vacations.

(vi) Competitive Bidding. Ensure that bid policies and procedures are thoroughly reviewed. Whenever possible, enforce competitive bidding.

(vii) Compensation. Buyers should be well-paid to reduce the motive and rationalization for fraud.

§6.4 Payroll and Personnel Cycle

(a) Operation of Cycle

The payroll and personnel cycle handles the hiring, firing, and payment of employees, along with timekeeping, expense accounts and travel reimbursement, and insurance matters.

(b) Functions

The functions of the payroll and personnel cycle are as follows:

- Personnel and employment;
- Timekeeping and payroll preparation;
- Payment of payroll;
- Payment of payroll taxes and other withholdings;
- Expense accounts and travel reimbursements; and

- Processing and payment of employee insurance, pension withhold-ings, and other employee benefits.

(c) Financial Statement Accounts

(i) Balance Sheet. The following balance sheet accounts are affected by the payroll and personnel cycle:

- Cash;
- Salaries payable;
- Payroll taxes payable; and
- Other withholdings payable.

(ii) Income Statement. The following income statement accounts are affected by the payroll and personnel cycle:

- Travel and entertainment;
- Salaries and commissions expense;
- Payroll tax expense; and
- Medical expenses/insurance.

(d) Perpetration

Payroll is particularly ripe for internal fraud. Common schemes include: nonexistent or ghost employees; fictitious hours and overtime abuses; over-stating expense accounts; and fictitious or overstated medical claims.

In one case, an individual responsible for payroll had control over per-sonnel documents, approval of amounts of wages, and verification of time cards. She also hired fictitious employees. She was discovered when she took time off for illness, and a replacement employee questioned the names of some employees later found to be phony. She was terminated, prosecuted, and placed on probation.

In another case, approximately one month after the payroll check date, Mr. Smith attempted to pick up his check from Ms. Doe, who was respon-sible for all departmental check distributions. Ms. Doe stated that the check was lost and that she would process the necessary data to obtain a new check. She then entered false payroll data in order to generate the check. Within a few weeks, Mr. Smith received a new check. However, upon checking his year-to-date earnings, he discovered that the "lost" check amount was included as his earned income. When confronted with the situation, Ms. Doe admitted to her supervisor that she had forged Mr. Smith's name and cashed the check for personal reasons. Ms. Doe, 43, had been with the company 7 years. She was terminated.

Expense accounts are easily and frequently abused. For example, a subsidiary president submitted requests for travel and entertainment advances with a business purpose. The chief accountant issued the checks. After $1\frac{1}{2}$ years, the president had not paid back the advances. When pressed he could not support the advances with proper business receipts. He confessed that he had none. The 45-year-old male, with 10-years' service, was terminated. The amount involved was $120,000.

(e) Detection

Ghost employees are typically discovered when payroll checks are hand delivered, and extra checks are left. In situations of proactive payroll fraud detection, significant computer and statistical analysis can be performed. For example, time card approvals, which are the same as signatures and endorsements on checks, can provide items for further investigation. Computer-generated detection methods could include:

- Payments to employees versus master lists;
- Payments to employees versus payroll authorization;
- Write-offs of employee accounts;
- Duplicate payments to employees;
- Overtime by employee;
- Password use with vacation;
- Social security numbers by descending or ascending order;
- Employees with no withholding;
- Each type of withholding in descending order;
- Salary expense in descending order;
- Hours worked in descending order;
- Time card hours versus job order;

- Hours worked by employee by pay period;

- Pay rates in descending order;

- Dates of employment with dates of payment;

- Travel reimbursement by employee overtime;

- Travel reimbursement compared to other employees;

- Travel reimbursement for specific function by employee;

- Travel reimbursements by type of expense, i.e., rental car, hotel, airfare;

- Date of travel reimbursements compared to date employee worked; and

- Numerical sequence of employee travel reimbursements.

(f) Prevention

(i) Proper Documentation. Proper documentation in the payroll area includes time cards for appropriate employees; prenumbered travel reimbursement forms and payroll checks; and verification of medical services.

(ii) Proper Approval. Proper approval would include those involving hours worked and wage rates; hiring and terminations; overtime; medical benefits; and travel allowances.

(iii) Separation of Duties. At a minimum, the following duties should be separated to reduce the possibility of one employee acting alone:

- Accounting for work and check processing;

- Processing and distributing paychecks;

- Hiring and firing from timekeeping;

- Claims processing, approval, and payment; and

- Approval and payment of travel.

(iv) Independent Verification. Independent verification is especially important in the prevention of payroll and personnel frauds, and includes the following:

- Using time clocks wherever possible, and verifying the hours worked against the clock;

- Insuring hours worked are approved by someone other than the employee; and

- Conducting surprise audits of the personnel and payment cycle.

§6.5 Inventory and Warehousing Cycle

(a) Operation of Cycle

The inventory and warehousing cycle handles functions relating to the purchase and warehousing of merchandise for manufacture and resale. Because of the volume of activity and funds involved, fraud represents a significant risk.

(b) Functions

The functions of the inventory and warehousing cycle include:

- Processing purchase requisitions;
- Receiving raw materials and finished goods;
- Storing raw materials and finished goods;
- Cost accounting;
- Processing goods for shipment; and
- Shipping finished goods.

(c) Financial Statement Accounts

Inventories on the balance sheet and cost of goods sold on the income statement are affected by the inventory and warehousing cycle.

(d) Perpetration

The more common frauds in the inventory and warehousing cycle include: ordering unneeded inventory; appropriating inventory for personal use; theft of inventory and scrap proceeds; and charging embezzlements to inventory.

For example, in one case, a dock employee and route driver were able to steal $300,000 of inventory over a 6-month period through collusion. The load sheets at the dock either were not filled out or inaccurately completed by both employees (control procedures required the dock employee and route driver to verify quantities loaded and sign a load sheet). The products were then transported to an independent distributor and subsequently sold. The defalcation surfaced when outside sources informed the company that certain products were being stolen as the result of collusion between certain employees and an independent distributor.

And in another case, a large international construction company had a remote project in the U.S. Southwest. The project was understaffed with respect to supervisory personnel, and as a result one individual ordered, received, and supervised the warehousing of a variety of materials. This longtime employee misappropriated building materials, auto parts, and other goods over a period of about 6 months. He ordered excess material, which he received and removed from the site. The project staff were all longtime employees but apparently did not question the excess inventory. During a regular audit, a relatively new employee brought the excesses to the attention of the audit department.

In a case involving a theft of inventory, an inventory records supervisor and a security guard colluded to steal $400,000 from a jewelry warehouse over a 2-year period. The security guard stole the merchandise, and the supervisor covered the theft up by manipulating inventory records. The theft was eventually discovered by an undercover investigator who was hired because of a significant increase in year-end inventory shortages. In view of this experience, it was recommended that the company perform surprise physical inventories at various times during the year.

(e) Detection

The three main ways inventory and warehousing frauds are detected include the statistical sampling of documents, computer analysis, and physical counts. Statistical sampling includes looking for inconsistencies and discrepancies in purchase requisitions, receiving reports, perpetual inventory records, raw material requisitions, shipping documents, job cost sheets, and similar documents.

A computer analysis can be conducted to include the following items:

- Purchases by item;

- Purchases by vendor;

- Inventory levels by specific types;

- Inventory shipped by address;

- Costs per item over time;

- Direct labor per inventory item;

- Direct materials per inventory item;

- Overhead per inventory item;

- Disposals followed by reorders;

- Shortages by inventory item; and

- Shipments by address.

(f) Prevention

Prevention is critically important in the case of inventory and warehousing frauds because of the amounts of money involved and the relative ease with which these frauds can be concealed. Prevention includes prenumbered and controlled requisitions, receiving reports, perpetual records, raw material requisitions, shipping documents, and job cost sheets.

Approvals should be made by someone independent of the purchase or warehousing function and should include the purchasing and disbursement of inventory.

Separation of duties becomes critical in preventing these frauds. Authorization to purchase should be handled by someone not in the warehousing function. Receipt of inventory should be handled by someone other than the person in charge of inventory.

Independent checks on performance are also important prevention measures. Physical observation of inventory should be conducted by someone independent of the purchasing or warehousing function.

Physical safeguards include insuring merchandise is physically locked and guarded, and that entry is limited to authorized personnel.

§6.6   Capital Acquisition and Repayment Cycle

(a)   Operation and Functions of Cycle

The capital acquisition and repayment cycle is used to borrow money and account for debt of the entity. Its functions include: to borrow funds and account for debt; to account for and pay interest; equity financing and accounting for stock transactions; and accounting for and paying dividends.

(b)   Financial Statement Accounts

The following balance sheet and income accounts are most often associated with the capital acquisitions and repayment cycle: cash, notes/mortgages payable; accrued interest, capital stock, capital in excess of par value, retained earnings, dividends, dividends payable, and interest expense.

(c)   Perpetration

The common schemes in this cycle include borrowing for personal use; misapplication of interest income; and theft of loan and stock proceeds.

(d)   Detection

Most frauds in the capital acquisition and repayment cycle involve tracing the proceeds of loans to ensure that all of the proceeds go to the benefit of the company. This can be accomplished by tracing loan proceeds to the bank deposits, and tracing authorization for borrowing from the minutes of the board to the loan ledgers. In addition, computer analysis can be done as follows:

- Compare addresses of interest payees;
- Match borrowings versus repayments;
- Schedule of late repayments;
- Schedule of authorization of loan proceeds;

- List of loan recipients; and
- List of addresses where loan proceeds were delivered.

(e) Prevention

Proper documentation of loan documents, journal entries, interest coupons, and stock certificates can aid in prevention of capital acquisition and repayment frauds.

Proper approvals include approval by the board of directors for borrowing, paying dividends, and refinancing of debt. Physical safeguards include keeping stock certificates and loan documents under lock and key. Independent checks should also be done on the transfer agent and registrar.

Segregation of duties is also important in prevention. The authorization to borrow should be separate from handling cash and accounting. Authorizations to issue stock should be divided from the handling of cash, and accounting should be separate from handling cash and dividends and interest.

§6.7 Cash Misappropriation

While not a cycle, cash is the focal point of most entities. All other cycles flow through the cash account. Because there are so many different ways to misappropriate cash, it is dealt with separately.

Most organizations can divide their cash into two major categories. Petty cash consists of cash on hand that is accounted for separately. It is reimbursed periodically, and the expenditures therefrom are then booked to the various accounts. Demand deposits consist of checking accounts maintained by the entity, savings or interest bearing accounts, and certificates of deposit and all other liquid investments that can be easily converted to cash.

(a) Perpetration

Below is a list of common frauds perpetrated with the cash account. It should be noted that these frauds are normally committed in conjunction with other cycles.

(i) Theft of Petty Cash. Theft of petty cash is usually accomplished by forging or preparing fictitious vouchers for reimbursement from petty cash.

As an alternative, perpetrators frequently "borrow" from the petty cash account, and fraudulently represent that the petty cash account is intact.

For example, petty cash was in the custody of the head security officer. He had altered legitimate receipts to higher amounts—primarily for postage, which is an overhead item and was loosely monitored. At a surprise count of the fund, only about $700 in currency and receipts were on hand of the $4,000 fund. Polygraph examinations were given to all security officers, but the head officer resigned before his test. A promissory note for the approximately $3,300 shortfall was executed by the terminated officer. He had been with the company for 7 years. The company estimated the loss at $12,000, but could not prove it.

(ii) Theft of Bank Deposits—Common Schemes. Receipts prepared for deposit are frequently stolen by employees. In some instances, they change the amount reflected on the deposit. In still other instances, they make no attempt to conceal the theft.

In one case, an employee in food services received daily receipts from sales along with the cash register tapes from two or three cashiers. The employee (1) ensured that the tapes were mutilated and could not be read, (2) prepared the transmittal of funds to the comptroller but kept the difference between the amount transmitted and submitted to her by the cashiers, and (3) sent the mutilated tapes to the comptroller with the deposit. The comptroller's office did not compare the deposit with the cash register tapes. The fraud was detected when one of the cashiers noted that the transmittal to the comptroller was small for a comparatively busy day. When questioned about tracing the transmittal amount to the cash register tapes, the perpetrator could not show completed tapes. The employee, who had been with the company $2\frac{1}{2}$ years, was terminated but not prosecuted.

Checks, both blank and signed, can also be stolen by employees, officers, and even outsiders. In one case involving an employee, a grandmother was the sole bookkeeper for an electrical supply company in Omaha, Nebraska. She wrote the company's checks and reconciled the bank account. Over a 5-year period she stole checks totalling $416,000, which she spent on herself and her family. In the cash receipts journal, she would code the checks as inventory; in fact, however, she wrote the checks to herself using her own true name. When the checks were returned with the bank statements, she would simply destroy them. She confessed because she had a nervous breakdown from the continuous guilt of doing something she knew was wrong.

141

(b) Detection and Prevention

Because cash can be counted exactly, most detection methods involving cash relate to its timely counting. The proof of cash is a standard audit technique that compares cash in the bank to reported cash on hand. Properly done, the proof of cash can not only account for theft, but can show overstatements or understatements by expense classification.

Timely bank reconciliations by a person not responsible for handling cash will frequently turn up discrepancies. Good reconciliation methods include examining endorsements and dates. For example, in one case a misappropriation of funds was detected through a reconciliation of bank deposits with a collection log, which was normally kept by the accounting clerk who at the time was absent on sick leave. Since the accounting clerk prepared the collection log, the daily cash report, and the bank deposits, she was able to alter individual accounts receivable records and misappropriate almost $24,000. This was accomplished by preparing daily cash reports that reflected less cash receipts collected than were actually received and depositing the lesser amount in the company's bank account. The accounting clerk processed virtually the entire accounting transaction. After the discovery of missing funds, she was terminated, prosecuted, pleaded guilty, and was sentenced to 10-years' probation. She was 25, and had been with the company 3½ years.

Cutoff bank statements are frequently used by auditors to insure expenses and income are reported in the proper period. Surprise cash counts sometimes turn up situations of employees borrowing or floating small loans. It is critical that these counts be done on an irregular basis.

Cash thefts are sometimes reported by customers who have either paid money on an account and have not received credit, or in some instances when they notice they have not been given a receipt for a purchase. As an example, a branch of a large bank received a client complaint that there had been a $9,900 forged savings withdrawal from her account. The client indicated that she had recently made a $9,900 deposit at the branch and suspected that the teller who accepted the deposit may be involved. The employee was interviewed and admitted to forging and negotiating the savings withdrawal. The teller had obtained the client's mother's maiden name and birth place, fabricated a duplicate savings receipt book, and on an unscheduled work day went to the domiciling branch and posed as the client. The employee did not have any identification, yet was persistent enough to obtain an approval on the savings withdrawal. The employee who forged the withdrawal was only 17 years old.

Computer analysis of the following categories can sometimes turn up fraud in the cash account: missing checks, checks payable to employees; void checks; comparisons of deposit dates to receivables; and listing of cash advances.

It is absolutely imperative that tight control exist over cash, and that the duties of accounting, authorization, and custody be maintained. In one case, a fraud occurred at one of several campus cashier's offices maintained by a university for the collection and processing of student tuition bills and other related charges. The perpetrator was employed as a teller for approximately 5 years before being promoted to head cashier. This position called for the reconciliation of the daily cash register receipts to the cash transmittal and bank deposits, as well as the preparation of deposits for funds received from outside departments such as the bookstore or dining service operations. These deposits involved substantial amounts of cash. As head cashier, the employee also prepared the initial accounting documents that serve as the input to the various general ledger accounts, including accounts receivable.

The perpetrator's extensive knowledge and experience, coupled with the employer's trust, resulted in diminishing supervision, particularly of the cash register reconciliations. As a result, the perpetrator was able to manipulate the documentation and the control procedures necessary to conceal the continued embezzlement of funds. The employee, who had 6 1/2 years of service, was fired and prosecuted for stealing an estimated $66,000.

CHAPTER SEVEN

Frauds Perpetrated by Outsiders

§7.1 **Introduction**
§7.2 **Frauds By/Against Individuals and Small Businesses**
    (a) Finance-Related Frauds
        (i)   Credit Frauds
        (ii)   Bankruptcy Frauds
        (iii) Security Frauds
        (iv) Debt Consolidation Schemes
    (b) Property Improvement Schemes
        (i)   Product Substitutions
        (ii)   False Labor or Overhead Charges
        (iii) Absconding with Retainers and Down Payments
    (c) Land Frauds
    (d) Chain Referral Schemes
    (e) Merchandise Swindles
    (f) Coupon Redemption Frauds
    (g) Directory Advertising Schemes
    (h) Charity and Religious Frauds
    (i) Personal Improvement Frauds
        (i)   Diploma Mills
        (ii)   Correspondence Schools
        (iii) Modeling Schools
        (iv) Vanity and Song Publishing Schemes
§7.3 **Frauds Against the Government**
    (a) Income Tax Frauds

(b) Benefit Programs
(c) Contracts
    (i) Bid Rigging
    (ii) Inflated Costs
    (iii) Product Substitutions

§7.4 Frauds Against Insurance Companies
(a) Definitions
    (i) Insurance Fraud
    (ii) Grand Larceny (Theft)
    (iii) Offering a False Instrument for Filing
(b) Life Insurance Frauds
    (i) Homicide; Staged Death
    (ii) Double Indemnity
(c) Casualty Insurance Frauds
    (i) Staged Accidents
    (ii) Legitimate Accidents with False Claims
    (iii) Fraudulent Billings
(d) Property Insurance Frauds
    (i) A False Theft Is Staged
    (ii) Household Goods Are Repossessed
    (iii) Personal Property Is Pawned
    (iv) Arson
(e) Health Insurance Frauds
    (i) Mobile Labs
    (ii) Bundling and Unbundling Claims
    (iii) Collusion Between an Insured and a Provider
(f) Personal Injury Insurance Frauds
    (i) A Non-Job-Related Injury Is Reported
    (ii) A Fake Job-Related Injury Is Reported
(g) Mortgage Insurance Frauds

§7.5 Frauds Against Banks
(a) Introduction
    (i) Definition of Bank
    (ii) Legal Aspects of Bank Fraud
(b) Loan Fraud
    (i) Loans to Nonexistent Borrowers
    (ii) False Applications with False Credit Information
    (iii) Single-Family Housing Loan Fraud
    (iv) Borrower Misapplication of Funds

     (v) Linked Financing
(c) Commercial Real Estate Fraud
     (i) False Appraisals
     (ii) Land Flips
     (iii) Nominee Loans
     (iv) Double Pledging Collateral
     (v) Detection of Commercial Real Estate Fraud
(d) Bank Bribery
(e) Check Frauds
     (i)   Check Kiting
     (ii) Forged, Altered, and Stolen Checks
     (iii) New Account Frauds
(f) Money Transfer Fraud
(g) Advance Fee Fraud
(h) Money Laundering

§7.1 Introduction

In the realm of commercial frauds, there are essentially three types: those committed by the organization itself (organizational frauds or commercial crime as defined in Chapter 9 of this Handbook); those committed within the organization (internal frauds, dealt with in chapter 6 of this Handbook); and those committed by individuals outside the organization (external frauds). This chapter deals with the latter category; specifically, with frauds committed against individuals and small business (7.2), government (7.3), insurance companies (7.4), and banks (7.5). (The glossary also provides definitions for various external frauds.)

External frauds, depending on the circumstances and especially for certain industries, can be extremely costly. For example, some policyholders of insurance companies commit wholesale fraud by inflating the cost of auto and home accidents, and claiming reimbursement for property that does not exist. And the reason fraudsters loot financial institutions mirrors that of the infamous American bank robber Willie Sutton: "Why do I rob banks? Because that is where the money is, stupid!"

§7.2 Frauds By/Against Individuals and Small Businesses

It is not possible to determine the number of persons and bogus business operators engaged in crimes against other individuals and small businesses. Suffice it to say that the problem is extensive; by some estimates, nearly everyone at one time or another has been either the perpetrator or victim of such a crime. Some of the more common frauds falling into this category are listed below.

(a) Finance-Related Frauds

(i) Credit Frauds. Credit frauds can be generally divided into two types. In some instances, credit information from one individual is used to obtain credit for use by another. For example, John R. Smith, with bad credit, obtains the credit information of John Q. Smith, and applies for a credit card under the name of John Q. Smith, using John R. Smith's address. Charges are then made on the account. When John Q. Smith protests, the credit company attempts to locate the real user of the credit, John R. Smith, who has since absconded.

The other common credit fraud involves individuals who apply for credit, but who have no intention of paying the bill when it comes due. After the bill arrives, the fraudster refuses to pay, typically by denying receipt of the merchandise. The resulting bad credit rating is not an issue because of the high value of the merchandise: jewels, furs, and other items not easily found and repossessed.

(ii) Bankruptcy Frauds. Bankruptcy is designed to give every person encumbered by mountains of debt another chance. All assets and liabilities are listed on the bankruptcy petition, and a receiver or trustee is appointed by the courts to distribute the remaining assets of the bankrupt to the creditors, in a predetermined manner. Creditors secured by hard assets (automobiles, residences, and other items) generally receive priority in payment.

Two common frauds are committed by individuals filing bankruptcy: conversion of assets in contemplation of bankruptcy, and concealing assets. In the first category, the individual realizes he or she is going to file for bankruptcy. Before the bankruptcy petition is filed, the individual sells assets for cash and then spends or hides the money. In the second category, after the bankruptcy petition is filed, the bankrupt does not disclose all of the assets to the receiver/trustee or bankruptcy judge.

(iii) Security Frauds. Security frauds can involve a variety of schemes, but normally these frauds are committed in one of three ways:

- False or misleading information in financial statements of the traded business enterprise;

- Brokers and dealers selling and purchasing stocks and securities without the knowledge of their clients in order to generate commissions, which is known as "churning"; and

- Manipulation of the stock's price through the purchase or sale of large blocks of stock.

(iv) Debt Consolidation Schemes. People who find themselves hopelessly in debt frequently turn to debt consolidation agencies out of desperation. Debt consolidation agencies do not advance loans, but rather act as an intermediary between the debtor and creditor. Some are legitimate; many are not. Debt consolidation agencies make legitimate income by organizing the debtor's affairs and collecting a percentage of the money handled for the debtor.

In the typical scenario, the debtor contacts the agency, who gets a complete list of the creditors of the debtor and the amount of monthly payments currently owed. Then the agency usually writes letters to the creditors, requesting a debt workout plan at a lower monthly payment spread out over a longer period of time. The creditors are often motivated to accept the arrangement if they feel (1) the entire debt, or the major portion of it will be repaid promptly at a lower payment; or (2) the debt consolidation plan will forestall bankruptcy or default by the debtor.

Unscrupulous debt consolidation schemes are perpetrated when the agency collects money from the debtor and does not forward it to the creditor. In some instances, it is months before the debtor finds out the money has been misappropriated. The debtor is then faced with the specter of losing money to the agency and still owing the debt.

(b) Property Improvement Schemes

"Fly by night" operators promising repairs to property at bargain rates are a particular problem with elderly victims. The typical fraudster is a professional con artist who obtains business primarily from door-to-door solicitation. His tools of the trade are not hammers and saws, but bogus business cards and counterfeited or preprinted contracts involving up front money. The scheme is often one of the following variations.

(i) Product Substitutions. A typical example of this fraud is when a property owner requests or is charged for a particular product or brand, but the contractor substitutes an off-brand for an inflated price and keeps the difference.

(ii) False Labor or Overhead Charges. Many contracts call for labor or overhead charges at cost, and the contractor's profit is a percentage of that cost. Obviously the more the repairs cost, the more the contractor makes. By fraudulently inflating such cost through bogus labor charges or overbilling of materials, the fraudster not only increases the profit, but can also keep the difference between the actual and inflated costs. Inflated overhead—as well as the product substitutions described in the last section—are also the two most favored methods used by government contractors to defraud taxpayers.

(iii) Absconding with Retainers and Down Payments. The most preferred method by seasoned professionals is simply to negotiate money in advance, then disappear. This is essentially an advance fee swindle perpetrated specifically in the property improvement or repair market. The advantage of this method is that it obviously is the least capital intensive for the fraudster: no storefront, props, or other accoutrements are required; just "get the money and run."

(c) Land Frauds

In the United States during the 1960s and 1970s, overpriced land was sold by mail order to thousands of unsuspecting consumers. Typically, the potential buyer was interested in purchasing a lot to build a retirement home. To exploit this market demand, many crooked land dealers would purchase huge quantities of raw land in remote areas of retirement states: Florida, California, Arizona, and Colorado. Then they would create exotic sounding names—Pleasant Valley, for example—for their land stakes.

Typically, the raw land would be heavily advertised for sale on very easy terms: a small or token down payment followed by low monthly payments. Purchasers would frequently sign contracts for the land without ever seeing it. Later, when they discovered that they had purchased sagebrush, they would default on the purchase, and the crooked land dealer would often resell the land to some other unsuspecting victim.

A special type of land fraud has come into play involving borrowers in the savings and loan debacle: the "land flip." In this scheme, the same piece of property is sold back and forth by the borrower between dummy or shell corporations. Each time the land is sold, the price is inflated. To support each sale, the borrower secures an appraisal based on an unrealistic or favorable set of assumptions, or obtains one through a friendly, incompetent, or dishonest appraiser. Then the borrower goes to a financial institution and mortgages the property for its "appraised" value, keeping the grossly inflated loan proceeds.

(d) Chain Referral Schemes

Chain referral schemes are based on the same idea as the well-known "chain letter." Most people are familiar with the chain letter; its premise is to mail money to, say, 5 people. They in turn mail money to 5 other people, who in turn mail to 5 more. By the time the chain reaches the seventh or eighth level, the multiplier effect creates enormous wealth to those higher up in the chain, because they are receiving money from the lower levels.

Of course, things other than money can be the object of chain letters. Some involve recipes, Christmas cards, and other harmless items. As most people know, however, chain letters don't work. That is because someone in the lower level inevitably fails to mail out his or her 5 letters, and the chain is then broken; only those in the upper levels typically profit.

Chain referral schemes, also called *pyramids* or *Ponzi Schemes* (after the notorious Charles Ponzi who successfully employed the scheme in the early twentieth century) are based largely on the same principal. The difference is that some are legitimate and some are not. For example, many products sold exclusively in the home, such as Amway merchandise, can be legitimate forms of pyramids. Individuals are recruited to sell merchandise. They in turn recruit their friends and colleagues to sell, and get a cut of their commissions. This recruitment continues on down, with those in the upper levels receiving a portion of the commissions from several different layers of sales personnel. However, because of the turnover in sales personnel, most people fail to achieve a sufficient level in the chain or pyramid to make the touted commissions. They often get discouraged and quit, further depressing the chain.

Illegal pyramids exist as well. One example is a variation of an investment fraud. A company will open its doors as an investment firm, promising better than average return on investment. When they receive money from investors A through G, the money is diverted to the use of the principals. When additional money is received from investors H through L, those funds are used to pay off investors A through G. When funds are received from investors M through Z, this money is used to pay off investors H through L, or at least to pay interest, and so on.

Such a scheme, or variations of it, can go on indefinitely, as long as investments continue to grow at a rate to cover the diverted funds. When the investments fall below that level, there is insufficient cash to pay off old investors, and the scheme collapses. The chain referral schemes are not dependent on a particular product or service, but rather on the method of diverting funds. Common chain investment schemes include franchising, sales distributorships, investment and securities of various kinds, and merchandise.

Another common variation is for fraudsters to place mail order ads promising wealth for "stuffing envelopes." The victim responds to the ad, sending in money. In return, he or she receives a letter suggesting the victim place a similar ad and collect money in the same way, using the same letter. In other words, the fraudsters are telling the victims in effect, "do the same thing to others that we just did to you."

Many operators simply set up a mail or telephone operation, collect funds, then close the operation and move, only to reestablish a similar operation and repeat the scheme. Law enforcement officials acknowledge a significant problem with chain referral schemes, but readily admit that they are incapable of adequately controlling the problem.

Finally, it should be noted that many chain referral schemes involve small amounts of money that are taken from many victims. Because victims typically feel foolish about being fleeced, they frequently do not file charges. And even when complaints are made, the police do not give these crimes priority because of staffing and budgetary commitments. As a result, many chain referral operators stay around a long time.

(e) Merchandise Swindles

Merchandising frauds run the gamut of frauds perpetrated against purchasers of merchandise and services. If you have ever paid for an item and received something less than advertised, you have been the victim of a merchandising swindle.

Some perpetrators of merchandising frauds include door-to-door salesmen selling overpriced merchandise such as freezers of meat, encyclopedias, and similar items. The fraud is not perpetrated by the sale, but rather by the misrepresentation made; i.e., the purchaser is paying wholesale rather than retail prices.

These frauds are generally in the following categories: (1) representations that the purchase is at a bargain when in fact it is not; (2) collecting money for one product and substituting another of lesser quality or cost; (3) misrepresentation of the selling price; or (4) failure to deliver the product or service.

(f)   Coupon Redemption Frauds

Coupon redemption frauds involve the fraudulent collection and conversion of coupons designed to promote various kinds of merchandise. For example, a coupon for a box of cereal from the newspaper may require the purchaser to present it at the supermarket and receive 25 cents off on the purchase of the cereal. Normally, the manufacturer pays the supermarket a token fee, perhaps several cents, to process the coupon and return it to the manufacturer. Unscrupulous grocery and supermarket owners will collect coupons, in some cases from an intermediary, and redeem them as though merchandise has been purchased from them when in fact it has not. Although the individual amounts can be small, the volume in most consumables can make it profitable for stores to engage in these schemes.

(g)   Directory Advertising Schemes

Directory advertising schemes are usually perpetrated against businesses. The essence of the scheme is for the fraudster to sell advertising in a nonexistent magazine or directory, and abscond with the proceeds. Many directory advertising schemes are perpetrated out of storefront operations. A fake (or in some instances, real) directory is presented to the potential victim. The victim contracts for the display or classified advertising, which will appear some months hence. By that time, the fraudster has collected the funds and disappeared.

(h)   Charity and Religious Frauds

Jim Bakker, former head of the defunct PTL, has brought international attention to religious frauds. The essence of his scheme was to sell "lifetime partnerships" in a luxury hotel, which his followers could use for life. Prosecutors were able to show that Bakker's plan was completely unworkable, because many more partnerships were sold than could ever be accommodated. Bakker used the money to pay himself and his lieutenants millions of dollars in salaries and bonuses. He was convicted under federal mail fraud statutes, and sentenced to 45 years in prison (the sentence, but not the conviction, was subsequently overturned).

Other types of charity and religious groups resort to fraud as a way of obtaining "contributions." In the most common of the schemes, fraudsters operating in boiler rooms call unsuspecting victims and raise funds for allegedly good causes or for worthwhile organizations. The funds collected are not used for their intended purpose, or the fraudsters fail to disclose that they keep the majority of the funds raised for "administration" and give the sponsoring charity or religion only a token portion of the money collected.

(i)   Personal Improvement Frauds

Personal improvement frauds is a term used for many variations of schemes that prey on the natural tendency of people to want to improve their education, job skills, or position in life. Fraudsters in this category use primarily mail order as an integral part of the scheme. Some common forms of personal improvement frauds are set forth below.

(i) Diploma Mills. For a fee—usually a hefty one—a "diploma" can be granted to those persons who apply. The fraudsters usually claim the heavy fee is for processing the application, or for verifying the existence of the experience necessary to be granted a degree. The hallmark of a diploma mill is the ease with which the "degree" is obtained, and the related cost thereto. Victims usually apply for an advanced degree to enhance their career skills; however, diploma mills do not achieve accreditation, and their diplomas are therefore essentially worthless.

(ii) Correspondence Schools. Correspondence schools offering advanced education do exist. However, there are also many such schools with the

same modus operandi as diploma mills, providing substandard education at superior prices. They are generally not accredited, and they offer little hope of job advancement.

(iii) Modeling Schools. Modeling schools appeal to the natural vanity of some people. In the typical scheme, the modeling school tells the student that he or she must have a portfolio of portraits to send to potential customers, ostensibly to enhance the possibility of the victim getting modeling assignments. The victim is then charged greatly inflated prices for a photographer to take the pictures for the portfolio. Many modeling schools that are not legitimate tout connections to famous people, or they claim that they have placed famous people, when in fact they have not. These schools get most of their business through mail order or newspaper advertising. Once a particular area is fleeced, the "school" pulls up stakes and moves on.

(iv) Vanity and Song Publishing Schemes. Vanity and song publishing schemes are common, and rely on the victim believing that he or she has talent in a particular area, such as art or song writing. These schemes are normally advertised in magazines or by direct mail. They usually offer to evaluate, for free, the talent of the victim. Of course, the victim is told after the evaluation that he or she is the newest undiscovered artistic genius. And for a hefty fee, the talent company will promote the artist's work. The artist then remits the fee, and the fraudsters use the funds for their own benefit, providing little or no services in the process.

§7.3 Frauds Against the Government

Fraud against the government is a general term for several kinds of schemes perpetrated against federal, state/provincial, and local governments or government agencies. Typically, government is defrauded by one of the following schemes.

(a) Income Tax Frauds

According to some estimates, most taxpayers either (1) fail to disclose all their income, or (2) take deductions to which they are not entitled. The most common income tax frauds involve categories of individuals who receive their compensation in cash: waiters, bellhops, prostitutes, and drug dealers.

(b)   Benefit Programs

In addition to income tax fraud, many other types of fraud against the government are perpetrated. These frauds generally involve making false statements of various kinds in order to obtain funds. Targets include welfare, unemployment, and social security benefits, as well as student loan and housing programs. Often, there can be rings of fraudsters making application for government benefits, resulting in very high losses.

(c)   Contracts

Government and government agencies are particularly vulnerable to fraud in contracts. In many instances, the product or service required by the government is not available on the open market, and there is therefore little or no basis for price comparisons. Frauds in contracts generally are of the following types.

(i) Bid Rigging. Bid-rigging is the process of setting the price or terms of the contract between the various bidders without the knowledge or consent of the affected agency. For example, bidders on highway construction may secretly meet before bids are opened. During their meeting, they decide who will submit the low bid and what the bid should be. They may also decide who will bid on what jobs. This is known as *bid rotation*.

Bid rigging is usually characterized by the lack of a number of competitive bids or by prices that are too close together. In addition, they are obviously characterized by higher prices than could be obtained on the open market.

(ii) Inflated Costs. It is common for the government to contract on a cost-plus basis. That is, the contractor is paid the actual cost of the job, plus a certain profit based on a percentage of the costs. Clearly, the successful bidder has a vested interest in keeping the costs high: the more the cost, the more the profit.

Commonly, in order to obtain the maximum profit, the contractor falsifies the cost of the product or service. This can be done through simple or complex means. Examples of the former include adding bogus labor or material charges. In the more sophisticated schemes, the costs are inflated through overhead allocations.

(iii) Product Substitutions. Government contracts sometimes call for very exacting specifications on the materials used on the job. Contractors frequently believe the specifications are too rigid and that they are therefore justified in substituting a lesser product or service, and keeping the difference.

In one scheme, a contractor bid on a new runway for the airport authority and won the bid. The contract called for the depth of the concrete covering the runway to be a certain minimum. After hearing rumors from competitors that the contractor was pouring less concrete than the minimum, the auditors checked the work orders and discovered that the paperwork reflected the concrete depth to hundredths of an inch. The auditor reasoned that concrete could not be poured so exactly, checked the actual work, and found the depth to be less than the contract specified.

§7.4 Frauds Against Insurance Companies

(a) Definitions

(i) Insurance Fraud. The definition of insurance fraud may vary from jurisdiction to jurisdiction. A typical definition would be:

Any person, who knowingly and with intent to defraud presents, causes to be presented, or prepares with knowledge or belief that it will be presented to or by an insurer or purported insurer, or any agent thereof, any written statement as a part of, or in support of, an application for the issuance of, or the rating of an insurance policy for commercial insurance, or a claim of payment or other benefit pursuant to an insurance policy for commercial or personal insurance which he knows to (1) contain materially false information concerning any fact material thereto; or (2) conceal, for the purpose of misleading, information concerning any fact material thereto.

(ii) Grand Larceny (Theft). Insurance fraud may also fall under this crime category. In the United States for example, a person is guilty of grand larceny/theft when he or she steals property valued over a certain dollar value. This amount varies from state to state and may to be divided into degrees by dollar value.

157

(iii) Offering a False Instrument for Filing. An insurance fraudster may also be guilty of this crime in some jurisdictions; for example, when he or she knowingly files a false statement or files false information with the intent to defraud the state/province or any subdivision thereof, or presents it to a public servant with the knowledge that it will be filed with, registered or recorded in, or otherwise become a part of the records of such public office or public servant.

(b) Life Insurance Frauds

Life insurance is a policy that covers someone's life. In the event of the policy owner's death, the insurer pays the insured's beneficiary a predetermined amount of money. Following are the most common schemes.

(i) Homicide; Staged Death. A beneficiary of a life insurance policy may commit homicide to collect benefits, or an insured might fake his own death. A variation of the staged death fraud is where a policy is taken out on an insured who is already dead.

(ii) Double Indemnity. In some cases, a beneficiary of a life insurance policy will report the death as having been accidental in order to obtain twice the face value of the policy. A variation of this scheme occurs when a beneficiary attempts to make a suicide appear to have been accidental.

(c) Casualty Insurance Frauds

Casualty insurance is a policy that covers personal injuries one may sustain as the result of an accident. While accidents can occur anywhere and at any time, a large number of casualty claims involve injuries sustained in traffic accidents. Following are the common casualty insurance frauds.

(i) Staged Accidents. As an example, an individual will purposely pull out in front of an oncoming vehicle or will allow themselves to be rear-ended in order to cause a collision. A fraudulent claim is then made for insurance benefits.

(ii) Legitimate Accidents With False Claims. In many cases, an individual is involved in a legitimate accident and later exaggerates their personal

injuries (usually soft-tissue injuries) in order to bilk an insurance company for money.

(iii) Fraudulent Billings.   An example of this type of fraud would be where an insured seeks the cooperation of a scrap yard that has the capability to crush autos. The insured has his auto crushed and files a theft claim. If the auto is not recovered within a reasonable span of time, a claim is paid. The insured then pays the scrap yard for destroying the vehicle and not reporting the destruction to the Department of Motor Vehicles.

Another example is when an insured's auto is brought into a body shop for repair after a legitimate accident. The body shop inflates the claim, typically to cover the deductible. The body shop then overbills the claim and gives a cash bribe to the claims adjustor or does additional damage to the car to maximize the profit.

In still another variation, a wrecked vehicle is located and insured. A bogus accident is concocted and a fraudulent claim is filed. Using the same vehicle, this scheme is often repeated with different insurance companies.

(d)   Property Insurance Frauds

Property insurance is a policy that covers someone's property from loss (whether stolen or destroyed), up to a predetermined amount of money. Following are some of the most common property insurance schemes.

(i) A False Theft Is Staged.   In this scheme, an insured secrets property he or she owns and reports it stolen, or alternatively reports property stolen, which was never owned.

(ii) Household Goods Are Repossessed.   An example of this fraud is where household items (furniture, appliances, etc.) are repossessed, and the insured reports the property stolen in order to replace them.

(iii) Personal Property Is Pawned.   A fraudster may inflate the value of his or her personal belongings, insure them, pawn them for a lesser amount of cash, report them stolen, file a claim, recover the items with the insurance payment, and pocket the difference. These schemes can be risky to the perpetrator, however, because in most jurisdictions pawn shops are required to check customer identification and keep records of their transactions, in order to facilitate police investigations of reported thefts.

(iv) Arson. Arson is the purposeful destruction of property by fires, sometimes for profit. For example, an insured may be about to lose his or her house, car, or business due to an inability to make loan payments. The insured may set a fire to obtain capital to refinance the item, also saving his or her credit rating in the process. Alternatively, an insured may replace an item with something less expensive when he or she remodels after the fire.

(e) Health Insurance Frauds

Health insurance is a policy that covers someone's health in the event that the person is injured or becomes ill. Following are some common health insurance schemes.

(i) Mobile Labs. As an illustration of this scheme, a group of people set up a lab in a storefront located in a blue-collar, low-income area, where English is the second language. They then pass out fliers in the parking lot of a minimum wage manufacturing firm, offering free physicals to people who have medical insurance. After filling out a family history, the insured is subjected to extensive tests for a variety of maladies, and the average physical ends up costing the insurer $3,000–$4,000. When the insured returns for the results of the tests, the labs are gone.

(ii) Bundling and Unbundling Claims. In one case, an insured woman has a hysterectomy performed. While she is on the operating table, the physician also removes her appendix. When the bill comes in, she is charged $3,000 for an appendectomy.

(iii) Collusion Between an Insured and a Provider. In this type of collusion, the provider furnishes the insured with a bill for services not rendered. The insured makes an application for reimbursement to the insurance company, and the proceeds are divided between the insured and the provider.

(f) Personal Injury Insurance Frauds

Personal injury insurance is a policy that covers physical injuries someone may sustain while on the job. Following are common personal injury schemes.

(i) A Non-Job-Related Injury Is Reported. As an illustration, an insured is injured in a car accident at home and reports it as a job-related injury.

(ii) A Fake Job-Related Injury Is Reported. In this scheme, an insured pretends to sustain a job-related injury, in order to collect Worker's Compensation benefits while he or she stays home.

(g) Mortgage Insurance Frauds

Mortgage insurance is a policy that guarantees mortgage payments to the lender if the purchaser of the property defaults on those payments. In one common scheme, a mortgage company recommends the sale of a mortgage to an insurance company, fully suspecting that the home buyer will default on payments. For example, in times of slow property sales, an employee of a mortgage company (who earns a commission for every loan that is funded) and a real estate agent (who is also paid a commission on sales) conspire to sell inflated property to individuals who would not normally qualify for such a purchase. Both agents receive handsome commissions on the sale and the home buyer gets the dream house he or she always wanted, but could never before afford. The mortgage insurer ends up footing the bill once the purchaser defaults.

§7.5 Frauds Against Banks

(a) Introduction

(i) Definition of Bank

A bank may be defined as any organization engaged in any or all of the various functions of: receiving, collecting, transferring, paying, lending, investing, dealing, exchanging, and servicing (safe deposit, custodianship, agency, trusteeship) money and claims to money, both domestically and internationally. Under the broadest concept, the term *bank* may be applied to such institutions as cooperatives, export-import banks, investment bankers, and mortgage bankers.

(ii) Legal Aspects of Bank Fraud. Financial institutions in most jurisdictions are insured by an agency of the government and are governed by related criminal statutes. For example, in the United States the broadest of

all federal statutes is Title 18, U.S. Code, Section 1344. It covers all assets owned or controlled by a bank, as well as employees and outsiders. It prohibits any action that would defraud the financial institution, such as embezzlement, misapplication, false statements, and related fraudulent behavior.

Fraud committed externally against a financial institution can take many forms. The most common offenses are loan frauds and new account frauds, as well as various check schemes. These and other frauds against banks are described in the following sections.

(b) Loan Fraud

Borrowers sometimes provide false information to a lending institution in order to obtain funds to continue business activity, or simply to fraudulently get money that they have no intention of repaying. Some of the most common schemes include the following.

(i) Loans to Nonexistent Borrowers. In this fraud, the borrower uses a false identity to obtain a loan. This scheme can be carried out individually by the borrower or with the assistance of an insider, such as a loan officer. The fraud can often be detected by one or more of the following warning signs:

- No CA or CPA associated with the financial statements;
- Unrealistic inventory or other property valuations;
- Unusual loan terms requested;
- Application information does not check out;
- Loan officer's bonus is based on volume;
- No public credit report available;
- Borrower is unknown to bank personnel;
- Property collateral is outside market area; and
- Proceeds are distributed prior to loan closing.

(ii) False Applications with False Credit Information. False information on the credit application can include overstated assets, understated or omitted liabilities, or other necessary credit information such as appraisals. For example, a borrower with marginal net worth might inflate the asset and

income figures on his or her financial statements to convince the loan officer of the credit worthiness of the application. These schemes can often be detected by one of the following methods:

- Appraisals/valuations defy common sense and local knowledge;
- Appraisers are paid on basis of appraisal amount;
- Large loans beyond experience and expertise of the loan officer;
- Borrower defaults on first payment;
- Numerous payment extensions, or placed on nonaccrual status;
- No audit trail verifying application information; and
- Applicant reports loans from many other banks.

(iii) Single-Family Housing Loan Fraud. One variation of the loan fraud is the borrower who purchases single-family housing units, ostensibly for personal use but in reality as rental property or in some instances for resale. A misrepresentation is usually made to the financial institution on the borrowers' ability to finance the property and make payments. These frauds are usually detected by the following methods:

- Unrealistic change in commuting distance;
- High-income borrower has little or no personal property;
- New housing expense is 150 percent or more of previous expense;
- Bank deposits listed at round amounts on application;
- Borrower reports overlapping dates of current and prior employment;
- Prior employer listed as out of business;
- High-income borrower does not use a professional tax preparer;
- Appraisal shows a tenant as contact person on an owner-occupied house;
- Initial title report shows delinquent taxes; and
- Homeowner insurance policy names someone other than the borrower.

(iv) Borrower Misapplication of Funds. Borrower misapplication is most common when the borrower has little or no personal risk in the collateral, for example, real estate. The highest-risk real estate loans are those in

which the lender provides all the funding on a nonrecourse basis. The more common ways borrowers misapply funds are as follows:

- Kickbacks or profit interests in construction activities;
- Brokerage or real estate fees;
- Property management fees;
- Related party vendors;
- Settlement sheet prorations of rent, taxes, and other items;
- Land flips;
- Sale of property rights, such as laundry or cable TV;
- Misappropriation of operating proceeds or loan proceeds; and
- Misappropriation of escrow payments.

(v) Linked Financing. In some cases, large deposits (usually brokered deposits) may be offered to a bank on the condition that it make particular loans to persons affiliated with the deposit broker. High returns are promised, but the loans are longer term than the deposits (often "hot" money). Sometimes kickbacks are paid to the broker or banker.

(c) Commercial Real Estate Fraud

Commercial real estate fraud is essentially a specialized form of loan fraud. Financial institutions, especially the savings and loan associations in the United States, have been rife with fraud committed in the commercial real estate area. These schemes are often perpetrated in connection with the insiders of the financial institutions. Usually, the schemes take one or more of the following forms.

(i) False Appraisals. False and inflated appraisals have been used to support loans larger than the value of the property. Appraisers have been parties to the fraud, were paid off, or were merely unqualified—fooled by bogus transactions like land flips.

(ii) Land Flips. A land flip is the practice of buying and selling a parcel very quickly, often in a single day or month, at a successively higher price to related parties, until a lender (who believes the buyer is arm's length) takes everyone out with an unrealistically inflated loan amount.

(iii) Nominee Loans. Nominee loans are those made in the name of a straw borrower or agent—i.e., one having no substance—while the identity of the real borrower is undisclosed to the lender.

(iv) Double Pledging Collateral. This scheme involves fraudulently pledging the same collateral with different lenders, before the related liens are recorded and registered.

(v) Detection of Commercial Real Estate Fraud. Commercial real estate fraud can often be detected through one of the following warning signs:

- Multiple loans to the same borrower;
- Same appraiser on different properties;
- Successive appraisals at high values in short period;
- Property bought/sold many times in short period;
- Borrower is a shell or holding company whose substance lies in numerous subsidiaries;
- Buyer obviously shopping for a loan instead of a long-term banking relationship;
- Seller of property is another bank;
- Borrower has prior default history;
- Borrower has history of loan pay-offs by obtaining other, larger loans;
- Loan application requests several loans to different persons on same property; and
- Deposit broker requires the loan as condition of delivering large deposits (i.e., linked financing).

(d) Bank Bribery

Statutes (e.g., Title 18, U.S. Code, Section 201) prohibit any officer, director, employee, agent, or attorney of a bank from knowingly soliciting or receiving things of value in connection with transactions of a bank. In the usual scheme, an officer is offered an inducement by a borrower to grant a loan that would not otherwise be made. These schemes can be detected by one of the following methods:

- Bank officer's lifestyle is beyond the means provided by normal compensation;

- High productivity by the bank officer;

- Compensation is based on volume productivity;

- Loan agreements contain terms favorable to the borrower;

- Pattern of disbursements to particular agents, brokers, appraisers, finders, etc.;

- Multiple loans to same borrower with same agents involved; and

- Bank officer has financial interest in customer's project, or stockholdings in bank subsidiary profiting from the business.

(e)   Check Frauds

Check fraud is a general term for the attempted negotiation of bad checks at a financial institution. Frauds can range from a new account customer attempting to make a false deposit, to check kiting. Con artists prey on banks in attempts to negotiate fraudulent or fictitious instruments. The range of schemes are described below.

(i) Check Kiting. Check kiting is a term for building up large apparent balances in one or more bank accounts, based on uncollected or floated checks drawn against similar accounts in other banks. Although many individuals engage to some degree in kiting, the usual scheme is perpetrated by a commercial customer using several bank accounts to increase available cash reserves. One of the most significant kites in the United States was committed by the brokerage firm of E.F. Hutton. They engaged in a $20 million kiting scheme to decrease the cost of their funds during the late 1980s. The resultant bad publicity eventually led to the company's demise. A simple kite can be illustrated as follows.

In commercial bank accounts established over a period of time to avoid suspicion, a fraudster starts with little or no money in Bank A and Bank B, and writes $5,000 in checks on each for deposit in the other:

	Bank A	Bank B	Total
Apparent Balances	$5,000	$5,000	$10,000
Actual Balances	-0-	-0-	-0-

The process is quickly repeated (e.g., the next day) with $8,000 in checks:

	Bank A	Bank B	Total
Apparent Balances	$13,000	$13,000	$26,000
Actual Balances	-0-	-0-	-0-

A $6,000 down payment is made on a Mercedes from Bank A:

	Bank A	Bank B	Total
Apparent Balances	$7,000	$13,000	$20,000
Actual Balances	($6,000)	-0-	($6,000)

After the first day's checks clear, more are written, this time for $9,000 each:

	Bank A	Bank B	Total
Apparent Balances	$11,000	$17,000	$28,000
Actual Balances	($6,000)	-0-	($6,000)

The balances are paid to a travel agent, and the fraudster takes a long trip:

	Bank A	Bank B	Total
Apparent Balances	-0-	-0-	-0-
Actual Balances	($17,000)	($17,000)	($34,000)

Check kiting is usually detected by one of the following methods:

- Frequent deposits and checks in same amounts;
- Frequent deposits and checks in round amounts;
- Frequent deposits with checks written on the same (other) bank;
- Little time lag between deposits and withdrawals;
- Frequent ATM account balance inquiries;

- Many large deposits made on Thursday or Friday to take advantage of the weekend;

- Large periodic balances in individual accounts with no apparent business explanation;

- Low average balance compared to high level of deposits;

- Many checks made payable to other banks;

- Bank willingness to pay against uncollected funds (note that not all payments against uncollected funds are check kites, but all check kites require payments against uncollected funds);

- Cash withdrawals with deposit checks drawn on another bank; and

- Checks drawn on foreign banks with lax banking laws and regulations.

(ii) Forged, Altered, and Stolen Checks. Many rings, led by drug dealers and underworld figures, are engaged in defrauding banks through (1) checks prepared with forged names of makers, endorsers, or payees; (2) altered checks to raise amounts; and (3) counterfeiting of checks and stolen checks passed by others. These schemes can be detected by:

- Obvious written alterations on checks;

- Illegible maker, endorser, officer signatures;

- Checks with maximum amount, void, or nonnegotiable imprinting;

- Unprofessional printing; and

- Business checks presented for cash instead of deposit.

(iii) New Account Frauds. Check fraud is much more likely to occur in new accounts than in established accounts. Special efforts must be taken to properly identify the potential new customer, without offending customers. Screening criteria must be established and enforced by everyone handling new accounts. Prompt, decisive action must be taken to manage and/or close apparent problem accounts.

Most new account fraud is perpetrated by the use of false identification [e.g., birth certificates; passports; duplicate social security numbers; voter registration cards; stolen credit cards; stolen driver's license; stolen paycheck; front (shell) businesses; student identification card; and disguised identities (post office box mail address, lock box rental, mail forwarding, telephone answering service, and rented office space)].

New account criminals are professionals. They use false identification to open new accounts and steal money before the funds are collected by the bank. New account fraud is normally detected by one of the following methods:

- Well-defined procedures for increasing employee's awareness of new account frauds;

- Specific guidance about acceptable identification and its reporting;

- Customer resident outside bank's trade area;

- Rush to open account/obtain loan;

- Dress and/or actions inappropriate for the customer's stated age, occupation or income level; and

- Requirement for detailed verification of customer's information:
  —previous checking account history (internal and external investigation);
  —credit reports and credit scoring systems;
  —Dun & Bradstreet;
  —Better Business Bureau;
  —special requests for no mail; and
  —post office box or hotel address.

(f) Money Transfer Fraud

Wires totaling two to three times a bank's assets may be processed every business day. It is rare that they do not equal a bank's total assets, and they can sometimes be ten times the assets for banks that have a large correspondent network. The process is highly automated at most banks.

In the most common money transfer fraud, funds are stolen by an outsider or bank employee who has access to the correct identification numbers needed in order to wire transfer funds. In one case in Chicago, a bank insider with knowledge of the wire transfer codes and procedures conspired with his friends to wire nearly $70 million out of the country. The scheme was detected (early enough to avoid a loss to the bank) when the transfer was made from a customer's account, thereby overdrawing the account balance.

Warning signs for this type of fraud include:

- Actual processing is done by clerks rather than more senior personnel;
- Frequent overrides by managerial personnel of established approval authority;
- Wires to and from bank secrecy countries;
- High volume, high dollar amounts are routine;
- Frequent wires for persons with no account at the bank;
- Access to wire room is often not properly restricted; and
- Employees become very comfortable with routine of job and their co-workers.

Variations of these schemes involve the misrepresentation of the identity of the customer. The fraudster will use pretext telephone calls to obtain correct account information from the bank. Then the codes are obtained from an insider. Thereafter, the funds are transferred out of the bank with a telephone call.

(g) Advance Fee Fraud

In a fraud related to linked financing described earlier in this chapter, banks are sometimes the victim of phony brokers offering to deposit large amounts of money in the bank at lower than market rates. The catch is that the bank must pay an up-front finders fee to a person who claims to have access to the money. Once the fee is paid, the person disappears. In some cases, desperate institutions are offered access to illegal money, and they typically do not report the loss of the advance fee when the deal falls through. These schemes are normally detected by one of the following methods:

- Deals too good to be true often are not true;
- Agent requests documents on bank stationery, and/or signatures of officers;
- Bank is asked to give nondisclosure agreements to protect the agent or other parties;

- Agent asks for an irrevocable agreement to pay a fee, commissions, and expenses;

- There are several complex layers of agents, brokers, and other middlemen; and

- Foreign agents, banks, and sources are involved in the deal—often an unnamed wealthy person or government.

(h)   Money Laundering

Money laundering is a means of concealing the existence, source, or use of illicit money by disguising it to make it appear legal and thereby avoid detection. Examples of illicit sources include:

- Narcotics trade;

- Corporate bribes and kickbacks;

- Illegal political contributions;

- Bribes to public officials;

- Loansharking;

- Prostitution; and

- Illegal gambling.

The most common method of laundering money is to open a legitimate front business that handles a great deal of cash—a casino, restaurant, parking lot, vending machine company, or pawn shop—and then deposit the ill-gotten gain along with the legitimate income of the business. The "cleaned" money is then withdrawn or wire transferred to a final destination. These schemes are usually detected by one of the following methods:

- Accounts accumulate deposits, which are subsequently transferred out;

- Large cash shipments;

- Large volume of wire transfers to and from offshore banks; and

- Large volume of cash deposits from a business not known before for such deposits.

A variation of the money laundering scheme is to use couriers, called *smurfs,* to make smaller deposits and withdrawals. For example, cash deposits in excess of $10,000 must be reported to the Internal Revenue Service on a special form called a Currency Transaction Report (CTR). In order to avoid the reporting mechanism, smurfs will make smaller deposits or withdrawals. These schemes are usually detected by:

- Withdrawals made in numerous transactions under $10,000;
- Noncustomers exchanging large amounts of small bills for large denomination bills;
- Inquiries as to policies of the bank regarding reporting currency transactions;
- Large dollar volume of cashier's checks and money orders sold for cash to noncustomers;
- Large volume of wire transfers to and from offshore banks; and
- Persons shown as unemployed and self-employed on CTR form.

In still another variation, the money launderer conspires with a bank insider, who agrees to make deposits for the money launderer and forego the reporting mechanisms. The bank gets free use of the deposited funds, or in some instances, the bank officer is compromised through a bribe or kickback. These schemes are usually detected as follows:

- An account has many different individuals making deposits, and only a few making large withdrawals;
- Accounts accumulate deposits and subsequently transfer them out;
- Large cash shipments;
- Large volume of wire transfers to and from offshore banks;
- High dollar limits and large numbers of bank customers exempted from CTR requirements; and
- Incorrect or incomplete CTRs.

CHAPTER EIGHT

Computer Crime and Computer Criminals

§8.1 **Introduction**

§8.2 **History and Evolution of Computer-Related Crime**

§8.3 **Nature and Extent of Computer-Related Crime**
  (a) Computer-Related Crime Typology
    (i) Input Tampering
    (ii) Throughput Tampering
    (iii) Output Tampering
  (b) The Most Common Computer-Related Crimes
  (c) The Trend in Computer-Related Crime

§8.4 **The Computer Criminal**
  (a) Typical Profile
  (b) Dispelling Myths
  (c) The "MOMM's" Concept
  (d) Personal Motivations
    (i) Economic Motives
    (ii) Egocentric Motives
    (iii) Ideological Motives
    (iv) Psychotic Motives
  (e) Environmental Motivations

§8.5 **The Control Environment: Key to Prevention**
  (a) Factors That Encourage Computer Crime
    (i) Motivational Environment
    (ii) Personal and Personnel Inducements
  (b) Factors That Discourage Computer Crime

       (i)   Prevention Measures
       (ii) Detection Measures
    (c) Security Countermeasures to Computer Crime
       (i)   Computer and Terminal Access Controls
       (ii) Data Communications Controls
    (d) Suggested Improvements to Prevent Computer Crime

§8.6 Some Selected Computer Crimes
    (a) A State University's Hospital
    (b) A Manufacturer of Magnetic Peripherals
    (c) A Top Oil Company
    (d) A Netherlands Bank
    (e) An Insurance Company
    (f) A University in Michigan
    (g) A Transportation Authority
    (h) A Diversified Corporation
    (i) California Welfare Department
    (j) Australia Betting Agency

§8.7 Some Final Thoughts

    "The computer hasn't really changed anything—it's just a replacement for the tools and techniques we've always used. Yesterday, it was a pen and paper; today, it's a keyboard and spreadsheet."—Overheard in a Large Accounting Firm

On the surface, the above statement might appear to be a reasonable one. However, it was made in a rather wishful and self-serving context by a partner who had very little computer knowledge, virtually no keyboard skills, and who, although reluctant to admit it, was uneasy about the advance of technology and the impact it might have on his career. Would younger staff, the future partners in the firm, pass him by? Would he become obsolete if he remained, relatively speaking, a computer illiterate? Such questions can raise our anxiety level and cause ulcers. It would be better to think of the computer as a glorified pencil, making this whole technology business seem a lot less threatening.

Of course, the evolution from pencil to computer was actually much more than a simple step up. It was a quantum leap. And just as the new technology has had a profound impact on society generally, and the business world in particular, so too has it changed the ways in which fraud and commercial crime are perpetrated. Although there are very few genuinely new frauds, the computer has dramatically changed the environment in which fraud is committed. In the same way that computer security deserves a separate chapter in this Handbook, even though it is a subset of internal control, computer crime also merits separate coverage.

This chapter covers the subject of computer crime and computer criminals as follows:

- The first and second sections provide a general introduction to the topic (8.1) and some historical background (8.2);

- The third section (8.3) describes the nature and extent of computer-related crime;

- The fourth section (8.4) deals with computer criminals;

- The fifth section (8.5) describes some of the control considerations that affect the risk of computer crime; and

- Finally, the last two sections present some brief case studies (8.6) and a summary (8.7).

§8.1 Introduction

[NOTE: *Much of the material in this chapter is reprinted and/or adapted from Chapter 5 of the* Computer Security Handbook, *a chapter entitled* Computer Crime and Computer Criminals *by G. Jack Bologna (Edited by Arthur E. Hutt, Seymour Bosworth, and Douglas B. Hoyt, Macmillan, 1988, pp. 58–75)*].

A computer-related crime may be defined as one in which a computer is used to commit a crime or as a crime in which a computer itself is the target. The usual crimes committed using computers include embezzlement, larceny (theft of property and proprietary information), fraud, forgery, and counterfeiting. Crimes committed against computers include sabotage, vandalism, electronic burglary, wire-tapping, and gaining illegal access, either by impersonating an authorized user, or by exceeding one's authority.

Computer crime is generally considered to be a white-collar crime when it involves an internal theft, fraud, or embezzlement by an employee or official of an organization.

Computer-related crime can be viewed as a phenomenon brought about by advances in information processing technologies. Before computers, there was no computer crime. But before computers there was crime—of both the white- and blue-collar variety. There were also crimes of violence against people and crimes against property. The computer did not usher in a new wave of crime; it merely changed the form of older crimes. Embezzlers could now steal by making electronic entries in magnetic books of account, rather than by pen and ink or in paper ledgers.

Computer-related crime today is mainly an occupational crime committed by people with requisite skills and knowledge. Yet, in addition to skills and knowledge, a computer criminal must also have access to a computing system. Access can be gained more easily by organizational insiders (employees) than by outsiders (intruders, hackers). Therefore, insiders represent a greater potential computer crime threat than do outsiders, despite the opinions of mass media commentators, who often suggest the opposite.

We might, therefore, conclude that computer-related crime is a phenomenon that involves knowledgeable people with criminal predispositions. Still the idea that certain people are born crime-prone is the subject of much controversy. Behavioral scientists suggest that cultural and environmental conditioning are equally significant factors in understanding crime.

The phenomenon of computer-related crime may be viewed from a number of perspectives:

- The incidence rate of computer-related crime and its longer term trend;

- The individual criminal and his motivations;

- The environmental factors that impact on the range of potential behavior patterns;

- The organizational cultures that minimize the probability of such crimes; and

- Security countermeasures to computer-related crime.

These and other perspectives are dealt with in the material that follows.

§8.2 History and Evolution of Computer-Related Crime

Electronic computers were first introduced for commercial use in the United States in the mid-1950s. Prior to that time, the few computers that existed were used for governmental purposes, i.e., for the tabulation of the national census, for military applications, and for scientific research.

Until 1958, no systematic tracking nor tabulation of computer-related crime existed. In 1958, Stanford Research International (SRI) began tracking publicly reported incidents of computer "abuses," some of which were criminal and others that involved the breach of civil laws such as the copyright and patent acts. SRI grouped these incidents into four categories.

- Vandalism against computers;
- Information or property theft;
- Financial fraud or theft; and
- Unauthorized use or sale of computer services.

Throughout the 1960s and 1970s, the number of such incidents never exceeded 100 per year. It was apparent that the number of publicly reported incidents bore no demonstrable relationship to the total number of incidents, and so SRI discontinued tabulating such abuses after 1978.

The real explosion in computer-related crime took place just after that time, with the introduction of the Apple II and, most significantly, the IBM microcomputer in 1981. Manual systems became less and less common throughout the 1980s, and by the 1990s even the smallest businesses had access to computing power that only the largest companies enjoyed during the 1960s and 1970s. Since virtually all organizations now operate in a computer environment, it is not surprising that many of yesterday's "manual" frauds are—at least in some sense—the computer-related frauds of today.

§8.3   Nature and Extent of Computer-Related Crime

Crimes such as embezzlement and employee thefts of funds were not unheard of before computers. Accountants attempted to discourage such crimes by requiring a separation of duties between persons handling cash or other assets and those making entries in the books of account. Accessibility to assets and accountability for the recording of transactions concerning such assets were thereby divided on the theory that forcing persons to conspire to commit a theft of assets would reduce the likelihood of theft.

An additional control measure relied upon by accountants was called the *paper trail*, or *audit trail*. In essence, that control measure required that all business transactions be entered into journals and be supported by source documents, such as vendor invoices, purchase orders, receiving reports, canceled checks, disbursement vouchers, sales receipts, and customer invoices.

Despite these control measures, employee theft, fraud, and embezzlement were still possible. Accounting systems were not designed to be foolproof or fraud proof. A determined criminal could still find ways to circumvent or override controls.

Computers have not changed the human disposition. Fraud, theft, and embezzlement are still possible in the computer era. It has been argued that such crimes are even more likely now because the classic accounting controls have been diluted. Paper audit trails have often been replaced by electronic audit trails, which are not as easily verified by traditional audit methods. Speed of processing has taken precedence over effective controls, or so it is claimed. Some traditionalists, therefore, recommend more intensive internal auditing for firms with computerized accounting systems, as an added measure of protection.

Despite auditors' concerns over the adequacy of internal controls in the computer era of accounting, there is little reliable data to support the claim that crime by computer (mainly employee theft, fraud, and embezzlement) is more prevalent than before computers. Individual losses from such crimes do appear much higher now, but the incident rate may not be higher than before. However, the risk or threat of loss is greater, particularly if the frequency and severity are considered as well as the new opportunities for misbehavior.

New opportunities for employee fraud, theft, and embezzlement have been created by computer technology itself. A whole cadre of new employees can now access accounting systems. Not only are such systems accessible by the so-called user community, i.e., employee and management personnel, who have a need for accounting information, but are also accessible to computer analysts, programmers, operators, and data entry clerks. In essence, computers have made financial information more easily accessible to more people for more purposes. With proper skills and criminal inclination, even outsiders can access the information and thereby manipulate or compromise the assets that lie behind the information.

§8.3 Nature and Extent of Computer-Related Crime

(a) Computer-Related Crime Typology

Computer-related crimes, and more specifically those crimes in which a computer has been used as a means or instrument to commit or abet a crime, can be grouped into three categories, which parallel the three stages of data processing: input tampering, throughput tampering, and output tampering.

(i) Input Tampering. An input type crime involves the entry of false or fraudulent data into a computer. Examples include data that have been altered, forged, or counterfeited—raised, lowered, destroyed, intentionally omitted, or fabricated. Thus, input tampering is euphemistically called *data diddling*.

While there are many reasons for entering spurious information into a computer, the main reasons are to overstate revenue and assets and to understate expenses and liabilities. These forms of manipulation of data input are sometimes directed by managers to deceive superiors, shareholders, and creditors. At lower levels, spurious data may be entered to commit a special fraud against the company as, for example, when an accounts payable clerk adds a phony vendor's name to the vendor master file, then submits invoices from that vendor to embezzle funds.

Input scams are probably the most common computer-related crime and yet the easiest to prevent with effective supervision and controls, such as separation of duties, audit trails, control totals, and access controls (authorization limits, terminal access controls). Internal controls are dealt with in greater detail in Chapters 2 and 5 of this book (*Managing the Risk of Fraud, Computer Security and System Recovery*).

(ii) Throughput Tampering. Throughput scams, accomplished by altering computer instructions, require a knowledge of programming. A typical example would be modifying a computer program so as to credit all fractional pennies arising from interest calculations to the perpetrator's account. Based upon publicly reported cases, there are far fewer incidents of throughput scams than of input scams.

(iii) Output Tampering. Output scams, such as the electronic theft of important information (customer mailing lists, R&D results, long-range plans, employee lists, secret formulas), seem to be increasing in this era of intense competition, particularly among high-technology manufacturers.

Such theft is much easier than it used to be before the advent of the micro-computer, because information can simply be copied onto a disk or stolen over data communication lines.

(b)   The Most Common Computer-Related Crimes

Among the publicly reported cases of computer crime, most have been of the input and output types. However, since throughput crimes are more difficult to detect, it cannot be said that their number is exceeded by the other two types. It is simply not known. Furthermore, throughput crimes may not be reported for other reasons. Proof is often quite complex, and admitting the occurrence may be an embarrassment to top management. These types of crimes have a greater probability of going undetected and, even if detected, are rarely brought to the attention of police or prosecutorial authorities. When reported, such crimes may be mismanaged by the authorities. Few police detectives know how to investigate com-puter crimes and few prosecuting attorneys know much about presenting such cases. They often recommend a case be handled by the civil courts rather than the criminal courts.

While computer hacking (electronic break-ins of computers by teenage pranksters) has received most of the recent media attention, the more seri-ous and most prevalent computer crime has been the fraudulent disburse-ment of funds, which is generally preceded by the submission of a spurious claim such as a:

- Vendor, supplier, or contractor invoice;
- Governmental benefit claim;
- Fringe benefit claim;
- Refund or credit claim;
- Payroll claim; or
- Expense claim.

Although such phony claims can involve anyone from data entry clerks to the company president, they most often involve an employee in the accounts payable, payroll, or the benefits section. They can either act alone or in collusion with an insider or outsider—depending on how tight the internal controls are. From an accountant's perspective, the claim is a fake debit to an expense, so that a corresponding credit can be posted to the cash account for the issuance of a cheque. Auditors assert such disbursement frauds represent more than half of all frauds by lower-level employees.

At higher levels of management the typical fraud involves the overstatement of profits by the fabrication of data such as sales, which are increased arbitrarily or by artifice (sales are booked before the sales transaction is completed), and the understatement of expenses, which are improperly reduced or disguised as deferrals to the next accounting period. There are numerous variations on these two main themes—overstatement of sales and understatement of expenses. One of the more common ploys to overstate profits is to increase the ending inventory of manufactured goods or merchandise held for sale. That ploy results in understating the cost of goods sold, thereby increasing the net profit.

The incentives to overstate profits are many and varied. Very often it is just a case of trying to meet or exceed "the plan." At other times, it is brought about by the executive compensation system. If bonus awards depend on profits, executives have an economic incentive to "fudge the numbers." They may also be tempted to do so if they own a great deal of company stock, whose value depends on investor perceptions of profitability. If profits are down, investors are not happy and may rush to sell, thus causing a lowering of the stock's price and depressing the value of the executive's own stock.

Manipulations of the above type often require the joining of both line executives and personnel in accounting and data processing capacities. The Equity Funding case—involving mass collusion in the setting up of phony insurance policies to inflate revenues and assets—is an example. Such conspiracies are becoming a recurring theme in business. The pressure on executives for high performance grows with each passing year. It is, therefore, likely that there will be more of such frauds in the future.

(c)   The Trend in Computer-Related Crime

As noted previously in this chapter, reliable statistics on the incidence of computer-related crime are hard to come by because the number of publicly reported incidents bear little or no relationship to the actual number. However, other sources do offer some insight. For example, in the late 1980s, the National Center for Computer Crime Data [1222 17th Ave., Suite B, Santa Cruz, CA, 95062, (408) 475-4457] conducted a study based largely on a survey of prosecutors and computer security professionals throughout the United States. Through extrapolation, the Center estimated that computer crime in the United States cost victims over $550 million in 1988.

In an earlier survey of 40 personnel directors during the early 1980s, the respondents ranked computer crime as number 6 for its frequency and seriousness.[1]

A sample group of personnel directors can hardly be called representative of the mass public, but they do tend to be more knowledgeable about such matters in industry. A ranking of the then-current prevalence of white-collar crime, as perceived by the survey respondents, appears in the following table.

Then-Current Rank	Crime Type
1.	Bribing political leaders
2.	Padding the bill on government contracts
3.	Employee theft, fraud, and embezzlement
4.	Polluting the environment
5.	Pilfering small tools and supplies
6.	Computer-related crimes
7.	Bribing union leaders
8.	Expense account padding
9.	Corporate income tax evasion
10.	Stock frauds and manipulations
11.	Falsifying time and attendance reports

Of course, it should be noted that in addition to computer-related crime being identified as sixth in the rankings, a number of other crimes on the list would today commonly require the use of computers—e.g., those ranked #3, 8, 10, and 11.

In the same survey, 67 percent of the respondents believed computer crime would rise in the future—in fact, they ranked computer crime as number one in terms of its future frequency. Their assessment no doubt took into consideration the fact that many more computers would be used in the future and that many more people would understand the technology and thus be able to compromise computer systems. In terms of the percep-

---

[1] Jack Bologna, *"Computer Crime: Wave of the Future,"* *Assets Protection Journal,* 1981, pp. 47–49.

tion of future white-collar crimes that were expected to occur with greater frequency, the rank ordering is set out in the table below.

One reason for the upward trend in computer-related crime is that—at least during the late 1970s and early 1980s—making computers more secure against tampering was not a paramount consideration in designing new computers. Security tended to be an afterthought, because it slowed down the speed of processing, required more memory capacity, and made operations more complicated and expensive.

Then-Expected Future Rank	Crime Type	Then-Current Rank
1.	Computer-related crimes	6
2.	Bribing political leaders	1
3.	Expense account padding	8
4.	Bribing union leaders	7
5.	Employee theft, fraud, and embezzlement	3
6.	Falsifying productivity reports	25
7.	Padding the bill on government contracts	2
8.	Corporate income tax evasion	9
9.	Bribing foreign officials (tie)	21
10.	Stock frauds and manipulations	10
11.	Polluting the environment (tie)	4

§8.4 The Computer Criminal

White-collar criminologists like Cressy and Sutherland suggest that white-collar criminals tend to be trusted employees of long tenure with unresolvable personal problems, usually of a financial nature, such as indebtedness for sickness in the family, or because of gambling, alcoholism, expensive tastes, or sexual pursuits. In police vernacular, these precedent conditions of dishonesty are usually referred to as the three Bs, "booze, babes and bets." However, it may be equally true that new employees have the same potential for surprising their employers with criminal acts.

Because of the relatively brief history of computer crime, it has yet to be demonstrated that computer criminals meet the above criteria; however, there is no reason to believe they do not.

(a) Typical Profile

The typical computer thief, as often described in the literature of computer crime in the United States, is or can be:

- Male; white; young, 19–30 years old;

- Has no previous criminal record;

- Identifies with his own technology far more than with his employer's business;

- Is employed in the data processing or accounting field;

- Is bright, creative, and energetic; outwardly self-confident and willing to accept challenge; adventurous; and highly motivated;

- Feels desperate because of economic problems resulting from high living, expensive tastes, family sickness, gambling, or drug or alcohol abuse;

- Feels exploited by his employer and wants to get even;

- Does not intend to hurt people; just a cold, indifferent, impersonal, and exploitative employer; and

- Sees self as a "borrower," not a thief.

Other motives ascribed to modern-day embezzlers, as reported in the media and in law enforcement and security journals, include:

- Resentment, brought on by being passed over for promotion; pay inequities, such as unequal pay for equal work, no distinction in pay for longevity, and bonuses paid on the basis of unfair performance criteria;

- Financial pressures, brought about by girlfriends, boyfriends with expensive tastes, or by gambling debts;

- Deceiving the "establishment" is fair game because the establishment is deceiving everyone else; and

- The challenge—beating the system is fun. The motive need not be economic. Perpetrators sometimes commit their crimes to prove how smart they are and how easily controls can be compromised by a dedicated and knowledgeable intruder.

In addition, there are symptoms that may indicate crimes in progress. These include:

- *High living:* beware of the programmer who shows up at the plant gate with a new Rolls Royce. If suspicions are aroused in more subtle ways, background checks can be used to determine if an employee is living beyond his or her means (e.g., a credit report, or checking title on an employee's house to see the size of the debt and any debt that was retired);

- *Super dedication:* beware of the bookkeeper or teller who has not had a vacation for 10 years;

- *The aging process:* beware of those employees, male and female, going through divorce or sporting young girlfriends or boyfriends; and

- *Chronic lateness:* beware of the employee who is always late with reports. They may be taking longer because they have to fabricate, cover up, or counterfeit the information.

The motives and symptoms are generalizations and cannot be applied with certainty to any specific instance. In fact, there is a lot more not known about computer crime and computer criminals than is known. The best tools available are a number of generalizations, common sense, and an investigative mentality. That realization should not embarrass us because there still is no single generally accepted theory of crime causality, even among the experts in criminology, after 100 years of research.

(b) Dispelling Myths

A false notion that should be dispelled is that fraud by or through a computer requires some special talent, particularly in the realm of programming skills. As previously noted, the typical computer fraud is not a throughput (programming) fraud but an input fraud, whereby false, fraudulent, or fabricated data are entered into a computer. Falsification was an underlying problem in the manual era of accounting, just as it is today. In that sense, not much has changed over the years. The form of the journal entry or input is the main distinction—machine-made versus handwritten.

Another notion with no statistical support is that the incidence of fraud has increased as a result of computers. There is also no conclusive evidence that the current incidence rate of insider computer-related business crimes—like employee theft, fraud, and embezzlement—is greater than it was in the past. However, it is true that computing systems may be more vulnerable to outsider attack by way of electronic eavesdropping and other improper or illegal access attempts by computer *hackers, time thieves,* and *information pirates* or predatory competitors.

(c) The "MOMMs" Concept

The why, when, where, and how of computer-related crime can be summed up in a concept called MOMMs, an acronym for Motivations, Opportunities, Means, and Methods. Each of these is briefly described below.

1. Motivations (Who and why?)
    Motivations for crime can be classified by a variety of conditions, caused by either internal or external conditions.

2. Opportunities (What, when, and where?)
    Opportunities to commit crime can exist wherever there are inadequacies that create an environment permissive of crime. Weaknesses in either system controls or management controls are the chief types.

3. Means (How?)
    The means for commission of computer-related crime usually involve the compromise of safeguards or ethics in some fashion. Where controls are improperly utilized, where personnel are disloyal, or where technology can be diverted to dishonest use are representative categories.

4. Methods (How much, how often?)
    The methods of committing computer-related crime are scams that entail the falsification or destruction or fabrication of information. The most convenient classifications are by input, by throughput, and by output.

The MOMMs concept is illustrated in Figure 8.1, which depicts computer-related theft as an iterative process.

Figure 8.1

The Computer Theft Iteration

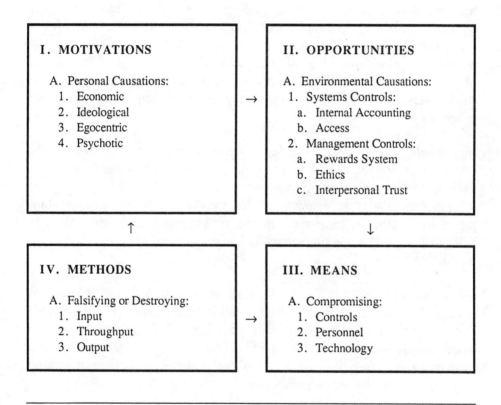

(d)   Personal Motivations

Motivations for computer-related crime can be distinguished by those that are personal to the crime perpetrator and those that are environmental.

The personal motives that can lead to the commission of a computer crime are economic, egocentric, ideological, and psychotic, as briefly described below.

(i) Economic Motives. The economic motive influences the perpetrator whose main purpose is the need or desire to secure financial gain from the crime—money or things that can be disposed of for money.

(ii) Egocentric Motives. The egocentric motive provokes the need or desire to show off the perpetrator's talent in committing what others may tend to see as a complex crime. Stealing money may be included in the criminal act, but it is not the primary purpose of the act. The stolen funds are a secondary consideration—the more funds the better, but only to demonstrate the prowess and ingenuity of the perpetrator. The youthful hackers of recent fame fall into this category. Their intentions are not generally to steal money, but information, so that they can demonstrate how bright and gifted they are.

(iii) Ideological Motives. The ideological motive incites the perpetrator who feels compelled to seek revenge against someone or something that he believes is oppressing or exploiting him or others. Terrorist bombings of computer centers is an example of that mindset. Sabotage against computers by disgruntled employees is another example. Such criminals may feel computer technology threatens their economic and political survival or well being.

(iv) Psychotic Motives. Psychotic motives include a distorted sense of reality, delusions of grandeur or persecution, and sometimes exaggerated fears or hatred of computers or their representative institutions to a point where bizarre behavior is directed against them to relieve anxieties. There have been few reported incidents of computer abuse where psychotic motives were attributed to perpetrators.

(e) Environmental Motivations

Environmental conditions that have provided motivation for computer-related crime and abuse include both the internal environment of the firm that operates a computer and the external environment, i.e., the world or market place in general. Internal influences that can aggravate the motives for computer-related crime and abuse include such things as:

- The work environment;
- The reward system;

- The level of interpersonal trust;
- The level of ethics;
- The level of stress (pressure for performance); and
- The level of internal controls.

Much thought and consideration continue to be given to the development of better internal and accounting controls to ward off or defend against computer crime and abuse. Other defensive measures include enhancement of the physical security of computer centers and protection of information and telecommunication systems from climatic disasters and outside intruders. Considerably less thought has been given to the enhancement of the work environment, the reward system, and the levels of trust, ethics, and stress. These factors are more difficult to assess as influences on risks, so they are often overlooked as defensive measures.

Externally, motives for computer-related crime and abuse may be provided by the current mores and social values of society, competitive conditions in the industry, and economic conditions in the country or the world.

§8.5   The Control Environment: Key to Prevention

If it could be assumed that all people are honest, there would be less need for internal controls. Some employees seem to steal under the best of employment circumstances; others would not consider stealing if they worked for Ebenezer Scrooge. The design of internal controls often reflects past experience; it has, for example, been said that a conservative is a former liberal who has been mugged. Rational individuals and societies tend to build or legislate constraints on human behavior by creating laws, norms of acceptable behavior, minimum standards of behavior, and even absolute prohibitions against certain forms of conduct.

Because not all people are prone to steal or are tempted to steal, it is counterproductive to build so many constraints on behavior that people begin to feel oppressed, distrusted, or under constant surveillance.

Much of Western society boasts of personal freedoms, such as freedom of speech, religion, and assembly. As a society these freedoms are kept in a state of creative tension by a set of countervailing rights. For example, while we have a right to speak our minds freely, we have no right to slander or libel another individual. And, while we have a right to select our own religious faith, we have no right to foist that faith on others or compel them to join our sect.

Ideally, internal controls should take into account a similar set of checks and balances. On one hand, consideration must be given to the risks, threats, and vulnerabilities that are faced in the marketplace, and how critical they are to survival and profitability. On the other hand, we must consider responsibilities toward employees, the value of their contribution to the success of the firm, and how their satisfaction with employment and working conditions may affect their performance and efficiency and the company's profitability.

A competent systems analyst or accounting systems designer can build controls upon controls in any firm. But controls must be balanced against the nature and extent of the risk. Controls must be cost effective and should not place undue burdens on the people who monitor them or work under them. So the internal control environment does not mean a "siege" mentality or a fortress environment. Internal control mindedness should be a matter of balance and equilibrium, not of paranoid fear.

The implications of this view of employee theft and the theft prevention process are as follows:

- Most prevention efforts concentrate or focus on building more accounting and access controls or physical security controls.

- It is necessary to recognize that there are limits to technological and procedural controls. It is difficult and costly to match the rate of growth of EDP technology with the rate of improvements in protection and detection mechanisms.

- An alternative for securing company assets in an EDP environment is to shift the concentration of effort and cost to decreasing the probability of commission of a crime. The technique for executing that strategy lies in strengthening management controls and improving the motivational and ethical climate and interpersonal trust in the firm.

One hypothesis, then, is that an organization's internal controls are optimal when two sets of opposing environmental conditions are counterbalanced. The environmental factors that encourage and discourage crime are itemized under the following two sections.

§8.5 The Control Environment: Key to Prevention

(a) Factors That Encourage Computer Crime

Factors that enhance the probability of the commission of internal theft, fraud, embezzlement, and corruption—including computer crime—can be either motivational (relating to the reward systems and corporate-wide policies that are in place) or personal (relating to the recruitment of an individual employee, that employee's character, etc.). Each of these are dealt with in the following sections.

(i) Motivational Environment. The motivational environment factors that enhance the probability of computer crime include:

1. Inadequate rewards:
   - Pay, fringe benefits, bonuses, incentives, perquisites, job security, meaningful work, promotional opportunities.
2. Inadequate management controls:
   - Failure to articulate and/or communicate expected minimum standards of job-related performance and on-the-job personal behaviors; and
   - Ambiguity or lack of clarity in job roles, relationships, responsibilities, and areas of accountability.
3. Inadequate reinforcement and performance feedback mechanisms:
   - Lack of recognition for good work, loyalty, longevity, and effort;
   - Lack of recognition for truly outstanding performances;
   - Delayed feedback or no feedback at all on:
     —Performance inadequacies; and
     —Unacceptable on-the-job behaviors;
   - Failure to counsel when performance levels or personal behaviors fall below acceptable levels; and
   - Lack of challenging job-related goals and objectives and acceptance of mediocre performance as the standard.
4. Inadequate support:
   - Lack of adequate resources to meet mandated standards; e.g., to complete tasks within quantity, quality, and cost parameters and within time frames for completion.
5. Inadequate operational reviews:

191

- Lack of timely or periodic audits, inspections, and follow-through to assure compliance with company goals, priorities, policies, procedures, and governmental regulations.

6. Condoning influences:

   - Unspecific or ambiguous corporate social values and ethical norms; and

   - Tolerance or indifference toward antisocial behavior.

7. Fostering hostility:

   - Promoting or permitting destructive interpersonal or interdepartmental competitiveness;

   - Promotion of a low interpersonal trust philosophy; and

   - Bias or unfairness in selection, promotion, compensation, or appraisal.

(ii) Personal and Personnel Inducements. The personal and personnel inducement factors that enhance the probability of computer crime include:

1. Inadequate standards of recruitment and selection.

2. Inadequate orientation and training on security matters and company policies with respect to sanctions for security breaches.

3. Unresolved personal financial problems.

4. Unfulfilled status needs.

5. Failure to screen applicants for sensitive positions before appointment:

   - Employment verification;

   - Educational verification;

   - Financial reliability; and

   - Character.

6. General job-related stress or anxiety.

(b)   Factors That Discourage Computer Crime

Factors that discourage acts of, and enhance the probability of *discovery* of, internal theft, fraud, embezzlement and corruption—including computer crime—are classified as either prevention or detection. Each of these measures is set out in the following sections.

§8.5 The Control Environment: Key to Prevention

(i) Prevention Measures. The prevention measures that discourage acts of computer crime include:

1. Internal accounting controls:
    - Separation of duties;
    - Rotation of duties;
    - Periodic internal audits and surprise inspections;
    - Development and documentation of policies, procedures, systems, programs, and program modifications;
    - Establishment of dual signature authorities, dollar authorization limits per signatory, expiration dates for signature authorizations, and check amount limits;
    - Off-line entry controls and limits; and
    - Batch totals, hash totals.
2. Computer access controls:
    - Identification defenses:
      —Key or card inserts;
      —Passwords and code names;
      —Exclusion / repeated error lockout;
      —Time activator/deactivator; and
      —Periodic code and password changes.

    - Authentication defenses:
      —Random personal data;
      —Voice, fingerprint, or palm geometry recognition; and
      —Call backs.

    - Establishment of authorizations by levels of authority or levels of security (compartmentalization and "need to know").

(ii) Detection Measures. The detection measures that discourage acts of computer crime include:

1. Exceptions logging systems:
    - Out of sequence, out of priority, and aborted runs and entries;
    - Out of pattern transactions: too high, too low, too many, too often, too few, unusual file access (odd times and odd places);
    - Attempted access beyond authorization level;

- Repeated attempts to gain access improperly—wrong password, entry code, etc.; and
- Parity and redundancy checks.

2. Management information system:
   - Monitoring operational performance levels for:
     —Variations from plans and standards;
     —Deviations from accepted or mandated policies, procedures, and practices; and
     —Deviations from past quantitative relationships, e.g., based upon ratios, proportions, percentages, trends, past performance levels, and indices.

3. Intelligence gathering:
   - Being aware of employee attitudes, values, and job satisfaction levels; and
   - Soliciting random feedback from or surveying customers, vendors, and suppliers for evidence of dissatisfaction, inefficiency, inconsistency with policies, corruption, or dishonesty by employees.

(c) Security Countermeasures to Computer Crime

A variety of methods has emerged as potential countermeasures to computer crime. Chapter 5 of this Handbook covers the topic of computer security in a general way. The following sections deal with the specific measures that are particularly relevant to the prevention of computer crime by unauthorized personnel and outsiders.

(i) Computer and Terminal Access Controls. Controls designed to ensure that only authorized users obtain access to computer systems include:

- *Passwords (alpha and numeric).*
- *Compartmentalization:* Restricts users to only those files and programs that they are authorized to use.
- *Error lock-out:* Shuts down the terminal's power after successive incorrect attempts to log on.
- *Voice print recognition.*
- *Finger print recognition.*

- *Palm geometry.*

- *Magnetic card access.*

- *Automatic shut-off:* After transmission is completed, if operator fails to sign off.

- *Time lock:* No messages can be received or transmitted at the terminal after normal working hours.

- *Call back:* Before user gains complete access, a phone call is made to the terminal site to verify the user's identity.

- *Random personal information:* Before the computer fully accepts an access request, it poses random personal history questions stored in its memory, such as: What is your mother-in-law's maiden name or date of birth? In what hospital was your oldest child born? When will you celebrate your 25th wedding anniversary? (Usually personal information, which is not carried in a wallet. If the wallet were stolen, the thief could not use the information therein to impersonate its owner to gain access to a computer.)

- *Personal identification number (PIN):* Used in conjunction with a magnetic card that has a coded authorization. He or she must present or insert both the card and his or her "PIN" number (a 4-digit or 5-digit number committed to memory) as proof of identity.

- *Personal signature recognition:* After logging on, the terminal operator writes his or her name with a light pen and the computer matches that signature with an authentic sample in its memory.

(ii) Data Communications Controls. Controls designed to ensure the security of data communications include:

- Cryptographic transmission and storage of data to avoid interception and casual perusal of sensitive information.

- *Scramblers*: To garble the computer message being transmitted.

- *Dial back devices*: The computer will not grant access unless terminal identification, user identification, password, and authority have been verified. Logs are kept and monitored of all access attempts. Those that were aborted for impropriety are further investigated. An alarm may be sounded when an improper access is being attempted.

(d)   Suggested Improvements to Prevent Computer Crime

Following is a list of some suggested improvements in internal and other controls, corporate policies, and laws, which should be looked at in order to reduce the risk of computer crime.

- Clear and explicit policies with respect to the proper and authorized uses of computers, and sanctions for abuses thereof.
- Better accounting controls.
- Better defensive countermeasures to ward off attacks and intrusions by outsiders.
- Better internal controls.
- Better supervision of employees with computer responsibilities.
- Better laws against criminal acts committed by computer and against computers.
- Better education of computer users with respect to the security and privacy of information.
- Better computer auditing methods.
- Better hardware protection.
- Better software protection.
- Better telecommunication systems protection.
- Better physical security of computer centers.
- Better proprietary information protection methods.
- Better personnel policies.
  - —Reward systems;
  - —Standards of performance;
  - —Recruitment standards;
  - —Confidentiality agreements;
  - —More trust and less pressure;
  - —Clearer job-related goals and objectives;
  - —More involvement in decision making; and
  - —More recognition for jobs that are well done.

§8.6   Some Selected Computer Crimes

Computer Protection Systems, Inc. (150 North Main St., Plymouth, Michigan, US 48170) has for the past several years published a monthly newsletter called *Computer Security Digest*. A review of that newsletter provided information on the computer crimes that follow.

(a)   A State University's Hospital

A computer operator at the hospital was charged with embezzling $40,000 by submitting false invoices that were processed through the hospital's computer. Another case involved a charge against the hospital's former assistant data processing manager, that he accepted a $41,000 bribe from a data processing consultant and conspired with another data processing consultant to steal $126,000 from the hospital by submitting false invoices for software services. Both the operator and the assistant data processing manager had previous convictions for computer-related crime. The hospital did not, as a matter of course, conduct background investigations on data processing employment applicants.

Conclusion: Conduct thorough background checks on all employees in sensitive data processing and related operations.

(b)   A Manufacturer of Magnetic Peripherals

A subsidiary of a major computer manufacturer was another victim of computer crime. An accounts payable terminal operator and her boyfriend conspired to defraud the company by fabricating invoices from a fictitious vendor firm, which they had earlier formed. Five checks totaling $155,000 were then issued to the phony vendor after which the terminal operator and her boyfriend left for sunnier climes. The operator finally turned herself in and disclosed the fraud to police when her boyfriend tried to effectuate a reconciliation with his estranged wife and began to physically abuse the terminal operator. The investigating police officer alleged that the company was too busy with all its business to build in any safeguards for its computer.

Conclusion: Verify the authenticity of large invoices and payments and spot check smaller transactions of this nature. Management must fulfill its legal responsibility to provide proper safeguards.

(c) A Top Oil Company

A former EDP employee and his wife were indicted for stealing $18,000 from the company in an accounts payable-type scam. The employee instructed the company computer to pay his wife rent for land she allegedly leased to the company by assigning her an alpha-numeric code as a lessor and then ordering that payment be made.

Conclusion: Never let a data entry clerk in accounts payable who processes payment claims also have access to the approved vendor master file for additions or deletions. Doing otherwise violates the separation of duties principle of internal controls.

(d) A Netherlands Bank

The head of the bank's foreign transfer department and his assistant were arrested on suspicion of forgery and embezzlement for a scheme that involved the taking of at least $65 million over a 2-year period. Police believe the money was embezzled by breaking the bank's computer code, allowing funds to be funneled into outside accounts. The alleged fraud was discovered through audit. The bank's management is also under investigation for tax evasion.

Conclusion: More trained EDP auditors, doing routine EDP audits, can detect this type of crime sooner.

(e) An Insurance Company

A guilty plea by an insurance company employee marks the second conviction under Florida's computer crime law. The employee, a benefits analyst with the insurance company, used her remote terminal in a Dade County field claims office to defraud the company of $206,000 over a period of almost 2 years. The employee used her position of trust and knowledge of claims systems to execute the fraud. She used false names to submit fictitious claims, but used the addresses of herself, her father, and her boyfriend. The repetition of the same addresses eventually tipped off the insurance company's security department. Under Florida's computer law HB.1305, she faces restitution of the $206,000, a fine, and a possible prison term of 1 to 5 years.

Conclusion: Blank claims forms should be kept under lock and key, preserialized, and under the strict control of an employee other than a data entry clerk.

(f)   A University in Michigan

The university's computer system was accessed by one or more people who damaged nearly 43,000 student records stored on the system. Many students' first names were changed to Susan, student telephone numbers were replaced with the phone number of the university's president, grade point averages were modified, and some files were deleted completely. The university's outside auditors reported that the computer's security system was penetrated either by someone who had extensive knowledge of the system or by misuse of the password used by the Admissions Office. The admission files were recreated by hiring a lot of temporary help.

Conclusion: Change passwords periodically, use individual (vs. departmental) passwords, make passwords more complex (i.e., alphanumeric, and monitor system users' security practices).

(g)   A Transportation Authority

A 31-year-old bus scheduler was acquitted of criminal charges involving extortion and violation of a state's computer crime law. The scheduler, who developed seven report generation programs for the transportation authority, attempted to collect $19,500 in payment for the programs after he was fired. The programs were developed with built-in security access blocks, which made accessing the source code difficult. The scheduler was said to have demanded the $19,500 before he would turn over the access codes needed to alter the source code. The programs were developed over a 2-year period in his free time. The scheduler's attorney contended that the programs saved approximately $150,000 over the past 2 years.

Conclusion: Make it clear to new hires (orally and in writing) that software applications designed by employees during their employment are the property of the employer. Establish programming standards, and monitor compliance via regular reviews of work in process as well as completed projects.

(h)   A Diversified Corporation

Criminal charges were filed against two former employees of a food corporation. The two allegedly programmed "logic bombs" that would erase inventory and payroll information processed by the company for 400 retail franchise operations. The programmed commands, one of which was set to activate on June 7, would also have shut down the computer system and erased all traces of the destructive commands. The motive is still unknown.

Conclusion: Use careful hiring practices and promote a positive working environment as basic preventive measures. Employ operating procedures that prevent and detect internal sabotage; for example:

- Authorized turnover of operational programs;
- Independent testing of new and revised programs; and
- Audits of program changes.

(i)   California Welfare Department

Although the exact amount of loss sustained by the Alameda County, California, Welfare Department is unknown, it is quite evident that over $300,000 has been lost owing to fraud committed by a supervisor and clerk. Again, this is a case of an input falsification fraud. A welfare department compliance unit supervisor and one of her former clerks falsified dozens of claims over at least a period of a year and collected unauthorized payments for the claims. The two were caught when one of the welfare department's data entry clerks discovered incomplete information on an input document authorizing a claims payment. The clerk then checked with the eligibility worker whose name had been forged on the document. When the eligibility worker denied authorizing the claim or signing the document, an investigation was started.

Conclusion: Rotate employees in sensitive positions. Do more intensive auditing of cash and disbursement functions.

(j)   Australia Betting Agency

An operator at a state-run horse betting agency was changing the time clock in the computer system by 3 minutes. After a race was run, the operator would quickly telephone his girlfriend—an input clerk—and give her the winning horses and the amounts to bet. The total loss is unknown. The fraud was detected when the operator's girlfriend became angry because he left her for another woman.

Conclusion: Any change in input parameters, even a change of time, should be logged by the system, preferably in an automatic manner, so as to create an audit trail of operational activities. Sensitive on-line operations may require the use of more than one operator at all times.

§8.7 Some Final Thoughts

One of the peculiar things about the field of computer-related crime is that one can say almost anything about it and not be challenged. One opinion tends to be as acceptable as any other. Since the field is new and generally unresearched, practitioners are free to make personal predictions, assessments, categorical statements, and generalizations. Rarely are they asked to support their judgments or conclusions with reliable facts.

One statement is repeated so often that it seems to have moved up from mythology to universal acceptance is that computer crimes are committed mostly by people with highly developed knowledge and skills (i.e., mainly programmers and analysts). A logical extension of that plausible but questionable rationale might naturally cause an uninformed person to wonder what it is about computer professionals that makes them so crime prone. In the absence of hard data, the mass media gives us the following answers:

- EDP technicians are more dedicated to their profession than to their employers;

- EDP technicians tend to be highly ambitious, energetic, naturally curious, creative, and challenge seeking; and

- EDP technicians tend to be young, psychologically immature, and easily frustrated when facing obstacles like unreasonable deadlines; programs that cannot be debugged quickly or simply; large backlogs of work; and demanding users who do not understand their technology, their jargon, or their value to the organization.

The speciousness of the rationale is not that the above circumstances do not exist in the EDP environment. Indeed they do. But the same thing could be said for other professions as well. Engineers, accountants, lawyers, and doctors suffer similar frustrations. They also tend to be more loyal to their profession than to their employers, clients, or patients. (If they were not, they might be sued more often or disciplined by their professional ethics board.) They likewise tend to be young, ambitious, energetic, curious, creative, etc., and they are professional problem solvers as well. But the mass media does not paint them as people who might use their positions of trust to violate their clients', patients', or employers' interests. What makes the EDP profession different or special?

It may be that EDP technology is more suspect because it is still relatively new and mysterious to many. Since the public does not understand it, they may be fearful about it and may believe negative allegations about computer technology and the people who work in the field.

The fact is that while most reported cases of computer-related crime involved at least one person with sufficient knowledge to gain access and manipulate data for personal economic gain, the inspiration for the scheme was, as often as not, an outsider or non-EDP employee. Most computer crimes involving the theft of company assets have been conspiracies. Internal controls, which require separation of duties, make conspiracies more likely than individual acts of computer-related theft. (But acts of sabotage against computers do tend to be individual acts, most usually by disgruntled EDP employees or terrorists.)

It is a simplistic and erroneous notion that EDP professionals, by virtue of their extreme youth and alleged lack of company loyalty, are more crime prone than other professionals. That myth is just too convenient to be true. Worse yet, it has discouraged research in computer crime motivations and has branded and labeled a large group of mostly innocent people.

Another cherished myth is that most computer-related thefts, frauds, or embezzlements are discovered by accident, not by audit or exceptions controls. If that were factual, it would be logical to conclude that criminals are more intelligent, more clever, or more cunning than noncriminals, particularly noncriminals who design systems, programs, and controls.

Frankly, very little is known about computer crime in an empirical sense. It is understood to involve substantial sums of money, to occur with some frequency, and is likely to increase in both frequency and amounts lost. These are conjectures based on two of the few realities in the field:

1. The proliferating use of computers will increase the probability of computer-related crime.

2. Our ability or willingness to design control mechanisms in computer systems has not kept pace with our ability to build more sophisticated hardware and software, and that also increases the probability of computer crime.

Therefore, the prudent businessperson will give appropriate attention to the maintenance of sound controls and will foster an environment that discourages criminal activity.

CHAPTER NINE

Commercial Crime

§9.1   Introduction
   (a) Definitions
        (i)   White-Collar and Economic Crime
        (ii) Commercial Crime
   (b) Victims of Commercial Crime
   (c) The Extent of Commercial Crime
   (d) Responsibility for Commercial Crime
   (e) Characteristics of Commercial Crime
        (i)   Tolerance
        (ii) Diffusion of Harm
        (iii) Rationalization
   (f) Causes of Commercial Crime
        (i)   Theory of Differential Association
        (ii) Criminogenic Organization Structures

§9.2   Forms of Commercial Crime
   (a) False Advertising
   (b) Industrial Espionage and Trade Secret Theft
   (c) Insider Trading
   (d) Securities Fraud
   (e) Organizational Bribegiving
        (i)   Political Bribery
        (ii) Commercial Bribery
   (f) Antitrust Violations
   (g) Crimes by Lawyers For/Against Their Clients
   (h) Other Commercial Crimes

§9.3   Prevention of Commercial Crime

(a) Deterrence: General Concepts
  (i) Severity
  (ii) Celerity
  (iii) Certainty
  (iv) General Versus Specific
  (v) Perceived Versus Real
  (vi) Effect of Deterrence on Commercial Criminals
(b) Formal Deterrence
  (i) Increasing Enforcement
  (ii) Sentencing of Commercial Criminals
(c) Informal Deterrence
(d) Ethics
  (i) Education
  (ii) The Tone at the Top
(e) A Prevention Strategy

§9.1 Introduction

(a) Definitions

The terms *white-collar crime, economic crime,* and *commercial crime* are not legal ones. They refer criminologically to a wide variety of offenses and behaviors, and are often used interchangeably. Accordingly, any definition of these terms is necessarily subjective.

Nevertheless, in developing working definitions for purposes of this Handbook, it is useful to point out the major common element of such behaviors, i.e., that they grow out of legitimate occupational efforts in business, politics, and the professions. Perpetrators typically do not seek out their jobs in order to commit crime: Their lawbreaking occurs after they are confronted with temptation or faced with what they believe are circumstances that they cannot satisfactorily resolve in any other manner. (Atypically, the perpetrator may actually seek out the opportunity to commit crime—for example, the professional con man).

In criminology, this common element was recognized almost a century ago. For example, in 1907 Edward Ross wrote about the "criminaloid"— someone who engaged in crime as a result of his or her occupation. He named examples such as corporate executives who embezzle, dishonest bank inspectors, and corrupt judges.

Another common element of these crimes was identified by Charles R. Henderson, an early twentieth-century criminologist, who wrote:

"The social classes of the highest culture furnish few convicts, yet there are educated criminals. Advanced culture modifies the form of the crime; tends to make it less coarse and violent, but more cunning; restricts it to quasi-legal forms. But education also opens up the way to new and colossal kinds of crimes, (such) as debauching of conventions, councils, legislatures, and bribery of the press and public officials."

Gary Green, in honing the white-collar crime concept, uses the term *occupational crime*, which he defines as "any act punishable by law which is committed through opportunity created in the course of an occupation which is legal." Green further delineates occupational crime into four categories, i.e., crimes committed:

- For the benefit of an employing organization (organizational occupational crime);
- By officials through exercise of their state-based authority (state authority occupational crime);
- By professionals in their capacity as professionals (professional occupational crime); and
- By individuals as individuals.

These various ways of looking at and categorizing white-collar crime illustrate that no one set of definitions can be considered uniquely correct. However, it is clear that an entirely separate branch of criminology has been well established.

The following sections set out the working definitions used for purposes of this Handbook.

(i) White-Collar and Economic Crime. Although scholars differ widely in their definition of white-collar crime, the *Dictionary of Criminal Justice Data Terminology,* published by the U.S. Bureau of Justice Statistics, defines white-collar crime as "non-violent crime for financial gain committed by means of deception by persons whose occupational status is entrepreneurial, professional or semi-professional and utilizing their special occupational skills and opportunities; also non-violent crime for finan-

cial gain utilizing deception and committed by anyone having special technical and professional knowledge of business and government, irrespective of the person's occupation.''

This definition is all-encompassing and appropriate for our purposes, i.e., it includes most if not all of the crimes and behaviors described in this Handbook. It could be applied equally to the term *economic crime,* although that is perhaps a poorer choice because many violent crimes could also be described as economic in their objective—for example, armed robbery.

(ii) Commercial Crime. This term is infrequently used as a substitute for white-collar crime and economic crime. For purposes of this Handbook, however, a more restrictive definition is adopted: *commercial crime is white-collar crime committed by or on behalf of a business or commercial entity.* In other words, the business or commercial entity is the perpetrator rather than the victim.

This distinction—i.e., between fraud committed against a business or commercial entity, and commercial crime committed by it—is a useful one. Historically, our legal system, institutions, and even the literature tended to focus more on conventional fraud. For example, auditors are alert to the possibility of an employee embezzling funds and their audit procedures—such as checking bank and accounts receivable reconciliations—may disclose such frauds.

In recent years, however—particularly during the 1980s—awareness has been heightened to the possibility of the business or commercial entity itself being the perpetrator. Frauds against investors and environmental crime are two examples that have received increasing media attention.

(b) Victims of Commercial Crime

Victims of commercial crime can include:

- Customers—e.g., through false advertising and price fixing;
- Competitors—e.g., through industrial espionage;
- Investors—e.g., through insider trading and securities fraud; and
- The general public—e.g., through environmental crime.

In addition, the practice of organizational bribegiving may victimize any one of the above or other groups, for example the general taxpayer where a bribe is given in the awarding of a government contract.

(c)   The Extent of Commercial Crime

Two decades ago commercial crime received much less media attention, largely being confined to a short paragraph or two in the business section of the nation's newspapers, if it was mentioned at all. Today's front-page stories testify to considerably greater public interest in and concern about commercial crime. Scholars attribute this growing emphasis to, among other things, a greater skepticism about the behavior of persons in authority. The splintering of American society during the Vietnam War undoubtedly contributed greatly to a mood of distrust and concern, while the crimes of Watergate, involving the President and his advisors and members of his cabinet, established a mood of distrust of the honesty of those in prominent places.

Statistics suggest that there is some reason for distrust. Clinard and Yeager (1980) found that 1,533 cases had been filed against the 562 Fortune 500 businesses (that is, the largest American companies) whose records were examined for 2 years, for an average of 2.7 violations for each company. About 60 percent of the companies had at least one case against them; for those companies, the average was 4.4 cases. The oil, pharmaceutical, and motor vehicle industries were the most likely to be proceeded against for violations.

In a study by Irwin Ross (1980), 1,043 companies were analyzed that at one time or another had appeared on the Fortune list of large industrial companies. Included in his study were five kinds of offenses: bribetaking or bribegiving by high-level executives; criminal fraud; illegal campaign contributions; tax evasion; and antitrust violations. One hundred seventeen, or 11 percent of the corporations, were violators.

(d)   Responsibility for Commercial Crime

Some scholars debate whether individuals should be held responsible for crimes committed on behalf of their organizations. Although some direct benefit accrues to the perpetrator, far more benefit accrues to the organization.

Regardless of whether the organization is held liable, the frauds are as a direct result of some human action or interaction. In the words of Parisi, "If (an organization) is like a gun, then there must be someone comparable to a triggerman."

Most criminal statutes require that the guilty person have the required criminal intent. However, in the case of organizations, they can be held liable even though they were unaware of or did not participate in the fraud. The law recognizes two theories, identification and imputation.

"Identification" assumes organizational liability when the employees and organizations can be viewed as one in the same; i.e., a small business owner who has incorporated. "Imputation" is where the organization is held responsible for the actions of its employees through the doctrine of *respondeat superiour,* a seventieth-century doctrine, which means "let the superior respond." The legal theory was developed from civil lawsuits to prevent employers from denying financial responsibility for their employees.

(e) Characteristics of Commercial Crime

While commercial crime can take many forms, it is often distinguished by one or more of the characteristics set out below.

(i) Tolerance. While awareness of commercial crime has increased in recent years, there still remains a somewhat greater tolerance for this form of crime as compared to violent crimes such as armed robbery, or those involving drugs. This greater tolerance may stem not so much from the nature of the crime itself, but rather from the perception of the perpetrator as being somehow more "civilized."

Elaborating on this idea, if the definition of economic and white-collar crime is confined to persons with the power to commit offenses in the course of their occupational work, it is obvious that the definition of commercial crime restricts the ranks of possible perpetrators even further. Anybody with strength, or decent aim, or access to poison, can commit murder, but only a limited number of "respectable" corporate executives or directors are in a position to violate antitrust legislation. People typically engage in forms of criminal behavior that are the most familiar, and seem to be the easiest and least likely to produce dire consequences. It is not surprising, in these terms, that a bank teller, short of cash, will try embezzling, while an unemployed minority youth, also without adequate funds, turns to armed robbery.

It seems that an often unheralded bonus of social status is access to opportunities for the less dirty, "more decent" kinds of crime.

(ii) Diffusion of Harm. Another notable characteristic of most kinds of commercial crime is that there are often a large number of victims, and they are frequently not aware that they have been harmed. Death from smog or asbestos poisoning is very likely to be slow and insidious, and its victims will be hard-pressed to relate their terminal illness to its precise cause, given the complicated nature of other possible contributing factors. A factory worker with cancer is not likely to be certain whether it was the toxic chemicals that he handled for 15 years, the fact that he smoked too many cigarettes, bad genes, or bad luck that will shorten his life.

In many other cases of commercial crime, the harm tends to be widely diffused and, for each person, rather insignificant. But these can still be significant crimes. Companies can earn millions over the course of a year by charging higher prices for products that do not meet the standards they are alleged to attain. Few people who pay for a package of 100 thumb tacks will take the time and energy to count the contents of the package to be certain that they have gotten their money's worth: it would be an easy and safe venture to put 92 tacks in each package, and some merchandisers find the temptation irresistible. Neither will a customer likely ever become aware that the gasoline pumps at a service station are calibrated so that they get fewer gallons than those for which they are charged. Even if they come to know about these kinds of peculation, most customers would shrug them off as not worth the trouble it would take to do something to remedy the situation; at most, they might take their business elsewhere.

The camouflaged nature of most commercial crime poses a particular law enforcement dilemma. Without complaining witnesses, policing has to be proactive instead of reactive; that is, the enforcement officials themselves have to decide where the offenses are being committed and how to go about stopping them. They often cannot, as with crimes such as robbery and burglary, rely on victim reports. Enforcers obviously cannot cope with all the violations and must decide on rules to guide their efforts. Should they go after the behaviors which cause the most harm? Should they take on the bigger offenders, or concentrate on the "smaller fry," where their chances of success are much better? They can readily accumulate ten convictions in a year against ten insignificant companies, whereas it might take three years to win a victory over one huge corporation. Besides, the resources of the large organization might allow it to win its case, regardless of the lawless nature of its behavior.

(iii) Rationalization. Economic offenders are known for providing elaborate excuses for their crimes, and the nature of such explanations may be a major distinguishing mark between them and street offenders. Cressey (1953) found that the embezzlers he studied typically insisted that they were only borrowing the money; that they intended to repay it once they had covered the bills and other financial demands vexing them. Commercial criminals will similarly rationalize their behavior; for example, antitrust violators usually maintain they are seeking to stabilize an out-of-control price situation when they conspire with others to fix prices, or psychologists arrested for phony and unauthorized charges against government medical benefit programs are likely to insist that they are being singled out by power-hungry prosecutors and investigators.

Rarely will there appear a commercial criminal with the refreshing honesty to admit that: "I was deliberately engaged in crooked business dealings. I was trying to do in as many people as I could. I am a rotten, dishonest person." If nothing else, malefactors will say that they stole from victims who could afford the loss, such as rich investors or big competitors, rather than widows and children, or will blame their violations on personal problems, such as alcoholism, drug addiction, or marital difficulties.

(f) Causes of Commercial Crime

(i) Theory of Differential Association. The theory of differential association is undoubtedly the best-known among all explanations offered to account for crime. Although it applies to all forms of crime—not just commercial crime—it is nevertheless useful for our purposes as well.

The theory first appeared in 1939 in the third edition of Edwin H. Sutherland's *Principles of Criminology*. Later, Sutherland would make his best-known contribution to criminology by coining the phrase *white-collar crime* and writing a monograph on the subject.

The theory of differential association begins by asserting that criminal behavior is learned. Expanding on that assertion, Sutherland specifies as a second point that criminal behavior is learned in interaction with other persons in a process of communication. If individuals acquiring criminal habits or propensities were exposed to situations, circumstances, and interactions totally of a criminal nature, it would be relatively easy to comprehend how this process of communication operates. In view of the enormous variation in standards and personalities to which any individual in our society is exposed, it becomes exceedingly difficult to discern the elements that induce criminal behavior without some additional principles.

Sutherland's third point is that criminal behavior is acquired through participation within intimate personal groups. This suggests that the roots of crime are in the socializing experiences of the individual. Unfortunately, the process of socialization is far from adequately understood. Sutherland's fourth point indicates that the criminal learning process includes not only techniques of committing crime but also the shaping of motives, drives, rationalizations, and attitudes. Crime techniques often can involve a high degree of skill: picking pockets (and not getting caught at it) demands considerable adroitness.

Fifth, Sutherland stipulates that the specific direction of motives and drives is learned from definitions of the legal codes as favorable or unfavorable.

Sixth, Sutherland establishes the principle of "differential association." According to this postulate, a person becomes criminal because of an excess of definitions favorable to violation of the law over definitions unfavorable to violation of the law. Sutherland states his seventh point, that differential association may vary in frequency, duration, priority, and intensity. But there is no suggestion regarding which of these elements is apt to be more important than the others.

Sutherland's eighth point is that learning criminal and delinquent behavior, involves all the mechanisms that are involved in any other learning. As his next to last proposition, Sutherland stressed that learning differs from pure imitation.

The last point is a worthwhile reminder that, while criminal behavior is an expression of general needs and values, it is not explained by these general needs and values because noncriminal behavior is an expression of the same needs and values. This means that the generalizations sometimes employed to account for crime—that people steal because they crave "esteem" or are "greedy" or kill because they are "unhappy"—have little scientific merit.

In other words, criminals and noncriminals are motivated by much the same needs and values. They become or do not become criminals on the basis of their unique responses to common drives for prestige, happiness, success, power, wealth, and other human aspirations. One person with a pressing need for money may take an extra weekend job pumping gas, or try to borrow from a friend. Another person, feeling the same need, may hold up a fast-food outlet.

(ii) Criminogenic Organization Structures. Edward Gross has asserted that all organizations are inherently "criminogenic" (prone to committing crime), but not necessarily criminal. Gross makes this assertion because of the inherent reliance of the organization on the bottom line. Without necessarily meaning to, organizations inherently invite commercial crime as a means of obtaining goals. For example, criminologist Oliver Williamson noted that because of a department's concern with reaching its goals, managers may well tend to maximize their department's own interests to the detriment of the organization.

Organizations can also be criminogenic because they encourage loyalty. According to Diane Vaughan, the reasons are that:

1.   The organization tends to recruit and attract similar individuals;

2.   Rewards are given out to those who display characteristics of the "company man";

3.   Long-term loyalty is encouraged through company retirement and benefits;

4.   Loyalty is encouraged through social interaction such as company parties and social functions;

5.   Frequent transfers and long working hours encourage isolation from other groups; and

6.   Specialized job skills may discourage company personnel from seeking employment elsewhere.

This in turn causes company personnel to sometimes perceive that the organization might be worth committing crime for.

§9.2 Forms of Commercial Crime

Some of the most common forms of commercial crime are described in the following sections.

§9.2 Forms of Commercial Crime

(a) False Advertising

Today, the realm of commercial crime can be said to primarily involve offenses against laws that regulate the marketplace and/or establishing standards of conduct for professional and political life. This category includes such matters as false advertising. For example:

- Claims have been made that shoes for sale are alligator when in fact they were made of a plastic product;

- Department stores often raise the price of a product significantly one day and then the next day drop it back to where it had been, maintaining in their advertising that it now is "on sale" and reduced "by seventy percent.";

- In bait and switch tactics, stores will advertise a specific product at a strikingly low price, but then, when the customer tries to buy the item, indicate either that it no longer is available, or demonstrate that it is much inferior to the thing that the store really wants to sell. It is the customer's presence and attention they want to attract: once they have him or her listening, they assume that slick salesmanship can accomplish the rest of the deceit; and

- In one of the more blatant advertising frauds, a company selling glass "demonstrated" in television commercials that its car window product was so perfect that when you looked through it you could hardly believe that there was anything between you and the outside scene. It was later proved that the company was using films taken from inside a car with the window rolled down.

(b) Industrial Espionage and Trade Secret Theft

Industrial espionage is a term that is broadly applied to activities engaged in to achieve one main purpose—the obtaining of information and/or related assets from competitors or potential competitors. The classic form of industrial espionage is *trade secret theft*.

There are three basic elements to a trade secret: novelty, value, and secrecy. The last item has to do with whether an organization handled its alleged "secret" in a protective manner. If it did not do so, it will not win judicial support if it charges theft of that secret by an employee or an executive.

215

Patent laws seek a compromise between capitalistic self-interest in a trade secret and social well-being by granting (in the United States) a 17-year monopoly to developers of innovative ideas. The U.S. Supreme Court, in its only ruling on trade secrets (*Kewanee Oil Co. v. Bicron Corp.*, 1974), declared the likelihood "remote indeed" that a company would not patent valuable information that it had developed. The Court, however, overlooked the advantage, well known to most companies, that trade secrets can be hoarded far beyond the 17-year patent limitation, a matter well documented by the success and secrecy of the formulas for Coca-Cola and Kentucky Fried Chicken, among others.

Leakage of trade secret information is said to be particularly likely from employees who go to work for competitors, careless secretaries, gregarious field sales personnel, and high-tech computer whizzes who often are more loyal to their equipment than to their fellow employees. Temporary help is regarded as especially vulnerable: in-and-out employees do not have any company loyalty and can be planted for purposes of theft. It is claimed that having at least two persons in an organization cooperate when dealing with sensitive materials is likely to reduce the compromising of such information. It is also recommended that secret mailing lists used by a business include at least one decoy address so that, if the list is compromised, whoever uses it will be sending material to a fictional person, at an address that actually is a company drop.

A review of the appellate court cases on trade secret theft show the defendants as persons who have been working for a business in the range of 6–10 years. Most purloiners obviously did not join the company with the intent to steal information, but rather formed (or were led to form) that resolve after they had been at work for the better part of a decade. The court materials suggest the illegal behavior probably is not predictable from background investigations or from psychological tests.

Typically, the defendants are smaller companies that have hired scientists from larger organizations. There also appears to be an unusual amount of theft from family-owned businesses, with the defendants saying that they believed, as outsiders, that their chances of advancement were hopeless. The sense conveyed by the court cases is that the resources of the large companies allow them to develop secret processes that threaten to swamp smaller organizations that are dependent upon maintaining a competitive position, and that a certain felling of desperation drives the offenders to try to pry the information loose.

(c) Insider Trading

Insider trading involves the use of nonpublic information to make stock trades on the market.

Criminal charges for insider trading have become the trademark of economic crime enforcement efforts during recent years. These efforts seek to encourage the confidence of investors that they are sharing satisfactorily in the information about the performance of companies.

A surge of prosecutions for illegal insider information transactions began in the late 1980s when stock transactions were first subjected to sophisticated computer review, enabling investigators to identify unusual stock movements. Soon afterwards, when some meaningful piece of financial information about the company was released, investigators could determine quickly who had traded the stock heavily before the news release. If, for instance, the transaction was made by the firm's president, it seemed likely, (though not assured), that he or she had acted on the information before it was publicly disseminated.

Cases also arose involving auditors selling stock when their examination of a company's books convinced them that it was in financial trouble, and brokerage houses unloading stock they held and advising preferred customers to do the same, while at the same time they pushed the same securities onto their less important clients. In a particularly egregious case, a young columnist for the *Wall Street Journal* conveyed information to a speculator concerning the content of the column he would be writing. The speculator bought up stocks and made millions of dollars, sharing a small part of his profits with the journalist (Winans, 1984).

Of course, the notable cases of Ivan Boesky and Michael Milken remain the most infamous and illustrate the staggering sums of money to be made from illegal stock trades. Boesky, the Wall Street arbitrage king, was sentenced to 3 years in prison and fined $100 million. In his plea agreement, he gave information that led to the indictments of so-called junk bond king Michael Milken, who eventually pled guilty to insider trading and was fined $600 million.

(d) Securities Fraud

Another scheme involving securities is the practice of "churning," whereby a broker buys and sells stock for a client to generate fees, rather than for what is in the best interests of the client. Broker discretion accounts are especially ripe for churning. In one case, two sisters gave brokers $500,000 each in discretionary accounts. The brokers traded stocks more than 1,400 times, allegedly giving themselves $400,000 in commissions, leaving the sisters with $70,000.

Other schemes involve mixing client funds with the broker's. Sometimes brokers will use the client's stock as collateral for personal loans and even post the winning trades to themselves, while posting the losses to their clients. Some brokers also resort to out-and-out embezzlement of their client's money and stock.

(e) Organizational Bribegiving

There are two main kinds of bribes that benefit organizations: (1) bribing politicians and giving illegal campaign contributions; and (2) commercial bribery including most types of purchasing frauds. The second category also includes bribes for industrial espionage—i.e., paying someone to reveal trade and other secrets about competing firms.

(i) Political Bribery. In his book *Political Corruption and Public Policy in America,* Michael Johnston defined three conditions that were normally present in political bribegiving:

- The fruits of governmental action are often extremely valuable (or, in the case of penalties and sanctions, extremely costly), with demand for benefits frequently exceeding supply;

- These benefits and sanctions can often be gotten or avoided only by dealing with the government; and

- The routine process through which benefits and sanctions are conferred is time consuming, expensive, and uncertain in its outcome.

Gary Green says the most common form of political bribe-giving is illegal campaign contributions. The companies he lists who have participated at one time or another include some very well known businesses: Exxon, Standard Oil, American Airlines, Carnation, Firestone, General Tire and Rubber, Goodyear, 3M, and Singer.

Paying foreign politicians and governments abroad was (and perhaps still is) common in order to do business in many countries. In the mid-seventies, a scandal erupted when it was disclosed that several airplane manufacturers routinely paid foreign officials huge sums to insure orders. In the wake of these scandals, the U.S. Congress passed the Foreign Corrupt Practices Act in 1977 outlawing bribes to foreign officials except in cases of national security.

(ii) Commercial Bribery. Commercial bribery involves the paying of firms for purchasing products and/or for industrial espionage.

Several federal and state/provincial laws address the practice of commercial bribery, which in some instances may also be a violation of restraint of trade. For example, certain industries in the United States— notably the liquor industry—are outlawed specifically from paying for business. Several major firms, according to Irwin Ross, have been guilty of commercial bribery: Anheuser Bush, Beatrice Foods, R.J. Reynolds Industries, and Joseph Schlitz Brewing, to name a few.

Industrial espionage can involve direct payments to third parties to secure valuable competitive information, or can be accomplished indirectly, e.g., through the hiring of a competitor's employees. For example, in the United States in 1988, several military procurement agents were charged with giving defense contractors information on more than $500 million in Navy purchases.

(f) Antitrust Violations

Antitrust activities are those that restrain trade or free competition. Practices outlawed (e.g., under the 1890 Sherman Anti-Trust Act in the United States) include: price fixing, bid rigging, discriminatory pricing, rebating, trusts, and related agreements.

In both the United States and Canada, successful prosecutions in this area have been rare. According to Gary Green, there were only 26 jail sentences meted out in the 79 years between 1890 and 1969. Of those, 22 included charges that were for other offenses such as racketeering, meaning that only 4 persons were sentenced to prison terms exclusively relating to anti-trust.

However, in the U.S. since 1970, primarily because of the precedent set by former President Jimmy Carter, antitrust violations have been prosecuted somewhat more aggressively.

(g) Crimes by Lawyers For/Against Their Clients

Offenses committed by lawyers include:

- Overbilling for time;

- Embezzlement of trust funds; and

- Fraud committed for the benefit of their clients (e.g., preparing false documents for admission in legal proceedings).

Fraud is easy to commit for a lawyer, in large part because of the nebulous nature of the services provided. As Blumberg states:

"Legal service lends itself particularly well to confidence games. Usually a plumber will be able to demonstrate that he has performed a service—clearing up a stuffed drain, repairing a leaky faucet or pipe—and therefore merits his fee. In the practice of law there is a special problem in this regard, no matter what the level of the practitioner or his practice in the hierarchy or prestige. Much legal work is intangible either because it is simply a few works of advice, some preventative action, a telephone call, negotiation of some kind, a form filled out and filed, a hurried conference with another attorney or an official of a government agency, a letter or opinion written, or a countless variety of seemingly innocuous and even prosaic procedures and actions."

(h) Other Commercial Crimes

Other commercial crimes include:

- Environmental pollution;

- Violations of occupational health and safety laws; and

- Marketing of drugs that have not been adequately tested or for which the test results have been falsified.

For example, Braithwaite's study of the pharmaceutical industry documents in detail "abominable harm" caused by drug companies. He finds bribery and extortion to be widespread and offers a case study of blatant falsification on MER/29 (triparanol), a drug designed to reduce blood cholesterol. The company was fined $80,000 for flagrant deceptive practices;

had its reports not been controverted, the owner stood to gain more than $4 million annually on the product.

§9.3 Prevention of Commercial Crime

Three internal personal forces can operate to reduce commercial crime:

- *Formal deterrence:* the fear of formal, officially imposed sanctions (conviction and punishment by the government);

- *Informal deterrence:* the fear of informally imposed sanctions, such as the loss of respectability or a career; and

- *Ethics:* the internalization of values that discourage violations of legal codes.

(a) Deterrence: General Concepts

Deterrence theory assumes that humans are rational in their behavior patterns, seeking profit and pleasure while avoiding pain. The assumption of deterrence is that an individual's propensity toward lawbreaking is in inverse proportion to his or her perceived probability of negative consequences. Under the deterrence theory, the difference in criminal and non-criminal behavior is that the criminal has a lower fear of the perceived consequences. That fear may come from a real threat, or a perceived one.

There are three dimensions of perceptions about the probability of suffering negative consequences: severity, celerity, and certainty. Consciously or subconsciously, rational potential perpetrators assess these three dimensions when plotting to commit commercial crime. In fact, most are quite calculated.

Two other factors, incapacitation and rehabilitation, which are generated by formal and informal sanctioning, also act to inhibit illegal behavior. Green cautions, however, that the formal and/or informal sanctions should not be more severe than the offense warrants.

(i) Severity. The more severe the punishment, the greater the deterrence. However, there is a limit to how severe the punishment can be for most commercial crime, because more severe sanctions must be reserved for the most undesirable behaviors (e.g., first-degree murder). This is because

some people will commit more heinous crimes than they ordinarily would have if they perceive the consequences to be the same regardless.

(ii) Celerity. The more swiftly the punishment is meted out, the greater the deterrence. If an aging commercial criminal believes that the worst case scenario is that his or her prosecution will be tied up for years in the courts and subject to endless appeals, deterrence is reduced.

(iii) Certainty. Certainty is generally thought to impose a greater fear-inducing dimension than either severity or celerity. If perpetrators know there is absolutely no chance they will get away with it, they are very unlikely to commit the crime.

Despite constant calls from some quarters for tougher sentencing practices, some argue that such sentences are not necessary or even desirable, because society does not have the jails or courts to accommodate all the offenders for extended periods of time. They argue that a better plan would be to sacrifice severity for certainty, with a reasonable degree of celerity.

(iv) General Versus Specific. Deterrence can also be categorized as general or specific.

- General deterrence refers to one person or group of persons being deterred from the commission of crime because they are aware, through an example, of negative consequences. If A is sentenced to prison for a commercial crime, then B through Z will be aware of the consequences and therefore be discouraged from similar actions.

- Specific (or special) deterrence refers to A being discouraged from committing an inappropriate behavior because he or she has committed such an offense in the past and is aware of the consequences.

(v) Perceived Versus Real. Finally, deterrence can be real or simply perceived as real. Green says that to deter an individual generally and specifically, his or her probability of receiving negative consequences need not be realistic; it need only be perceived as realistic. As an example, Green says:

"If executions were faked on television and, in fact no person was actually executed, there would still be the possibility of a general deterrent emanating from the program."

(vi) Effect of Deterrence on Commercial Criminals. Chambliss (1967) points out that commercial crimes are more instrumental and less expressive than street crime, and therefore should be deterred more easily. In addition, most commercial criminals, compared to more traditional offenders, perceive the informal sanctions of the loss of career and prestige to a greater extent, and are therefore theoretically more deterred by those consequences.

(b)   Formal Deterrence

(i) Increasing Enforcement. A crime control strategy has little chance of success unless offenders are sanctioned. However, formal levels of current enforcement are, by all measures, extremely low.

Braithwaite advocates a novel approach: enforced self-regulation. Under his idea, the government would compel each company to write rules for themselves or their employees, unique to the particular circumstances. A governmental agency would then be formed to monitor compliance. He points out several successes in the noncriminal area—e.g., the Federal Aviation Administration monitors self-regulation for the U.S. airline industry, and the Federal Trade Commission monitors rules that the U.S. advertising industry has largely set for itself.

However, there are problems with self-regulation, and the industries that attempt to regulate themselves have spotty records at best. In one study of the 320,000 physicians in the United States, an average of only 72 medical licenses per year were revoked.

It may be that increased enforcement can only come at the expense of a complete and total revision of the criminal justice system. Many commercial criminals have little fear of detection because of the constant barrage of information that shows the police and courts simply cannot keep up with the pace of criminal offenses. Until potential offenders have the perception that they will be caught and punished, we should not expect a reversal of the crime trend.

(ii) Sentencing of Commercial Criminals. Several major studies of sentencing practices have been conducted on economic and white-collar criminals. The first studies indicated that, contrary to Sutherland's intuitive belief, white-collar offenders appear to be sentenced more harshly than persons convicted of other felonies.

Hagan, Nagel, and Albonetti defined white-collar criminals as persons with a college education who committed one of a roster of specific offenses. They compared the sentencing of members of this group with that of persons of less education who commit the same offenses, those with less education who commit nonwhite-collar crimes, and those with college education who commit nonwhite-collar offenses. Their finding was that sentences generally were tougher for college graduates.

Wheeler, Weisburd, and Bode analyzed only sentences for white-collar offenders, holding constant other variables such as age, harm inflicted, the sentence options available to the court, and previous offenses. They concluded that the following two conditions associated with white-collar offenses were most likely to lead to imprisonment:

- *The allowed maximum sentence.* More than three-quarters of those who could have done 15 years or more were sentenced to prison. Only a third of the persons who could have been sentenced to a year or less actually received time.

- *The financial impact of the crime.* Those who take under $500 are less likely to go to prison than those whose offenses create more substantial losses.

The sentencing studies were careful to note their possible shortcomings. Most important is the fact that certain offenses and offenders have been siphoned off much earlier in the judicial process. Judges may get only the most difficult economic offenses and may be responding to these.

(c) Informal Deterrence

Informal sanctions—the loss of job or prestige—can be powerful deterrents to commission of crime. In certain instances, they may be even more powerful than the fear of formal sanctions such as going to prison. For example:

- In one case, a bank president, who was told he was about to be indicted, spent most of his time asking whether the charges were going to be made public. When told that indeed the charges would be public, the banker committed suicide that evening.

- In one study (Cameron, 1964) middle-class housewives who were caught shoplifting were more worried about others finding out than about going to jail.

Informal sanctions often exist without formal sanctions. However, the imposition of formal sanctions will usually lead to additional informal sanctions.

(d)   Ethics

(i) Education.   Green points out that teaching people that certain behaviors are illegal and therefore inappropriate is uncomplicated and extremely effective in reducing crime. Moral education that discourages illegal behavior must be continuous. Simply put, persons must be informed as to what behavior is acceptable and what is not so that they can alter their actions appropriately.

However, appealing simply to the morality of the offense is usually insufficient. Persons must also be told of the punishment or pain that accompanies the commission of a crime (i.e., the deterrence threat).

(ii) The Tone at the Top.   Behaviorists generally conclude that one of the single most important factors influencing group behavior is the attitude of management. In one survey conducted by S.N. Brenner and E.A. Molander, about half the sample believed there was pressure from superiors to engage in unethical behavior.

One prime example is the famous Equity Funding Case, which occurred in the early 1970s. For nearly 10 years, massive fraud was perpetrated by the Equity Funding Corporation through manipulation of financial statements. More specifically, Equity Funding falsified more than 56,000 life insurance policies and overstated their assets by $120 million. It was estimated that 50 to 75 employees, who managed to keep the scheme a secret for several years, were involved. The trustee appointed to sort out the massive fraud, Robert Loeffler, said, ''Of almost equal importance was the surprising ability of the originators of the fraud to recruit new participants over the years.''

The Equity Funding scheme was uncovered when a disgruntled former employee went to the authorities.

(e) A Prevention Strategy

Clinard and Yeager endorse the following remedial steps to deal with commercial crime:

1. The strengthening of consent agreements and decrees (under which companies do not admit that what they were doing was wrong, but agree to stop doing it) to provide substantial remedies for violations and to include systematic follow-ups;

2. Increases in fine ceilings, with fines to be assessed according to the nature of the violation and in proportion to the company's annual sales;

3. Stiff criminal penalties for violations of health and safety or environmental regulations that "recklessly endanger" the public or employees;

4. Stronger statutes to prohibit companies that previously had violated federal laws from receiving federal contracts;

5. Mandatory publicity for corporate civil and criminal violations;

6. More extensive use of imprisonment with longer sentences. Community service in place of incarceration should be prohibited by law, except for unusual circumstances;

7. Convicted corporate offenders should be prevented from being indemnified by their companies;

8. Management officials convicted of criminally violating corporate responsibilities should be prohibited for 3 years from assuming similar management positions in their company or others;

9. Directors should be liable, but not criminally, for being derelict in their duty to prevent illegal corporate actions; and

10. A new commercial bribery statute should be enacted to help prosecute corporate executives who receive kickbacks from their customers or suppliers.

§9.3 Prevention of Commercial Crime

However, as previously noted, many researchers believe there are better deterrents to commercial crime than incarceration of the individuals who are directly involved. They argue that the most effective deterrence threats are:

- Monetary penalties;
- Adverse publicity; and
- Incarcerating executives.

PART IV

Crisis Management

CHAPTER TEN

Dealing with a Known or Suspected Fraud

§10.1   **Introduction**

§10.2   **Forensic and Investigative Accounting Defined**

§10.3   **Skills and Attributes of the Forensic Accountant**

    (a) Professional Skills and Attributes

        (i)   Accounting and Audit Knowledge

        (ii)   Fraud Knowledge

        (iii) Knowledge of Law and Rules of Evidence

        (iv) Investigative Mentality and Critical Skepticism

        (v)   Understanding of Psychology and Motivation

        (vi) Communication Skills

        (vii) Understanding of Computers and Information Technology

    (b) Ethics

        (i)   Independence and Objectivity

        (ii)   Respect for Access to Information and Privacy Laws

§10.4   **Tools of the Forensic Accountant**

    (a) Interview Techniques

    (b) Information Gathering Techniques

    (c) Use of Private Investigators

    (d) Search and Seizure Mechanisms

    (e) Investigative Software Packages

§10.5   **Categorization of Services Offered**

    (a) Proactive Versus Reactive

    (b) Civil Versus Criminal
       (i)   Typical Civil Actions
       (ii)   Typical Criminal Matters
    (c) Other Categorizations
§10.6   The Five-Step Investigative Approach
    (a) Identification of Major Issues
    (b) Investigation of Issues
    (c) Financial Analysis and Synthesis
    (d) Communication of Findings
    (e) Presentation of Financial Evidence

§10.1 Introduction

The purpose of this chapter is to provide the reader with an understanding of forensic and investigative accounting as it relates to fraud investigation. In doing so, this chapter will:

- Identify the skills of forensic and investigative accounting practitioners, particularly those attributes falling outside the area of the traditional accounting profession;

- Identify the tools that forensic and investigative accountants have developed and that are applied in their engagements;

- Detail the types of services offered by forensic and investigative accountants, including both proactive and reactive services; and

- Offer an overview of a typical 5-step approach to carrying out a forensic accounting investigation.

§10.2 Forensic and Investigative Accounting Defined

Forensic and investigative accounting is the application of financial skills and an investigative mentality to unresolved issues, conducted within the context of the rules of evidence. As a discipline, it encompasses financial expertise, fraud knowledge, and a strong knowledge and understanding of business reality and the workings of the legal system. Its development has been primarily achieved through on-the-job training, as well as experience with investigating officers and legal counsel.

The term *forensic* can be defined as "belonging to, used in, or suitable to courts of law." It follows then, that forensic accounting is a discipline that deals with the relationship and application of financial facts to business problems, conducted in a legal setting.

An analogy may assist the reader in understanding the forensic accounting concept. Several years ago, the central figure in the television series *Quincy* was a Los Angeles coroner who was called upon to investigate suspicious or unexplained deaths. He ultimately presented his findings in testimony before the courts. His work was that of a forensic medical expert. Likewise, accountant practitioners concentrating their professional practice on matters requiring them to testify in court as to the findings of an investigation of accounting and financial evidence are termed *forensic accounting experts*. The ultimate test for the forensic accountant is acceptance by the courts of law—both criminal and civil—as an expert witness providing testimony in the area of accounting and financial matters.

The National Association of Certified Fraud Examiners (NACFE) provides courses of instruction in the area of forensic accounting. While the accounting profession currently does not prescribe any standard specifically related to forensic accounting, it is clear that the standards for such a practice are determined by the "courts of law." At the same time, a professional accountant (in the United States, a certified public accountant; in Canada, a chartered accountant, certified general accountant, or certified management accountant) is required to meet the general standards of professional practice as stipulated by the body governing his or her profession.

§10.3 Skills and Attributes of the Forensic Accountant

The forensic accountant practitioner must possess a range of skills to be able to professionally carry out financial investigations. These include not only expert accounting knowledge but also knowledge of business and an awareness of the process of law. With these skills, the forensic accountant is able to investigate, analyze, document, report on, and testify as to financial aspects of an investigation into fraud or other so-called white-collar crimes.

In many instances, the forensic accountant may be requested to quantify the amount of a fraud in a criminal matter or the financial damages in a civil matter. While a criminal matter must be proven beyond a reasonable doubt and a civil matter must be proven on the balance of probabilities, both require similar techniques and skills of the forensic accountant.

(a)   Professional Skills and Attributes

The professional skills and attributes of a forensic accountant fall into seven main categories:

- Accounting and audit knowledge;
- Fraud knowledge;
- Knowledge of law and rules of evidence;
- Investigative mentality and critical skepticism;
- Understanding of psychology and motivation;
- Communication skills; and
- Understanding of computers and information technology.

Each of the above is briefly described in the following sections.

(i) Accounting and Audit Knowledge. Professional training in accounting and audit provides not only accounting and audit knowledge but also a practical understanding of business in general: business operations, financing, corporate structure, industry practices, and standards of conduct.

The majority of those who identify themselves as forensic accountants are certified public accountants, chartered accountants, certified general accountants or certified management accountants with audit backgrounds; these individuals have sought and found careers for themselves in an area that allows them to use their skills as accountants, together with other personal attributes that are necessary in investigating business fraud and commercial crimes.

Audit skills are an important foundation for a forensic accountant. Due to the sensitivity of the work involved, forensic accountants must be able to focus on the need for a 100 percent substantive examination of all documentation related to a particular matter.

Related to audit skills is the requirement for complete and accurate documentation, which in turn means that the auditor must be able to catalogue the information that is available. He or she must also be able to determine what other sources exist for information that may not be available at first but that can, with research and diligence, be uncovered, obtained, and utilized. With his or her accounting and audit skills, the accountant is able to inquire about, locate, and identify documents—whether they are present initially or obtained during the course of the investigation—that are relevant to the issues under investigation.

For most professional accountants, audit experience includes both audit and nonaudit engagements covering a wide cross-section of business enterprises and their operations, ranging from small sole proprietorships to large multinational corporations, both public and private. This familiarity with business enterprise is an important element in the forensic accountants investigation of business frauds and similar matters.

(ii) Fraud Knowledge. In addition to professional training in accounting and audit, the most important aspect of the forensic accountant skills mix is exposure to and knowledge of many different types of fraudulent transactions. This will allow him or her to identify "red flags" and to piece together patterns and theories that may otherwise elude an accountant who has not had the same degree of exposure to fraud.

Forensic accountants do not merely compute, they analyze. The analytical process is not an easy one, as each case is unique and therefore calls upon the experience of the forensic accountant, the formal training, and other important attributes. Specifically, he or she must be able to identify accounting problem areas, prioritize these problem areas or issues as required, and appropriately refine the focus of the investigation or refocus the investigation as new information is obtained and assessed. Often, an original theory may be only the beginning of an investigation, or it may be refined to a specific issue warranting further review. In providing assistance to the courts, this ability to properly focus the investigation is an important one for the forensic accountant.

The importance of experience cannot be overemphasized. The forensic accountant must also be able to look beyond the form of the documentation, to understand its substance and foundations, and to assess whether it is consistent with other business realities. The forensic accountant must understand the nature of the documents that he or she is reviewing and question their business reality. More than anything, a forensic accountant is distinguished by having "been there before." Knowledge of many different types of fraud, based on first-hand investigative experience, means a more effective plan of investigation, knowing when, how, and who to interview, and how to communicate findings in reports to clients and if necessary to the court.

(iii) Knowledge of Law and Rules of Evidence. It is important for the forensic accountant to be knowledgeable about both criminal and civil law, since these laws have a direct impact on matters involving the forensic accountant. Specifically, a forensic accountant must be able to understand both criminal and other statutes that may have been contravened in order to identify possible issues. There is also a need to understand the rules of evidence to ensure that all findings are admissible in court, if necessary. Specifically, the following understanding of the rules of evidence for both civil and criminal matters is important for the investigative accountant:

- What evidence is;

- How it is obtained;

- How it is preserved;

- How it is presented before the courts; and

- How the forensic accountants own work can become part of the evidence brought before the courts or before some other tribunal responsible for determining what has occurred.

To provide accounting assistance in a matter involving fraud, the forensic accountant must possess a general understanding of the issues by which the courts of law judge an act to be fraudulent. He or she must be knowledgeable as to the courts tests for fraud—for example, the presence of dishonest intent as seen in the perpetrator's actions, or more particularly, the 'mens rea' or state of mind of the perpetrator at the time the act occurred. He or she must review and analyze accounting, banking, financial, and other business records, and identify both specific acts and patterns of conduct that are suggestive of dishonest intent to deprive a victim of an asset.

(iv) Investigative Mentality and Critical Skepticism. The forensic accountant must be instilled with an investigative outlook, the tenacity of a detective, and the ability to identify indicators of fraud. These attributes could be termed *investigative mentality*. This mentality encourages the forensic accountant to seek substance over form—to identify and analyze data and

to conduct interviews in order to determine what has actually occurred in a business transaction, rather than what simply appears to have occurred.

The investigative mentality is sometimes manifested by the 'smell' test—the ability to assess relevant transactions or events to determine their reasonableness and to the extent possible, their veracity. In other words, in light of all the known facts, does a particular action appear reasonable and logical? Is the action and/or pattern of behavior plausible in the circumstances, or is there an 'odor' that begs further investigation.

Investigative mentality can also be thought of as professional, critical skepticism. It is not a shotgun approach; rather, it is a specific and precise set of judgmental procedures, suitable for the circumstances, that allows the forensic accountant to identify and assess all relevant facts and develop hypotheses. These hypotheses can then be researched further and tested more extensively as the investigation proceeds. The forensic accountant never discounts any aspect of an investigation on face value; only after examining all available evidence and weighing its totality will he or she determine an item to be not relevant to the issues at hand.

Another analogy—that of the watchdog/bloodhound—further illustrates the forensic accountants investigative mentality attribute. A normal auditor is a watchdog—he/she does not look for fraud in the course of an audit, but will respond if warning signs appear through audit procedures. The forensic accountant, however, is more of a bloodhound—actively seeking out the presence of evidence, all of which when viewed together may indicate the occurrence of a fraudulent act.

While the investigative mentality requires a disciplined approach and a methodology, it also requires creativity in being able to identify and seek out further sources of evidence and to analyze this new information. A forensic investigation is not restricted by issues of materiality or sampling, which are relevant in guiding an audit assignment. Such restrictions may cause fraudulent acts to be overlooked, and they are inadequate in establishing evidence.

(v) Understanding of Psychology and Motivation. Another attribute of the forensic accountant is an understanding of the human element. Documents do not commit fraud; computers do not commit fraud; rather, people commit fraud. In assessing information, documentation, and accounting records, one of the seasonings, which the forensic accountant can apply to the mix, is his or her understanding of individuals, including what motivates an individual to commit fraud and the attributes of an individual who

commits fraud. This understanding, together with the ability of the forensic accountant to examine information not just from an accounting viewpoint, but also within the context of the overall picture or business reality, is important.

In general, it can be said that individuals react to satisfy needs. The forensic accountant must recognize the presence of such needs during his or her investigation, whether it is the need of an employee for greater income to maintain an extravagant lifestyle or the need of a sales manager to maintain sales volumes in a declining market so as to ensure his or her continued employment. Such needs often provide the motivation for acts, which an employee may label differently, but that are, in essence, fraud.

In a situation where an individual has both the need and the opportunity, a fraudulent act may be the result.

(vi) Communication Skills. A forensic accountant, as an expert witness to the court in findings of fact, must be able to clearly communicate such information. This means that they must be able to communicate without bias in written form, including the use of accounting schedules, charts, and exhibits. They must also be able to communicate to others the nature and extent of the work undertaken and the findings which have evolved from that work, so that it can be understood both in a court of law and in other venues.

When the forensic accountant testifies as an expert witness in court, he or she must be able to explain their procedures, analyses, and findings in such a way that the basis for their expert testimony—both facts and, if necessary, opinion—is understood. The forensic accountants knowledge of the available evidence and possible alternate explanations of the events must be as complete as possible, to ensure their findings are not compromised through cross-examination.

(vii) Understanding of Computers and Information Technology. The ledgers of yesterday have been replaced by computers today and in fraud investigation it is important to be as up-to-date as the alleged perpetrators of fraud. Thus, an ability to understand the opportunities computers provide to potential perpetrators of fraud as well as an ability to use computers in analysis and documentation of an alleged fraud are important skills for the forensic accountant.

A knowledge of computer graphics is also helpful. The forensic accountants findings often include quantitative analyses that are conducive to being presented in the form of graphs and charts that depict and summarize the information. Typical graphs and charts include summaries of the source and use of funds, as well as flow charts showing the movement of assets at various times.

(b) Ethics

(i) Independence and Objectivity. Independence and objectivity are integral concepts in the ethical training of professional accountants. While the need for these attributes is well established in the audit area, they are extremely important in investigative work. The forensic and investigative accountant is not an advocate; rather, he or she provides the skills and input of an independent expert. Even a bias with respect to a single, small matterwhether actual or perceivedmay call into question in the eyes of the court otherwise unbiased evidence presented by the forensic accountant. He or she must therefore report as objectively as possible.

(ii) Respect for Access to Information and Privacy Laws. One factor that must not be overlooked in the role of investigator is that the information that is gathered must be collected in an ethical and legal manner. One cannot misrepresent ones self when gathering information, nor can the process of collecting information be abused. Most importantly, the rights of an individual whose activities are being reviewed must not be abused.

§10.4 Tools of the Forensic Accountant

(a) Interview Techniques

One of the more important tools for the forensic accountant is the interview process, which enables him or her to obtain nondocumentary evidence in a clear and concise manner. Clarity is important so that explanations can be assessed, without ambiguity figuring in the assessment. The forensic accountant must be able to differentiate between an inarticulate explanation by a nervous individual and the evasive explanation frequently offered by an individual who does not want to have his or her actions or motives identified and examined more closely.

The forensic accountant must be able to control and direct the interview process to draw out further evidence, often from hostile or adversarial interviewees. Effectively, the forensic accountant applies his or her own knowledge of the human element to assist in this process.

(b) Information Gathering Techniques

The forensic and investigative accountant is not a police officer. He or she does not have the resources of a police officer and, even when working to assist the police, must work with his or her own expertise. Among the most important investigative tools are those that enable the forensic accountant to gather and analyze information available in the public domain, in conjunction with other information gathered during the investigation.

For example, in investigating an individual, background information can be gathered concerning the individuals credit rating, secured debts, professional qualifications, and other details. For a company, information about the industry can be gathered from government statistics, computerized news data bases, and information on file from governmental offices. Corporate information such as jurisdiction of incorporation authorized share capital, and the identity of all officers and directors since incorporation can be obtained from the appropriate registry office in the jurisdiction where the incorporation took place. Obviously, private off-shore corporations have less information available than publicly traded companies in North America.

Public domain information may also assist in the analysis of a companys financial results. Comparison of a companys statistics and trends to those in the related industry may identify unexplained variances that alert the forensic accountant to possible questionable activities that warrant further investigation.

There are many sources of public information about organizations, industries, and institutions. Very often a university reference library or a governmental resource center can provide access to documents, reference textbooks, computerized data bases, and other sources of information that can assist in understanding and analyzing a case.

(c) Use of Private Investigators

It may also be necessary to engage private investigators to conduct surveillance of individuals, e.g., to observe their activity and record their presence at various locations and times, including meetings with certain individuals. The forensic accountant with ready access to those providing such services in a professional manner is providing a more complete service to clients.

(d)   Search and Seizure Mechanisms

In criminal matters, a search warrant is often utilized by the police to obtain documentary evidence. The forensic accountant may assist the police in specifying on the search warrant those accounting, banking, and other records that are to be seized as evidence of fraudulent activity. In Canada, the forensic accountant must also be named on the warrant to attend upon its execution at the premises to be searched in order to help identify those documents that are to be seized as evidence.

In civil matters, search and seizure mechanisms may also be available. For example, in Canada the forensic accountant may provide assistance in obtaining evidence through the use of an 'Anton Pillar' order obtained pursuant to a court application. Such an order permits the recovery of documentary evidence by counsel, under the court's supervision, from the other party. Such evidence could otherwise have been subject to destruction or concealment.

Along a similar vein, if there is a concern that the assets of an individual under investigation may be dissipated, a Mareva injunction may be obtained from the court. This injunction prohibits the individual under investigation from conducting his or her affairs in a manner that would financially prejudice the other party in a case prior to the court rendering its decision.

Under the rules of civil procedure, there are requirements for examinations for discovery (answering of questions under oath) and production of documents. In the process of discoveries, the forensic accountant can assist counsel in requesting documents to be produced by the other party and in determining questions to be put to the witnesses for the other party.

(e)   Investigative Software Packages

The forensic accountant assembles evidentiary support for his or her testimony or opinion. This support often takes the form of a written report accompanied by various supporting information—e.g., document briefs, chronologies of events, accounting schedules (either summaries or analytical schedules), graphs, and charts. This material, in aggregate, is often voluminous.

In recent years, computer software packages have been designed to assist in complex investigative efforts. Investigative software packages include programs that allow data to be retained in a computer and analyzed for example, to identify sources and/or references to various documents.

Various data base programs may also be utilized for retaining evidentiary information. These packages enable information to be easily accessed, and allow different fields of this information to be selected, compared, analyzed, and ordered to facilitate the investigation.

§10.5 Categorization of Services Offered

(a) Proactive Versus Reactive

Forensic accounting services can be proactive or reactive. Proactive services include training on fraud awareness and fraud prevention activities, presented elsewhere in this Handbook. Reactive services are investigative and analytical in nature and are rendered after the event. Much of the information in this chapter addresses reactive services.

(b) Civil Versus Criminal

Another way to identify the types of services that a forensic accountant renders is to consider the venue in which a dispute is finally resolved. For example:

- A criminal forum must establish guilt beyond a reasonable doubt;
- A civil matter, which has less onerous restrictions, must determine its finding of facts based on the balance of probabilities;
- A nonjudicial tribunal can have a different standard, being either stricter or more lenient than a court of law; and
- Finally, if the circumstances are such that no reference is made to an outside tribunal, but rather two parties are to resolve a matter on their own; then the level of proof required is only what the other side will accept.

§10.5 Categorization of Services Offered

Using the most frequently applied divider—civil versus criminal—typical cases can be grouped as set out in the following sections.

(i) Typical Civil Actions.

Typical matters that involve civil actions include:

- Insurance claims relating to property damage or business interruption;
- Claims for loss of income arising from personal injuries or fatalities;
- Breach of contract claims;
- Breach of fiduciary duty; and
- Fidelity insurance claims.

(ii) Typical Criminal Matters. Criminal matters include:

- Money laundering, that is conversion of the proceeds of crime;
- The receiving or offering of secret commissions;
- Planned bankruptcies;
- Criminal breach of trust;
- Computer viruses, being criminal mischief;
- Employee theft;
- Sale of confidential information;
- Fraud upon a company by its management;
- Fraud upon a company by its employees;
- Fraud of customers by a company;
- Fraud of suppliers by a company; and even
- Murder for profit.

(c) Other Categorizations

Services of a forensic accountant can also be categorized in other ways, for example by the type of procedures performed. These procedures can include:

- Initial review of documentation to determine whether further research or investigation is required or necessary;
- Providing an affidavit outlining the results of a review of documentation;
- Providing a report identifying the scope of work and findings;
- Assisting counsel in obtaining a search warrant; and
- Providing expert testimony in court.

The industry that the forensic accountant is investigating can be another method of classification. For example:

- Service industries could include transportation, banking, brokerage, retailing, real estate, construction, professional services (including services of professional accountants and lawyers), mortgage brokerage, and telecommunications.
- Manufacturing industries could include construction, farming, food processing, manufacturing, mining, petroleum, and publishing.

The above classifications could then be further refined, and other areas added. For example, government and nonprofit sectors are other areas where forensic accountants are called upon to provide their services.

§10.6 The Five-Step Investigative Approach

There are usually five major steps or aspects to a forensic accounting engagement. These are:

- Identification of the major issues;
- Investigation of the issues;

- Analysis of the data and syntheses of information;
- Summarization and communication of findings; and
- Presentation of financial evidence.

(a)   Identification of Major Issues

In a forensic engagement, it is important first of all to identify the objectives and the areas of uncertainty that need to be clarified. This includes:

- Determining the major strengths and weaknesses of the evidence and supporting material in order to identify what additional research, documentary evidence, investigation, and/or analysis is required; and
- Developing an understanding of the issues and the surrounding information so that preliminary decisions can be made on how additional information will be acquired and the type of analysis that will be undertaken with the available material.

The identification of issues can be achieved through a review of various evidentiary material, for example:

- Statements of claim or counter claim;
- Statements of defence;
- Examinations and/or productions relating to a civil matter or search warrants;
- Witness "will says"; and/or
- Police witness interview notes.

Once this step is complete, the nature and extent of the required forensic accounting assistance can be determined. However, it should be noted that the issues identified initially are often revised as the forensic investigation proceeds.

(b)   Investigation of Issues

One of the forensic accountant's important objectives is to determine what eventual use will be made of the information he or she obtains. In particular, the forensic accountant must be able to understand the difference between relevant and irrelevant information, and the standards of evidence required by the eventual tribunal or court.

Once areas of relevant information have been identified, the general objectives of the investigation must be translated into specifics; e.g., identifying the documents and other information to be analyzed, and/or the interviews and third-party information that are required to address the issues. Additionally, the forensic accountant may carry out research to identify any precedents that may assist the issue investigation process. In this phase, the forensic accountant also seeks to identify possible logical alternative interpretations for the issues that have been identified.

(c)   Financial Analysis and Synthesis

During this stage, the financial issues being investigated are evaluated in detail. Appropriate conclusions are then drawn, either in terms of a quantum or quantification of the issue, or a finding of facts—e.g., whether or not a particular transaction or event took place and its resulting effect.

(d)   Communication of Findings

The forensic accountant must be able to present his or her findings in a way that is understandable, and do so in an appropriate format. The appropriate format can be:

- An affidavit, which is a sworn statement of findings with supporting documentation;
- A reporting letter, which is a communication to counsel outlining the scope of the review and its findings; or
- A report, being a formal communication to the court.

(e)　Presentation of Financial Evidence

Forensic accountants must be prepared for examination of all their activities under oath at any stage—from an affidavit, to examination for discovery, to trial. They must be able to qualify as an expert witness based on their education, experience, and knowledge as a professional accountant, as well as their knowledge as a forensic accountant.

Finally, the forensic accountant must also be prepared to respond to cross-examination and to the submission of different financial evidence and alternatives produced by the other side.

Bibliography

Set out below is a selected list of books on the subject of fraud, commercial crime and related areas, by author.

August Bequai. *White Collar Crime: A Twentieth Century Crisis.* Lexington, Mass.: D.C. Heath, 1979.

Jack Bologna and Robert J. Lindquist. *Fraud Auditing and Forensic Accounting.* New York: John Wiley & Sons, 1987.

Jack Bologna. *Corporate Fraud—The Basics of Fraud Prevention and Detection.* Stoneham, Mass.: Butterworths, 1984.

Michael J. Comer. *Corporate Fraud,* (2nd ed.) London and New York: McGraw-Hill, 1985.

Robert K. Elliott and John J. Willingham. *Management Fraud: Detection and Deterrence.* New York: Petrocelli Books, 1980.

J.J. Grau and B. Jacobson. *Criminal and Civil Investigation Handbook.* New York: McGraw-Hill, 1981.

Gary Green. *Occupational Crime.* Chicago, Ill.: Nelson-Hall, 1990.

Douglas Hoyt et al. *Computer Security Handbook,* (2nd ed.). New York: MacMillan Publishing Company, 1988.

Paul L. Kirk and John I. Thornton (eds.) *Crime Investigation,* (2nd ed.). New York: John Wiley & Sons, 1974.

Leonard I. Krauss and Aileen MacGahan. *Computer Fraud and Countermeasures.* Englewood Cliffs, N.J.: Prentice-Hall, 1979.

Larry J. Siegel. *Criminology,* (3rd ed.). St. Paul, Minn.: West Publishing Company, 1989.

Charles Wagner. *The CPA and Computer Fraud.* Lexington, Mass.: Lexington Books, 1979.

Glossary

(Note: Much of the material in the glossary has been abridged, reprinted, and/or adapted from the Fraud Examiners' Manual *[National Association of Certified Fraud Examiners, 1989), which in turn based its Glossary on* The Investigation of White-Collar Crime *(Edelhertz, 1977)].*

Abuse of Trust. The misuse of one's position and/or of privileged information gained by virtue of that position in order to acquire for oneself (or for another in whom one has an interest) money, property, or some privilege to which one is not entitled. Abuse of trust often involves as well a violation of fiduciary duty.

The victims of such abuses are those who rely to their detriment (i.e., who have placed their trust in) the individual or group that misuses a trusted position.

The abuse of trust can occur in many areas, but is a situation that arises most frequently in the following four white-collar crime areas.

1. Banking; e.g., where abuse of trust can involve self-dealing in connection with loans or credit to oneself, one's friends, or business associates.

2. Securities; e.g., where insider information may be used for personal benefit at the expense of clients, stockholders, and others.

3. Commercial bribery; e.g., where the procurement and competitive bidding processes may be manipulated.

4. Embezzlement and fiduciary violations; e.g., where trustees and others may misuse property or funds in their custody.

Remedies for abuses of trust include criminal, civil, and regulatory remedies, enforceable under federal and state/provincial laws.

See also: BANKING VIOLATIONS, COMMERCIAL BRIBERY, COMPETITIVE PROCUREMENT FRAUDS, EMBEZZLEMENT AND FIDUCIARY FRAUDS, INSIDER SELF-DEALING, SECURITIES FRAUD.

Advance Fee Schemes.   Schemes in which assurances of some future benefit are made with full compensation to the promisor/perpetrator who has no intention of performing, but rather is interested in obtaining the partial payment requested as a service fee or an advance good faith deposit (often called a *returnable deposit*).

Typical victims of advance fee schemes are businessmen who cannot obtain customary banking or credit sources. They thus pay deposits or fees to others to arrange loans or credit for them. In the United States, these frauds are customarily prosecuted under the federal mail fraud statute and state larceny and fraud statutes, and are investigated frequently by the Postal Service.

Antitrust Offenses.   Combinations in restraint of trade, price fixing, or other schemes to unlawfully drive competitors out of business; and/or agreements among competitors to share business according to some agreed formula (such as bid-rigging conspiracies and discriminatory pricing agreements); and/or domination of a business area by one or a few enterprises. Victims of antitrust offenses are businessmen and purchasers of goods or services who pay higher prices.

Antitrust offenses constitute violations of federal and, in the United States, state criminal and civil laws. In the United States, check with local prosecutors, state attorneys-general, U.S. Department of Justice and regional offices of the U.S. Federal Trade Commission.

See also: COMPETITIVE PROCUREMENT FRAUD, PRICE FIXING, RESTRAINT OF TRADE.

Auto Repair Fraud.   A form of consumer fraud involving maintenance services to automobiles.

Auto repair frauds fall into several categories:

1. Overcharging for labor or parts or use of shoddy or substandard parts.

2. Failure to perform promised services or repairs.

3. Charging for services not performed or parts not used.

4. Performing services or repairs that are unnecessary or unwanted.

Remedies usually involve state/provincial fraud or larceny laws, and state/provincial and local licensing laws. Many law enforcement agencies have adopted proactive detection techniques, such as the use of decoy vehicles.

See also: CONSUMER FRAUD, REPAIR FRAUD.

Bait and Switch. A form of consumer fraud involving misleading advertising. The substance of the bait and switch is where a store advertises a "bargain," which is no more than an inducement (i.e., bait) to lure a customer to the store where he or she is presented with similar but higher-priced items (i.e., the switch). Thus the advertisement does not constitute a bona fide offer for sale of the merchandise in question. This may be because (1) the advertised item is not available on the premises or is available in unreasonably short supply, or (2) acts are undertaken to prevent the customer from purchasing the advertised item in favor of higher-priced merchandise (i.e., by downgrading or "knocking" the advertised goods). Such sales tactics are only sometimes sufficiently blatant to support criminal fraud prosecutions and/or false advertising charges. More frequently they are dealt with through civil remedies invoked by local consumer protection offices and district/crown attorneys (where they have civil jurisdiction), consumer divisions of state/provincial attorneys general offices, and, in the United States, the Federal Trade Commission.

See also: FALSE AND MISLEADING ADVERTISING.

Banking Violations. Violations by insiders or by customers of banks, savings and loan associations, or credit unions. Insider violations generally involve embezzlements or self-dealing (where insiders lend money to themselves or to businesses in which they have an interest), or take bribes or special favors to make loans or to refrain from collecting loans. Violations by outsiders would include false financial statements to induce a bank to make a loan, the use of fraudulent collateral, check kiting, and similar offenses.

Victims are depositors and shareholders, bank stockholders, creditors, the federal government as the insurer of deposits, and surety companies who bond bank employees and officials.

These violations are prosecuted under federal and state/provincial statutes for embezzlement, false entries in books and records of banks (including computerized records), and misapplications. In the United States, violations in state-chartered institutions are often federally prosecuted because deposits are federally insured.

See also: ABUSE OF TRUST, CHECK KITING, COLLATERAL FRAUDS, COMMERCIAL BRIBERY, INSIDER SELF-DEALING.

Bankruptcy Fraud. Frauds involving financial insolvency.

Victims of bankruptcy frauds are usually creditors and suppliers of the failed or failing business, although "silent partners" and stockholders can also be victimized by managers of the business who operate fraudulently. There are two major types of bankruptcy fraud:

1. The scam or planned bankruptcy, in which the assets, credit and viability of a business are purposely and systematically milked to obtain cash which is hidden by scam operators.
2. Fraudulent concealments or diversions of assets in anticipation of insolvency, so the assets cannot be sold for the benefit of creditors (i.e., squirreling away assets when bankruptcy appears imminent).

Planned thefts and fencing activities may be associated with either types of bankruptcy fraud as a means by which assets can be diverted and converted to cash.

Bankruptcy fraud is primarily a federal violation. In the United States, some forms of bankruptcy fraud, such as scams, would also be violations of state fraud and larceny laws.

Bid Rigging. see COMPETITIVE PROCUREMENT FRAUD.

Boiler Room. A technique used to promote fraudulent sales of securities, charitable donations, etc.

The "boiler room" technique involves the use of telephone solicitors, operating locally or by use of long distance lines, who call lists of victims and solicit them to buy. The telephone salespersons work on high commissions using preplanned sales pitches. Their services, particularly in charitable solicitations, are sometimes sold to otherwise legitimate enterprises, which rarely see very much of the collections. The technique depends primarily upon glib misrepresentations.

In the United States, the use of this technique exposes the perpetrators to criminal prosecution under federal wire fraud and mail fraud laws and under fraud and nonregistration provisions of the Securities Acts administered by the U.S. Securities and Exchange Commission. It also exposes the users to criminal or civil action at the state and local levels under state fraud statutes, state "blue-sky laws" regulating securities sales, and local and state laws, requiring licensing and filing of information in connection with charitable solicitations.

See also: CHARITY AND RELIGIOUS FRAUDS, SECURITIES FRAUD.

Business Opportunity Schemes. One of the most prevalent and multivaried forms of fraud in which victims are offered the opportunity to make a living, or to supplement their income, by going into business for themselves (full- or part-time), or by purchasing franchises or equipment to manufacture some item, sell merchandise, or perform some service.

Victims are generally individuals with some small pool of money they have saved and to whom the prospect of the promised independence and/or income is attractive. Such schemes range from being total shams to being opportunities whose promised returns are highly illusory. The operators of these schemes have essentially one goal, which is to acquire the money of the subscriber or investor victims. Work-at-home merchandising schemes (knitting machines, raising minks, etc.) or the sale of distributorships (cosmetics, special rug cleaning processes, etc.) are common examples of the kinds of opportunities pitched in this type of fraud. The opportunity presented by the fraud operator often includes the promise of "guaranteed" markets for the goods or services to be produced. Often the schemes induce the victim to enlist other victims, creating a pyramid scheme.

In the United States, these schemes are generally prosecuted under federal mail fraud laws, and state laws which proscribe larceny, false pretenses, etc. Check with U.S. Postal Inspector, U.S. Federal Trade Commission, state attorneys general offices, and local prosecutors.

See also: FRANCHISING FRAUDS, PYRAMID SCHEMES, SELF-IMPROVEMENT SCHEMES.

Chain Referral Schemes.   Any scheme in which the victim is induced to part with money or property on the representation that he or she will make money through inducing others to buy into the same deal.

First-tier victims usually believe that those whom they involve in the scheme (second-tier victims) will themselves make money-but since second-tier victims can only make money by involving third-tier victims, and so on, the scheme must eventually collapse. Generally only the fraud operators who manage the scheme make money on it; few first- or second-tier victims (especially if they are honest) have a sufficient number of victimizable friends and acquaintances to come out whole.

One common type of chain-referral scheme is the chain letter; more sophisticated is the "pyramid scheme," in which (for example) the victim is sold a franchise to sell both merchandise and other franchises, with the promise of profits on merchandise sold and commissions, or overrides, on merchandise sold by any second or later-tier victim who buys a franchise. The profits appear, therefore, to be in selling franchises rather than in selling merchandise. These schemes ultimately collapse of their own weight.

In the United States, chain-referral schemes are criminally prosecuted under federal and mail fraud statutes, and state fraud laws. Civil actions have been undertaken by the U.S. Federal Trade Commission, state attorneys general offices, and local prosecutors.

See also: MERCHANDISING FRAUDS, PYRAMID SCHEMES.

Charity and Religious Frauds.   Frauds arising out of the fund-raising activities of charitable and/or religious groups.

Almost anyone can be the victim of such frauds often without knowing it, but even where the victim may later suspect the fraud, his or her individual loss may be so small that there is little desire to pursue the matter. Three types of fraud situations are observed in this area.

1. The bogus charity or religious group, e.g., where money is solicited for a nonexistent organization or cause, or for a charitable front created for the sole purpose of soliciting funds, which will end up in the collector's pockets.

2. Misrepresentation of association with a charity or religious group, e.g., where money is solicited on behalf of a legitimate organization or cause by those with no ties to such organization or cause, and who have no intention of giving to the group.

3. Misrepresentation of the benefits or uses of contributions, e.g., a situation in which those solicited for donations to a legitimate charity or religious organization are not aware that most of the money collected reverts not to the charitable cause, but rather is used to cover the cost of professional fund raisers and/or administrative overhead expenses. (This is a grey area since professional fund raisers perform a legitimate service for which they may properly and legitimately be compensated).

In some instances charitable organizations themselves are the victims of con men who use them as a front, keeping the lions share of the collections, as in the case of boiler room operations (see "Boiler Rooms"). In other instances the solicitation falls into a grey area where otherwise legitimate charities and causes will cover up the fact that most of the monies collected go to salaries, fund raisers, and so on. Depending on the blatant nature of the operation, or where in the grey area a con falls, there may be federal criminal violations (i.e., mail fraud, wire fraud in the United States), violations of state/provincial statutes, violations of local licensing laws dealing with charitable solicitations, or in the United States of state laws requiring filing of information with state agencies and full disclosure as to funds collected, costs of solicitation, monies provided charitable beneficiaries, etc.

See also: BOILER ROOM.

Check Kiting. Any of a variety of frauds against banks which depend for success upon the time it takes to clear checks.

The most common form of check kiting involves the opening of two or more accounts. Balances are built up in each by deposits from the others. Checks are circulated between accounts, with no money taken out of any account, until at least one of the banks develops confidence in the depositor. Then the depositor takes money out of that bank, depending on the circulation of checks between the two or more banks, and the several days it takes to clear checks (especially between different cities), so as to prevent detection.

Banks are victims of check kites. When first discovered, check kites appear far more costly than when all transactions are analyzed, since hundreds of thousands of dollars in checks may be circulated to steal only a few thousand dollars. In some instances, however, massive amounts have been stolen. In many instances businessmen employ check kites when they cannot get loans from banks to tide themselves over a temporary business situation, and intend to (and often do) put the money back into the accounts before the check kite is discovered. In such instances that bank has been fraudulently induced to unwittingly grant what amounts to an interest-free loan.

Check kites are generally prosecuted under federal fraud and banking laws. Local law enforcement investigations should carefully consider signs of check kites in cases investigated, since they may play a part in other, broader fraud schemes.

See also: BANKING VIOLATIONS.

Collateral Frauds.   Frauds involving the holding, taking, or offering of collateral pursuant to a financial transaction.

In many instances these will be banking transactions (see "Banking Violations"). Beyond this, however, such frauds may be encountered in connection with any transaction in which security is provided, such as security for private loans, non-existent accounts receivable sold or pledged to factors, and the like. In some cases collateral used as security may not belong to the person offering it. It could be stolen (e.g., stolen securities), borrowed, or already subject to an undisclosed lien or other encumbrance. Alternatively, there may be some gross misrepresentation as to the collateral's value.

Collateral frauds are typically violations of federal fraud and banking laws. There may be elements in banking or corporate violations involving self-dealing, as where a bank officer makes a loan knowing the collateral is bad. Collateral frauds may also be involved in organized crime activities, e.g., obtaining proceeds of stolen securities not by an attempted sale, which would precipitate discovery when title was transferred, but by their use as collateral for loans.

See also: BANKING VIOLATIONS.

Commercial Bribery.   A form of insider fraud or abuse of trust in which an employee or officer of a private enterprise or government entity is given a bribe or some other valuable consideration, to induce the employee or official to make a purchase, or grant a contract or some special privilege (such as a zoning variance, license, etc.).

Commercial bribery is a violation of specific statutes in a large number of jurisdictions, and falls within the proscriptions of more general criminal statutes in other jurisdictions. It may violate numerous federal statutes, depending on the manner in which it is executed.

Competitive Procurement Fraud.   Unlawful manipulation of the public or private contracting process.

Victims are competitors not participating in the fraud; the public or private entity soliciting bids (which are believed to be competitive); and customers or constituents of those entities who do not realize benefits that would be derived from a truly competitive procurement process.

Three main forms of competitive procurement frauds are:

1. Bid rigging, i.e., a form of illegal anticompetitive conduct in which bidders in a competitive procurement collusively set their bids so as to deprive the bid solicitor of a competitive process. The effect is an administered bidding process in which the winner and the terms and prices of the goods and services involved in the procurement are set by the conspirators rather than by the competitive process. Parties to the conspiracy are thus able to divide among themselves a set of procurement contracts and to fix prices for goods and services at the same time.
2. Bid fixing, i.e., a form of illegal manipulation of the procurement process whereby one bidding party is provided with inside information (by the bid solicitor or an agent thereof), which enables said bidder to gain an unfair advantage over other bidders.
3. Bribery/kickbacks, i.e., a situation in which procurement contracts are let on the basis of the payment of bribes and kickbacks to procurement officials rather than on the basis of competitive procurement guidelines.

Competitive procurement frauds are prosecuted under federal and state/provincial criminal laws proscribing mail fraud, criminal conspiracy, bribery, kickbacks, etc. Proof in these cases usually involves (1) the most painstaking analysis of bidding patterns, (2) the examination of relationships between bids to the entity whose defrauding is being investigated, and bids by the same bidders to other entities for possible broader patterns of trade-offs, and (3) close scrutiny of performance on the jobs done pursuant to contracts.

See also: COMMERCIAL BRIBERY, FALSE CLAIMS, KICKBACKS, PUBLIC/OFFICIAL CORRUPTION.

Computer Fraud.   Frauds arising out of the increasing use of the computer to maintain business and government records, such as those relating to inventories, accounts payable and receivable, customer and payroll records.

Most computer frauds are really old frauds that are committed in a computer environment. True computer frauds do exist—such as those involving unauthorized changes to a computer's programming—but these are relatively less common and are most often committed by technical computer people.

Consumer Fraud.   Frauds of the marketplace involving seller misrepresentations to buyers. Victims are consumers of all kinds, individual and institutional, public and private.

Common forms of consumer fraud include:

1. Selling of useless goods or services, represented as beneficial; e.g., "miracle face creams."
2. Misrepresentation of product performance, benefits, or safety.
3. False and misleading advertising.
4. Failure to service items after sale, including reneging on warranties.
5. Repair fraud.
6. Hidden charges with respect to financing, necessary follow-up services, etc.
7. Weights and measures violations.

See also: BAIT AND SWITCH, FALSE AND MISLEADING ADVERTISING, MERCHANDISING FRAUDS, REPAIR FRAUD, WEIGHT AND MEASURES FRAUDS.

Coupon Redepmtion Frauds.   Frauds that involve cheating manufacturers or merchandisers who promote sales of their products by offering coupons that return part of the purchase price when the products are purchased.

Many manufacturers, primarily in the food business, place coupons in newspaper and magazine ads offering, for example, "15 cents off" if the product is purchased. The grocery store is supposed to redeem the coupon and will customarily receive a service charge of about 5 cents for handling the transaction. Frauds are committed against the manufacturers by amassing large numbers of coupons and submitting them to manufacturers without any bona fide purchases of the products.

The modus operandi of this type of fraud involves two basic steps: (1) collecting coupons, and (2) processing for redemption. Collecting coupons may be done by going through large numbers of old newspapers and magazines; sometimes this is done by trash collection or waste disposal companies as a side venture. Processing for collection requires the collaboration of retail merchants and is most efficiently done with the cooperation of officials of food retail chains, frequently without the knowledge of their companies.

These frauds have involved organized criminal syndicates. In the United States, they have usually been federally prosecuted under the mail fraud statute, though they could be prosecuted under numerous state fraud statutes.

Credit Card Frauds.   Frauds arising out of the application for, extension, and use of credit cards. Victims are the issuers of the credit cards. Common credit card abuses include:

1. Use of stolen credit cards.
2. False statements in the application for a credit card, including application under a false name.
3. Buying with no intention to every pay, by use of a credit card, which was originally legitimately obtained.

Credit card cases are usually referred to prosecutive agencies by credit card company investigators who have completed major portions of the investigation. In the United States, prosecution can be undertaken under the federal mail fraud statute, and under state fraud, larceny, and forgery laws.

Credit Rating Schemes.   Frauds arising out of the application for, extension of, and use of credit. Victims are generally the providers of credit. Common credit-related schemes include:

1. Sale of good credit ratings to high-risk applicants.
2. False statements in application for credit.
3. Creation of false credit accounts for purpose of theft.

The modus operandi of such schemes vary widely. In recent periods employees of credit rating organizations have altered credit ratings for payment, sometimes using computer techniques. False financial statements are another common method. On a smaller scale is a fraud, which operates like shoplifting—opening a charge account with false information in order to purchase and take away goods on the spot, simultaneously with the opening of the accounts.

Cases involving sales of credit ratings and alteration of computerized ratings are commonly prosecuted in the United States under the federal mail fraud statute, since they have been nationwide in scope. They would also be prosecutable under state laws proscribing fraud, false pretenses, and larceny.

See also: LOAN OR LENDING FRAUDS.

Debt Consolidation or Adjustment Swindles. Swindles perpetrated against people who are heavily in debt, and against their creditors, by purporting to provide a service that will systematically organize the marshaling of the debtor's assets and income to repay all creditors over a period of time, with creditors refraining from pressing for immediate payment of all sums due.

Some such services are provided by legitimate private agencies, and in many jurisdictions provision is made for such processes in nonbankruptcy proceedings in bankruptcy courts.

The modus operandi of this fraud is to often use heavy TV and newspaper advertising to lure debtors into signing up. Sometimes they talk creditors into waiting for their money; in other instances they falsely tell the debtors they have done so. They then take the debtors' assets and a portion of their weekly or monthly earnings, paying themselves first, and (usually only after they have their entire "fee") doling out the remainder to creditors. Frequently creditors receive little or nothing, and the debtors are left minus their fees and still in debt.

In the United States, these schemes have been prosecuted under the federal mail fraud law, state general fraud, larceny, and false pretenses statutes.

Directory Advertising Schemes. Frauds arising from the selling of printed mass advertising services.

These schemes are of two basic kinds: (1) impersonation schemes, in which con men send bills to business enterprises, which look like those customarily received; e.g., from the phone company for yellow-page advertising, with directions to make checks payable to entities, which look like legitimate payees of such bills; and (2) schemes in which it is promised that advertising will appear in a publication distributed to potential customers but where, in truth and in fact, distribution will be limited to the advertisers themselves, if the directory is printed at all.

In the United States, these cases have been federally prosecuted under the mail fraud statute and can be prosecuted under state general fraud laws, larceny, and false pretenses statutes.

Embezzlement and Fiduciary Frauds. The conversion to one's own use or benefit the money or property of another over which one has custody, to which one is entrusted, or over which one exerts a fiduciary's control.

These crimes are prosecuted under specific statutes, such as those dealing with embezzlement, banking misapplications, etc., the federal fraud statutes, federal and state/provincial laws regulating brokers and investment services, and in the United States, general fraud or larceny statutes at the state level.

Victims are institutions, businesses in general, pension funds, and beneficiaries of estates being managed by fiduciaries.

See also: ABUSE OF TRUST, BANKING VIOLATIONS, INSIDER SELF-DEALING, LOAN OR LENDING FRAUDS.

Employment Agency Frauds. Fraudulent solicitations of money or fees in order to find employment for, to guarantee the employment of, or to improve the employability of another.

Victims are generally individuals seeking jobs or hoping to improve skills in order to obtain better-paying employment opportunities. Variations of employment related frauds include:

1. Phony job agencies, i.e., where an agency solicits advance fees in order to find employment for the victim when in fact the service is neither performed nor intended to be provided.
2. Job training frauds, i.e., where money is received from victims to train them for specific employment and (1) the training is not supplied; (2) guaranteed job opportunities on completion of training are not supplied; or (3) the training is misrepresented as being ''certified'' or

"recognized" by employers when it is not and does not qualify the victim for anticipated employment.

In the United States, these frauds are prosecutable under the federal mail fraud statute and state general fraud statutes. Substantial recoveries have been made for victims of such frauds by the U.S. Federal Trade Commission.

Energy Crisis Frauds. Frauds arising out of the sale of goods or services related to energy or fuel use, saving, and production.

Victims are generally individual consumers interested in stretching their dollars spent on energy sources and/or saving energy. Energy schemes include the following types of frauds.

1. Merchandise schemes: sale of worthless or bogus items, which do not deliver the specific benefits promised or the degree of benefit promised; e.g., carburetor gadgets to save gasoline or phony solar heating systems. Often these frauds occur because of the novelty of the items involved combined with the naivete of the victims.

2. Weights and measures violations: short weighing or measuring of fuels to customers; e.g., manipulation of gas pump measuring devices, or misrepresentation of fuel by changing octane ratings on fuel pumps.

3. Discriminatory allocation of fuel by distributors to subdistributors and retailers, in consideration of commercial bribes to distributors' executives or special payments to companies with the power to make distribution in the form of under-the-table payments or required purchases of other items—useful or not needed—in violation of antitrust or other laws.

These cases can be prosecuted in the United States under special state statutes; e.g., those dealing with weights and measures, or violations of specific administrative regulations promulgated to deal with energy crises, and (in appropriate situations) as commercial bribery or antitrust violations.

See also: ANTITRUST OFFENSES, COMMERCIAL BRIBERY, MERCHANDISING SCHEMES, WEIGHTS AND MEASURES VIOLATIONS.

False and Misleading Advertising. Use of untrue or deceptive promotional techniques, resulting in consumer fraud.

Victims are consumers relying to their detriment on the false or misrepresented advertising or promotion. The following kinds of practices are prominent among those that fall under the heading of false and misleading advertising:

1. Advertising as a sale item an item that is actually at the regular or higher price.
2. Misrepresentations concerning the size, weight, volume, or utility of an item.
3. Falsely claiming an attribute that a good or service does not in fact possess.
4. Misstatement of the true costs of a good or service through the use of confusing payment provisions or otherwise.

These violations are prosecutable in the United States under the federal mail fraud statute, state general fraud statutes, and specific statutes dealing with false advertising.

Administrative and other civil remedies are frequently invoked against these offenses, and local consumer protection offices provide mediation remedies since these offenses frequently fall into grey areas with respect to wrongful intent.

See also: BAIT AND SWITCH, CONSUMER FRAUD.

False Claims. Fraudulent written claims for payment for goods or services not provided as claimed, to public or private entities. False claims may involve activities such as:

1. Presentation of a bogus claim or claimant; e.g., the ghost payroll situation.
2. Misrepresentation of the qualifications of an otherwise ineligible claim or claimant; e.g., welfare fraud.
3. False representation of the extent of payment or benefits to which claimant is entitled; e.g., overtime pay frauds.
4. Claims for reimbursement for goods and services allegedly provided to nonexistent recipients; e.g., Medicaid/Medicare fraud, by service providers.

The false claim will carry all the trappings of a legitimate claim and is most successfully undertaken by individuals with a thorough knowledge of the system being defrauded. The false claim is one of the basic implementing tools of the white-collar thief and can run the gamut from the elaborate computerized creation of fictitious claimants to the simple manipulation of numbers on a time card. False claims will sometimes involve the cooperation of executives or officials of the private or governmental entity to which such claims are submitted.

Violations are prosecuted under both general and specific fraud statutes, e.g, those dealing specifically with false claims submitted to the federal government. Such violations are also generally a basis for civil action, whether or not the proof is sufficient to meet the criminal standard of proof.

See also: COMMERCIAL BRIBERY, FRAUDS AGAINST GOVERNMENT PROGRAMS, GHOST PAYROLL, MEDICAID/MEDICARE FRAUD, OVERTIME PAY FRAUD, WELFARE FRAUD.

False Statements.   The concealment or misrepresentation of a fact material to the decision-making process of an entity. The false statement is often the means by which a fraudulent scheme to obtain money or benefit is effected either because (among other things):

1. The false statement constitutes the underlying documentation for a false claim; or

2. The false statement impedes discovery of the fraudulent scheme; i.e., covers up the fraud. These statements often provide the opportunity for conditioning the victim to unquestioningly accept and approve a false claim.

On the federal level in the United States, false statement prosecutions under 18 U.S.C. 1001 and 1014 have been a major weapon against white-collar crime directed at the federal government. Even where such statutes are not present as part of the arsenal of state statutes, their use for the purposes outlined above will be valuable in showing the manner and means by which frauds were perpetrated, in prosecutions under state general fraud, larceny, and false pretenses statutes.

See also: FALSE CLAIMS, FRAUDS AGAINST GOVERNMENT PROGRAMS, GHOST PAYROLLS.

Franchising Frauds. Frauds arising out of business opportunity situations in which individuals invest time, talents, and money to obtain a business enterprise, relying on others (i.e., the franchisor) to supply at prearranged rates specified goods and services such as necessary business structures, the goods to be sold or materials with which goods can be made, advertising, and an exclusive territorial market or market area for the franchisee's output.

Victims generally invest their major assets in what are fraudulent franchise opportunities. Frauds in franchises generally arise because one or more of the following occurs.

1. Franchisor has no intention of performing on any of his obligations; i.e., the franchise is a complete ruse to acquire victim-franchisee's initial investment monies.

2. Franchisor fails to provide promised goods or services essential to success of franchise.

3. Franchisor makes success for franchisee either difficult or impossible by extending too many franchises in a given locale or market area.

4. Franchisor has misrepresented the market or demand for goods/services central to the franchise, or has misrepresented the level of skills needed to realize franchise profitability.

Scenario 1 is outright fraud, while 2–4 represent variations ranging from fraud to shady dealing, to failure to fulfill contractual obligations.

Franchise frauds in the United States are federally prosecuted under the federal mail fraud statute, and under state statutes proscribing frauds, larceny, or false pretenses. In some instances, where success depends not on the victim's own labor, the franchise agreement may be considered a "security," and enforcement may be possible under securities acts, for example in the jurisdiction of the U.S. Securities and Exchange Commission or state securities regulatory agencies.

See also: BUSINESS OPPORTUNITY SCHEMES, CHAIN REFERRAL SCHEMES.

Frauds Against Government Benefit Programs. Unlawful application for and receipt of money, property, or benefit from public programs designed to confer money, property, or benefit under specific guidelines.

Victims are federal, state/provincial and local governments, their taxpayers, and qualified, intended beneficiaries of such programs. Typical kinds of frauds suffered by government programs include:

1. Misrepresentations of applicants' qualifications concerning program eligibility; e.g., welfare received by ineligible persons.

2. False billing/vouchering in which public programs make good on false claims for services not rendered or for nonexistent beneficiaries; e.g., physician's claims under Medicaid/Medicare programs for patients not treated, or for specific treatments not provided.

3. Inflated billing/vouchering/claiming, by which public programs are charged more than allowable costs; e.g., housing fraud where cost of construction is inflated so that the builder/owner receives more than the total cost of land and buildings and avoids making the investment required by law and administrative guidelines.

4. Embezzlement, by which employees or officials of public programs convert funds, property, or benefits to their own use (often via their custodial or fiduciary relationship to the program); e.g., in the United States licensed dispensers of food stamps converting funds to their own use.

5. Misuse of properly obtained funds, in which money, property, or benefit conferred under very specific guidelines concerning end use are received and utilized for unauthorized ends; e.g., receipt of federal loan funds (such as student educational loans) with failure to use such for specified purposes.

These frauds are prosecutable under specific enforcement sections of statutes setting up government programs, as well as statutes proscribing false claims, false statements, and conspiracy. In the United States they will also be violations of general fraud and larceny statutes, on the state level.

See also: EMBEZZLEMENT AND FIDUCIARY FUNDS, FALSE CLAIMS, FALSE STATEMENTS, MEDICAID/MEDICARE FRAUD, WELFARE FRAUD.

Funeral Frauds.   Class of guilt inducement frauds relying for success on the emotional stress of victims who have lost, or are about to lose, loved ones through death. Victims are the relatives or friends of deceased or terminally ill persons.

Funeral-related frauds often take the form of consumer and merchandising frauds and generally involve one or more of the following practices.

1. Relying on the guilt or anxiety of bereaved relatives. Victims are persuaded to contract for unnecessary or unduly elaborate funeral services or merchandise.

2. Billing for funeral expenses to include charges for services not performed (here fraud artist relies on victim anxiety or guilt to preclude memory of whether service was performed or not and/or to preclude victim's challenge of the bill for payment.)

3. Services or goods in connection with burial are represented as legally required, when in fact they are not.

4. Contracts are made for future provision of goods or services in connection with funeral and burial arrangements which fraud operator has no intention or no capacity to provide; e.g., sale of nonexistent cemetery plots.

Since many such abuses fall into grey areas of consumer fraud and misrepresentation, state/provincial attorneys-general and consumer protection agencies often undertake to provide civil mediation remedies. In addition, the U.S. Federal Trade Commission has expressed considerable interest in fraudulent activities in this area.

See also: CONSUMER FRAUD, GUILT-INDUCEMENT FRAUD, MERCHANDISING FRAUD.

Ghost Payrolls.   Form of false claim in which fictitious employees are added to a payroll and payments to these employees revert to the payroll manipulator(s). Fictitious employees are commonly referred to as *ghosts*.

Victims are generally public and private entities responsible for honoring payroll claims. Often the ghost payroll is a device used to defraud government programs designed to provide employment for the unemployed or disadvantaged. This is closely related to welfare and unemployment insurance frauds. This device can also be used in cost-plus contracts to cheat governmental entities, or by managers of subunits in private enterprises to steal from their parent organizations.

A variation on the ghost payroll is the overtime pay fraud in which false claims are made with respect to overtime work by bonafide employees.

In the United States, prosecution on the federal level would be under mail fraud, conspiracy, false claim, and false statement statutes. On the state level, such prosecution would be under general fraud, false pretenses, and larceny statutes.

See also: FALSE CLAIMS, FRAUDS AGAINST GOVERNMENT PROGRAMS.

Guilt Inducement Frauds.   Frauds perpetrated via the tactic of inducing guilt or anxiety in the victim concerning his or her relationship or obligations to another person who is significant to the victim (i.e., a child, parent, spouse).

Victims are individuals who, susceptible to the guilt or anxiety induced by the fraud operator, are persuaded to part with money or property in the belief that the questioned transaction will atone for any shortcomings or fulfill obligations they have toward another.

Because guilt inducement is a major tactic used to secure voluntary victim action, it cuts across many fraud areas. A few examples of the dynamics of such frauds are noted below.

1. Encyclopedia salesmen induce victims to enter into purchase contracts for books, having suggested to the victims that imminent scholastic failure of their children can be expected if such purchase is not made—here a merchandising fraud is consummated by the offender's capacity to induce parental anxiety in victims.

2. Children of deceased are persuaded to purchase elaborate and unnecessary funeral arrangements construed by the fraud operator to constitute a decent burial. The implication in such funeral frauds is that failure to buy the most expensive items or close checking of the details of bills are tantamount to lack of affection or respect for the deceased.

3. Unnecessary and imprudent expenditures for life insurance are made by many wage earners to whom it is suggested that failure to subscribe to such policies constitutes a failure to one's spouse and family.

4. Self-improvement merchandise and facilities are marketed to victims on the basis of such guilt inducements as ''you owe it to your spouse to

be as (lovely, successful, etc.) as you can be'' or ''you can only be a failure if you fail to take advantage of opportunities to improve your (looks, job, speaking ability).''

Depending on the level and quantity of misrepresentations involved in such frauds, remedies will range from criminal prosecutions (mail fraud, state general fraud statutes, etc. in the United States) to regulatory or administrative measures in federal, state/provincial and local levels to enjoin deceptive practices, and compel reimbursement of victims.

See also: FUNERAL FRAUDS, SELF-IMPROVEMENT FRAUDS.

Home Repair or Improvement Frauds.   Frauds arising out of the provision of goods and services in connection with the repair, maintenance, or general improvement of housing units.

Victims are generally homeowners, but may also include public agencies or programs that subsidize and/or underwrite home purchase and ownership. Home repair or improvement frauds include the following practices:

1. Shoddy or incompetent workmanship.
2. Sale of overpriced or unfit materials or services for home repair projects.
3. Failure to provide services or goods paid for by customer.
4. Submission of false claims for materials or work not provided.
5. Misrepresentation of the need for particular materials or services to be performed.
6. Misrepresentations or concealment of the costs of credit, or of the nature of liens securing the payment obligations.

The victim may be told that the home is in violation of building codes or in a condition substandard to the rest of the neighborhood, endangering the value of the home or the safety of the victim's family.

In the United States, these violations are prosecutable under a broad range of statutes, including mail fraud, statutes aimed at fraud against the federal government, state general fraud statutes, and local licensing laws, including those regulating door-to-door solicitations. This is a major area for administrative and mediational activities on the part of attorneys-general offices and municipal consumer protection offices.

See also: CONSUMER FRAUD, MERCHANDISING FRAUDS, REPAIR FRAUD.

Insider Self-Dealing.   Benefiting oneself or others in whom one has an interest by trading on privileged information or position. In the United States, insider self-dealing is a major cause of bank failures.

Typical violative situations include those where a corporate officer or director trades in the stock of his company on the basis of inside information as to prospective profits or losses; bank officers lending money to themselves or businesses in which they have an interest; corporate executives or purchasing officials setting up suppliers of goods and services to contract with their companies, and so on.

For nature of enforcement remedies, see also: ABUSE OF TRUST, BANKING VIOLATIONS, COMMERCIAL BRIBERY, SECURITIES VIOLATIONS.

Insurance Fraud.   Fraud perpetrated by or against insurance companies. Victims may be the clients or stockholders of insurance companies or the insurer itself.

Insurance fraud breaks down into the following categories and subclasses.

1. Frauds perpetrated by insurers against clients/stockholders include the following deliberate and intentional practices:
   a. failure to provide coverage promised and paid for when claim is made;
   b. failure to compensate or reimburse properly on claims;
   c. manipulation of risk classes and high-risk policy holder categories;
   d. embezzlement or abuse of trust in management of premium funds and other assets of insurance companies; and
   e. twisting, i.e., illegal sales practices in which insurer persuades customers to cancel current policies and purchase new ones from it.

2. Types of frauds perpetrated by insureds against insurance providers:
   a. filing of bogus claims for compensation or reimbursement, multiple claims for same loss from different insurers, etc.;
   b. inflating reimbursable costs on claim statements;

c. payment of bribes or kickbacks to local agents to retain coverage or coverage in improper risk category; and

d. failure to disclose information or false statements made in application for insurance.

Cases are often developed by insurance company investigators or state/provincial insurance departments and referred to investigative and prosecutive agencies. Federal prosecutions in the United States are generally under the mail fraud statute; state and local prosecutions under general fraud laws, larceny statutes, etc. Where the frauds are committed against insurers, assistance may be obtained from the Insurance Crime Prevention Institute (ICPI), Westport, Connecticut.

See also: ABUSE OF TRUST, FALSE CLAIMS.

Investment Frauds. Frauds in which victims, induced by the prospect of capital growth and high rates of return, invest money in imprudent, illusory or totally bogus projects or businesses.

Investment frauds generally victimize those with a pool of liquid or convertible assets, ranging from retirees or near-retirement-age people, widows and widowers, to high-income professionals and businessmen. Hallmarks of many such frauds are:

1. Higher-than-average promised rates of return.
2. Developmental nature of investment object; i.e., project or business is not a mature entity.
3. Sales made by strangers; i.e., through boiler rooms.
4. Generalized definition of nature and scope of project, and lack of detailed plans by which progress might be observed.
5. Object or site of investment geographically remote or distant from investors.
6. Failure to fully disclose facts material to investor prior to his commitment of money.
7. Nonregistration with U.S. Securities and Exchange Commission or comparable state/provincial regulatory agencies.
8. Promise of special advantages; e.g., tax shelters.

Examples of such frauds are too numerous to include here. In the United States they are generally violations of special statutes such as the federal

Securities Acts enforced by the U.S. Securities and Exchange Commission, state securities regulatory laws enforced by state agencies, the mail fraud statute, and state general fraud, larceny, and false pretenses statutes. Where land frauds are involved, the U.S. Department of Housing and Urban Development and state agencies that require full disclosure filings will have enforcement jurisdiction. In this area of enforcement, state and local investigatory and prosecutive agencies can anticipate major support and assistance from federal agencies that have overlapping or parallel enforcement interests.

See also: LAND FRAUD, PONZI SCHEMES, PYRAMID SCHEMES, SECURITIES FRAUD.

Land Fraud.   A type of investment fraud that involves the sale of land based on extensive misrepresentations as to value, quality, facilities, and/or state of development.

Victims are usually individuals buying land for retirement, investment, or both simultaneously. Land frauds usually consist of the sale of land or of interest in land

1. To which seller has no present title or claim of right; i.e., seller cannot properly transfer title or interest to buyer as represented at the time of sale;
2. About which a misrepresentation or failure to disclose a material fact has occurred;
3. At inflated or unjustified prices based on misrepresentations to purchaser;
4. On the promise of future performance or development, which the seller neither intends to provide nor can reasonably expect to occur. Misrepresentations usually involve presence of utilities, water, roads, recreational facilities, credit terms, etc.

Such frauds have been perpetrated for decades and resulted in numerous successful prosecutions on both federal and local prosecutive levels, as well as in extensive civil actions by regulatory agencies, which have resulted in both extensive restitution to victims and options to cancel improvident purchases. In the United States, federal prosecutions are undertaken under the mail fraud statute, and it may be anticipated that there will be increasing prosecutions for failure to comply with recently enacted registration and disclosure laws under the jurisdiction of the U.S. Department of Housing and Urban Development; there are parallel state registration and disclosure laws. Local prosecutions have been undertaken under general fraud laws, false advertising, and larceny statutes. There is substantial federal-state-local cooperation in this enforcement area.

See also: INVESTMENT FRAUD.

Landlord-Tenant Frauds.   Unlawful practices involving the leasing or renting of property. Common fraud practices by landlords include:

1. Keeping two sets of books; i.e., tax violations.
2. Schemes to avoid return of security deposits.
3. Rental of property to which one has no title claim or right.
4. Deliberate and persistent violations of safety and health regulations, and failure to provide heat, services, etc.

These white-collar crimes are usually misdemeanors and are violations of local ordinances. Frauds such as schemes to cheat tenants out of their security deposits should be prosecutable under state/provincial fraud or landlord-tenant legislation.

Loan or Lending Fraud.   Unlawful practices arising out of the lending or borrowing of money. Victims may be financial institutions, the stockholders of financial institutions, or borrowers.

Loan frauds generally involve either the failure to disclose relevant information, which would bear on the extension or granting of a loan, or the provision of false information, or both. When perpetrated by the lender, loan frauds may take the form of:

1. Lending to oneself through ghost accounts.
2. Lending to friends or entities in which one has an interest.
3. Commercial bribery; i.e., approving loans to those who would not otherwise qualify as borrowers, in exchange for kickbacks or other considerations.
4. Advance fee schemes, by which borrowers remit money to secure a loan that is not forthcoming or for which no payment was necessary.

When perpetrated by borrowers, loan frauds may take the form of:

1. False statements, whereby a loan to which one is not entitled is fraudulently obtained.
2. Improper use of legitimately obtained loans, where improper use was intended at the time the loan application was made.
3. Larceny by false pretenses, by which a loan is obtained with no intention of repayment.

A separate and important dimension of loan fraud involves the misuse or misrepresentation of items of collateral and collateral accounts.

These frauds are prosecutable in the United States under federal statutes proscribing mail fraud, banking frauds, securities frauds, and program frauds (such as those involving construction or repair loans, which are federally guaranteed). They are also prosecutable under general state fraud laws, false pretenses statutes, and larceny statutes.

See also: ABUSE OF TRUST, BANKING VIOLATIONS, COLLATERAL FRAUDS, FALSE STATEMENTS.

Medicaid/Medicare Fraud.   Fraudulent practices, arising in connection with the receipt or provision of health care services under government-financed programs. Such frauds are nearly always perpetrated by health care providers (both professionals and facility operators) against the government(s) financing the programs and/or the intended beneficiaries of such programs. Specific Medicaid/Medicare fraud practices include:

1. "Ping-ponging": referring patients to other doctors in a clinic in order to claim reimbursements for the "consultation" rather than for bonafide patient treatment or observation.
2. Upgrading: billing for services not provided.
3. Steering: sending patients to a particular pharmacy, medical lab, etc., for required prescriptions or services, and receiving kickbacks therefrom.
4. Shorting: delivering less medication; e.g., pills, than prescribed while charging for full amount.
5. Procurement abuses: establishment of supply/purchase arrangements with firms that pay kickbacks to health care facilities or are owned by those controlling the facility itself.
6. False claims: submission of claims for payment from government for patients that do not exist, or were never seen or treated.

These violations are prosecutable in the United States under federal fraud statutes, including mail fraud, false claim, and false statement statutes, as well as specific statutes in legislation authorizing such programs. Since many such programs are administered through state agencies and involve use of state funds, state general fraud, false pretenses, and larceny statutes will also be applicable.

See also: COMPETITIVE PROCUREMENT ABUSE, FALSE CLAIMS, FRAUDS AGAINST GOVERNMENT BENEFIT PROGRAMS, KICKBACKS.

Medical Frauds.   Unlawful activities arising out of the provision and sale of bogus, highly questionable or dangerous medical services, cures, or medications.

Victims are often individuals who have been given little hope of recovery or improvement by traditional medical establishments and desperately seek any promise of ameliorating their conditions. Also victimized are persons who are poorly informed and thus vulnerable to claims made by medical fraud artists, often in such areas as beauty treatments and cosmetics. Medical frauds generally include one or more of the following abuses.

1. Quackery: false representation of oneself as a legally trained and licensed health care professional.
2. Fake cures: sale of bogus or highly questionable cures for specific illnesses or diseases.
3. Misrepresentations of medication: misrepresentations as to the therapeutic value of medications, and/or omissions made regarding known side effects of medications.
4. Misrepresentations of treatment: false statements made with regard to the therapeutic value of a particular treatment protocol, with regard to its degree of ''acceptance'' or bonafide medical practice; and/or omissions of material information concerning known side effects of treatment that would affect patient's choice of treatment program.

Such frauds may operate through misrepresentations made to victims themselves, as well as to regulatory agencies such as the U.S. Food and Drug Administration. In the latter case the misrepresentations may involve the nature of test results or the methodology or procedures involved in conducting such tests.

In the United States, federal enforcement has been dominant in this field, through the mail fraud prosecutions, Food and Drug Administration efforts, and U.S. Federal Trade Commission proceedings. Local quacks should, however, be open to prosecution or control under general fraud statutes, larceny and false pretenses statutes, and vigorous exercise of licensing powers with respect to health and beauty services.

Merchandising Frauds. An umbrella term for a broad variety of consumer frauds involving misrepresentations inducing the victims to purchase merchandise, which either is not as represented or which in fact will never be delivered to them. The frauds usually involve one or more of the following aspects.

1. Representation that the item is sold at lower than usual price, whereas it is in fact sold at the usual retail price or higher.
2. Misrepresentation as to the quality or utility of the merchandise.
3. Misrepresentation as to the ultimate price, or credit terms.
4. Misleading information as to warranties, cancellation of transaction, returnability of merchandise, and validity of money back guarantees.
5. Solicitation of money with no intention to deliver the merchandise promised.
6. Bait and Switch frauds.

Victims customarily buy from door-to-door salesmen or are entrapped when they respond to newspaper, magazine, radio, or TV advertisements. Examples of such frauds include door-to-door magazine subscriptions sales, hearing-aid frauds, bulk sales of items falsely represented to be at wholesale prices (e.g., freezer food sales), and false sales (where items sold are falsely represented to be priced at less than regular prices, or sold pursuant to closeout of a business or replacement of inventory).

Enforcement with respect to these frauds has been successfully undertaken at federal, state/provincial, and local levels. Laws invoked in the United States have included federal mail and wire fraud statutes, the U.S. Federal Trade Commission Act, general state fraud and false advertising statutes, and local licensing laws governing door-to-door sales and solicitations.

See also: CONSUMER FRAUDS

Nursing Home Abuses.   A variety of frauds perpetrated by individuals who provide institutional nursing and convalescent care to patients, particularly the aged.

Victims of such frauds are the patients of such facilities, their families, and/or governmental entities who subsidize the cost of care provided to eligible patients. Forms of nursing home fraud abuses include:

1. Unlawful conversion or attachment of patients' assets.
2. False claims to patient, family, or government entity regarding services delivered.
3. False statements in license application or renewal.
4. Maintenance of fraudulent records as to general or overhead costs of operation of facilities as a basis for false claims to governmental entities.
5. Receipt of kickbacks from facility suppliers.
6. Employment of inadequate or unqualified staff in violation of licensing guidelines.

These frauds are prosecutable in the United States under federal false claim and false statement statutes, and state fraud laws. They generally require careful and painstaking audits to separate out extensive self-dealing, kickback arrangements, and concealments through sophisticated accounting techniques, etc.

See also: COMPETITIVE PROCUREMENT ABUSES, EMBEZZLEMENT AND FIDUCIARY FRAUDS, FALSE CLAIMS, FRAUDS AGAINST GOVERNMENT PROGRAMS, MEDICAID/ MEDICARE FRAUD.

Patent Fraud.   A form of self-improvement scheme, which most closely resembles vanity publishing frauds.

In patent frauds, individuals are solicited through newspaper advertisements, etc., to send "patentable" ideas or gadgets to fraud operator for "evaluation by experts." The "evaluation" of course usually involves a fee, or at least "further processing" of the submission may involve a fee, thus an advance fee situation evolves. The fraud operator generally has neither the intention nor the capacity to develop or process a patentable item.

For further information on remedies, etc., see also: ADVANCE FEE SCHEMES, SELF-IMPROVEMENT SCHEMES, VANITY PUBLISHING SCHEMES.

Pension Frauds and Abuses.   Thefts and fraudulent conversions of pension fund assets either by trustees, employers or employees.

Frauds perpetuated by trustees involve the violation of their fiduciary duty in the management of pension fund monies by:

1. Poor investments tied to self-dealing or commercial bribery.

2. Embezzlement.

Such frauds victimize those who have contributed to the fund and those intending to benefit from it.

Fraud perpetuated by employees include the accrual of abnormal overtime, etc., to form an inflated base period on which pension payment level is to be established (very often in local public sector employment situations). Victims are other employees whose potential benefits are reduced by fraud of their peers or bankruptcy of the fund, as well as employer contributors to the pension plan.

Prosecutions in this white-collar crime area have shown patterns of questionable union–employer agreements to permit widespread trustee fraud. In the United States, major violations have been prosecuted under the federal mail fraud statute, and this area is considered one in which there are major white-collar crime/organized crime interrelationships.

See also: ABUSE OF TRUST, EMBEZZLEMENT AND FIDUCIARY FRAUDS, COMMERCIAL BRIBERY, FALSE CLAIMS.

Pigeon Drop or Pocketbook Drop.   One of a large variety of street con games regularly perpetrated on gullible victims. It is a scheme in which the victim is persuaded to withdraw a large sum of cash from a bank account in order to show good faith or financial responsibility regarding the sharing of a "discovered" cache of money with two other persons (who are con artists). In the course of the con, both the discovered money and the victim's "good faith" money disappear as do the con artists.

Victims may be anyone, since perpetrators of this fraud have a remarkable ability to disarm their victims. Keys to the pigeon drop con are:

1. The con artists do not appear to be associated or know each other in any way.

2. A pocketbook, envelop, etc., is "found" by one of the confederates, and it contains a sizeable amount of money, no owner ID, and the suggestion that the money is illicitly generated, i.e., a gambler's proceeds, etc..

3. An agreement to share the money is made with the victim showing good faith (i.e., putting up money) to those involved. (Alternately, a deal is made for all to put up money in a pool to be held by the victim.)

4. A switch is made while the victim is distracted, and his or her money is stolen by one of the confederates.

In the United States, street cons of this type are generally prosecuted under state fraud, false pretenses, and larceny statutes. Police in most jurisdictions have had experience with one or more such street con games.

Pollution and Environmental Protection Violations. Many abuses in the environmental area involve more than violations of specific environmental/pollution control statutes and orders. White-collar crime abuses in this area consist primarily of the making or submitting of false statements concerning the degree of compliance with statutes and regulations for pollution control in order to cover up violations or lack of compliance with environmental standards. Falsification of test or sample data designed to measure compliance with standards represent another from of white-collar violation in this area.

See also: FALSE STATEMENTS

Ponzi Schemes. This is a general class of frauds in which the fraud operator uses money invested by later investor/victims to pay a high rate of return instead of making investments represented to them. Such schemes must inevitably collapse because it is mathematically impossible to continue them indefinitely. The length of time they can continue will depend upon the promised rate of return to investors, the amount of money the fraud operator takes out for himself or herself, and the costs of inducing victims to part with their money (e.g., sales commissions). Many such frauds have cheated victims of millions of dollars; some have operated over a period of years.

Ponzi elements are to be found in many varieties of investment frauds, under different guises and in different variations; e.g., long-term investments and short-term business financing.

In the United States, these schemes have been federally prosecuted under the mail fraud statute and as securities violations investigated by the U.S. Securities and Exchange Commission. On the state level they would be violations of general fraud, false pretenses, and larceny statutes.

See also: INVESTMENT SCHEMES

Price Fixing.   Illegal combinations by sellers to administer the price of a good or service, depriving customers of a competitive marketplace, restraining competition, and maintaining an artificial price structure.

Victims are customers of such combinations who are deprived of freely determined prices for the goods and services they purchase. Secondary victims may be competitors of the firms participating in the price-fixing agreement.

Frequently, when one thinks of price fixing, one thinks of a large nationwide conspiracy between industrial giants. While this is part of the problem, it is equally probable that many price fixing arrangements occur at the local level. For example, in Virginia the practice of a local bar association that set the price for title searches was held to be unlawful. In other locally prosecuted cases, druggists have been adjudicated for fixing prices on prescription drugs.

Price-fixing violations are most often the subject of federal enforcement efforts, but in the United States are also proscribed by many state antitrust statutes.

See also: ANTITRUST OFFENSES, RESTRAINT OF TRADE.

Procurement and Contracting Abuses.   See COMPETITIVE PRO-CUREMENT ABUSES.

Public/Official Corruption.   White-collar crime, which generally falls into the category of abuse of trust-type violations involving commercial bribery, collusion with bid-rigging, avoidance of the competitive process in connection with the purchase of goods and services by governmental entities, and self-dealing in connection with governmental purchases or grants of franchise to use public property and real estate.

Most public corruption has its parallel in the private sector. Thus conflict of interest is the public equivalent of insider self-dealing; and there is little distinction between public and commercial bribery situations, particularly where they overlap, such as in the government procurement area.

In the United States, these violations are federally prosecuted under federal mail fraud and organized crime statutes. On the local level there are numerous statutory provisions for prosecution involving bribery, taking of kickbacks, perjury, etc.

See also: ABUSE OF TRUST, COMMERCIAL BRIBERY, COMPETITIVE PROCUREMENT FRAUDS, FRAUDS AGAINST GOVERNMENTAL PROGRAMS.

Pyramid Scheme. The commercial version of the chain-letter scheme, used by fraud operators in the selling of phony distributorships, franchises, and business opportunity plans.

See also: CHAIN REFERRAL SCHEMES, FRANCHISING FRAUDS, INVESTMENT FRAUDS.

Referral Sales Schemes. See CHAIN REFERRAL SCHEMES, MERCHANDISING SCHEMES.

Repair Fraud. A form of consumer fraud, involving repairs or maintenance services performed on consumer goods. These white-collar crime schemes generally involve:

1. Overcharging for services performed.
2. Charging for services and parts not used.
3. Performing services or repairs not wanted or needed.
4. Failing to perform services or repairs promised.

This is a major area for proactive investigations, particularly decoy techniques. Where a sufficient pattern of deliberate violations have been developed and the decoy technique is successfully implemented, there have been convictions under state/provincial laws.

See also: CONSUMER FRAUD.

Restraint of Trade. Actions, combinations, or schemes that interfere with unfettered marketplace transactions. Examples are: price fixing, bribery and kickbacks for commercial advantage, interference with competitive bidding processes, dictation of price structure to customers or dealers, and exclusive buying arrangements.

In the United States, although the best known statutes in this area are federal, many abuses occur in local jurisdictions and are subject to state or local remedies, especially when interstate commerce is not involved. Many organized crime activities, aimed at monopolizing local markets to provide certain services or merchandise, may also involve restraint of trade. State antitrust statutes should be reviewed to determine their applicability in such situations.

See also: COMMERCIAL BRIBERY, COMPETITIVE PROCUREMENT ABUSES, PRICE FIXING.

Scam. See BANKRUPTCY FRAUD.

Securities Fraud. Fraudulent activities involving the sale, transfer, or purchase of securities or of money interests in the business activities of others.

Victims are generally securities investors who are not aware of the full facts regarding transactions into which they enter. Abuses cover a broad range and can include, for example, situations where:

1. Businesses or promoters seek to raise capital unlawfully or without proper registration and oversight.

2. Securities of no value are sold, or they are misrepresented to be worth far more than their actual value.

3. Purchasers are not advised of all facts regarding securities, and/or failure to file appropriate disclosures with federal and state/provincial regulatory agencies.

4. Insiders use special knowledge to trade in securities to the disadvantage of the general public, which lacks such knowledge.

5. Broker–dealers and investment advisers act for their own benefit rather than for the benefit of their clients.

6. False information is provided to security holders and the investing public in financial statements published or filed with securities regulatory agencies, or by payments to financial writers or publications.

7. Manipulation of the price of securities by purchases and sales occurs in stock exchange or over-the-counter markets.

8. There has been a failure to file registration or other reports with federal and state/provincial regulatory agencies.

Securities violations potentially exist wherever investors rely on others to manage and conduct the business in which an investment is made. It is not necessary that there by any formal certificates such as stocks and bonds. Any form of investment agreement is potentially a security.

See also: ADVANCE FEE SCHEMES, BOILER ROOMS, FALSE STATEMENTS, INSIDER SELF-DEALING, INVESTMENT FRAUDS.

Self-Improvement Schemes. Frauds that appeal to victims' desires to improve themselves (personally or financially) by the acquisition of social or employment skills.

Schemes in this category tend to run on a continuum from improving purely personal/social skills and attributes to those tied to an individual's employment opportunities. On the personal end of the scale are the dance studio or charm school schemes; on the employment end of the scale are fraudulent job training schemes and advance fee employment agencies.

Somewhere in the middle are modeling agencies that purport both to improve the "person" and his or her employment prospects; also courses on improving one's image or ability to communicate with others. Some business opportunity schemes, which hold out the prospect of financial improvement plus "being a respected community businessman," also fall into this category by appealing to the victim's desire to improve his or her finances and life style.

These abuses have been prosecuted in the United States under mail fraud and state fraud statutes, curbed by the U.S. Federal Trade Commission, and have also been the subject of enforcement efforts based on state and local legislation, licensing codes, and other codes governing the operation of schools or educational settings.

See also: BUSINESS OPPORTUNITY SCHEMES, EMPLOYMENT AGENCY FRAUDS, VANITY PUBLISHING SCHEMES.

"Sewer" Service. A term used to describe the kinds of activity noted below. Many merchandising, home repair, and other frauds rely on the use of litigation for ultimate collections of proceeds of the fraud. Likewise, many enterprises that are not strictly speaking fraudulent; e.g., those that sell much overpriced merchandise on credit, similarly depend upon litigation or the threat of litigation to squeeze money from victims.

In both these situations devices are often adopted to fraudulently deprive victims of the opportunity to defend against such litigation-usually by not informing them that litigation has been initiated against them (i.e., dropping the summons or subpoena "down the sewer") This is accomplished, usually, by false affidavits, filed in court, that a summons and complaint were served on the victim.

In the United States, such violations have been federally prosecuted for violation of the 1866 Civil Rights Act, but state violations are also clearly present where false affidavits are filed in court.

Short Weighting or Loading. Purposeful shorting of the volume or quantity of a cargo, accompanied by a false claim (invoice), demanding payment for the full amount.

Such frauds are easiest to perpetrate where the cargo is of such nature or bulk that it is difficult for the receiver to detect shortages. The reverse of the short weighting/loading fraud is often used as a modus operandi for diversions (thefts) of cargo. In this situation a transport vehicle is purposefully overloaded; the overage is not recorded (false statement by omission), and the overloaded amount forms the basis of kickbacks to scheme operators by the recipients of the shipments (often fences of stolen goods). Manipulation of the size or volume of loads must always be accompanied by false claims or false statements, since accompanying documentation or invoices do not reflect the fraudulent changes in the load size.

This violation involves either a false claim to a customer or a plain and simple theft from the shipper. Since insiders are frequently involved, it will often involve commercial bribery, kickbacks, etc. In the United States, it may also involve federal prohibitions on the interstate shipment of stolen property.

See also: WEIGHTS AND MEASURES VIOLATIONS.

Talent Agency Schemes. See SELF-IMPROVEMENT FRAUDS, VANITY PUBLISHING SCHEMES.

Tax and Revenue Violations. These are frauds perpetrated with the intent to deprive a taxing authority of revenues to which it is entitled or of information it needs in order to make a judgment regarding revenues to which it is entitled, or to avoid admission of involvement in illicit, though profitable, business activities.

Tax frauds may be perpetrated through the filing of false returns—as in personal income tax frauds; through the bribery of public officials—as may occur in property tax assessment frauds; or in the failure to file appropriately—as with an organized crime figure who may not be concerned with avoiding tax liability but rather with revealing the sources of his taxable income. Many white-collar crimes obligate the offender to commit tax fraud because of illicitly obtained monies he or she does not wish to report; e.g., assets due to bribes, larcenies, kickbacks or embezzlement proceeds. Common crimes, especially of a business nature, also result in tax violations; e.g., bookmaking and fencing of stolen goods (both income and sales tax abuses).

Tax avoidance through false statements may be a component of otherwise legitimate business enterprises, especially in areas of business and occupation taxes, inventory taxes, and sales taxes. Individuals and businesses will also seek to avoid or evade excise taxes (e.g., on cigarettes or in the case of tanker trucks by substitution of low-taxed home heating oil for higher-taxed diesel fuel).

Tax violations in the United States are usually prosecuted under special federal, state, and local tax statutes.

Vanity Publishing Schemes. Schemes that involve eliciting fees from individuals on the promise of promoting their creative talents (real or imaginary), or assisting them in the development of said talent.

Such frauds rely upon the vanity of the victim (i.e., his or her belief that he/she has a creative talent that has not as yet been discovered). Generally these schemes relate to creative endeavors in which clear performance standards regarding the talent are not available and are often a matter of taste, such as literary publishing or song writing.

The scheme operator will imply a promise of national advertising, book reviews, distribution, and special marketing services, but not so concretely that he or she will be held to any implied promise. The victims usually invest heavily and lose both their money and their hopes. They are left with a few copies of a printed and scored song arrangement or a number of copies of books, which established book review publications have not troubled to look at because of their publishing source.

It should be kept in mind that there is a legitimate private publishing market. General principles of fraud analysis should be applied to determine whether or not the line has been crossed in ways that make misrepresentations fraudulent.

See also: SELF-IMPROVEMENT SCHEMES.

Weights and Measures Violations.   Abusive practices involving the cheating of customers by failure to deliver prescribed quantities or amounts of desired goods. These violations usually involve false statements or claims in which the victim has relied on seller's representation of the delivered quantity in remitting higher payment. Examples of such white-collar crimes are:

1. Gas pump meter manipulation to show more gas pumped than received by the customer.
2. Butcher's thumb on the meat scale.
3. Odometer rollbacks in auto sales.

These frauds are most successful where one victim cannot easily verify weights or measuring devices, or where the victim has no reason to question the seller's claim or statement (e.g., when the products sold are bottled or packaged).

These abuses are usually detected on inspection by local agencies' personnel and prosecuted or enforced as violations of local ordinances. Purposeful, intentional, and continued activity of this kind should be considered as possibilities for violations of general fraud statutes.

See also: SHORT WEIGHTING OR LOADING.

Welfare Fraud.   Abuses associated with government income and family subsidy programs.

Government welfare programs are often exploited by a small number of applicants who apply for benefits to which they are not entitled, or continue to claim eligibility when they no longer meet the established criteria for such aid.

Receipt of monies from claimants by officials processing welfare claims represents another dimension of this fraud area. Such monies may be solicited as kickbacks in exchange for inflated claims filed; as bribes to certify claimants who are ineligible or to avoid reporting claimants' ineligibility, or as extortion for processing claims to which a recipient is fully eligible.

In some cases nonexistent recipients (ghosts) may be created to fraudulently siphon money out of such programs.

These violations are enforced under both specific provisions of welfare legislation and under general fraud statutes. Where general government funds are involved, there may be overlapping federal/state/provincial enforcement jurisdiction.

See also: FRAUDS AGAINST GOVERNMENT BENEFIT PROGRAMS.

Work-at-Home Schemes. see BUSINESS OPPORTUNITY SCHEMES, FRANCHISE FRAUDS, SELF-IMPROVEMENT FRAUDS.

Professional Studies and Pronouncements

§A.1 Treadway Commission Report Summary
  (a) Recommendations for the Public Company
    (i)   The Tone at the Top
    (ii) Internal Accounting and Audit Functions
    (iii) The Audit Committee
    (iv) Management and Audit Committee Reports
    (v)   Seeking a Second Opinion and Quarterly Reporting
  (b) Recommendations for the Independent Public Accountant
    (i)   Responsibility for Detection and Improved Detection Capabilities
    (ii) Audit Quality
    (iii) Communications by the Independent Public Accountant
    (iv) Change in the Process of Setting Audit Standards
  (c) Recommendations for the SEC and Others to Improve the Regulatory and Legal Environment
    (i)   New SEC Sanctions and Greater Criminal Prosecutions
    (ii) Improved Regulation of the Public Accounting Profession
    (iii) Adequate SEC Resources
    (iv) Improved Federal Regulation of Financial Institutions
    (v)   Improved Oversight by State Boards of Accountancy
    (vi) Insurance and Liability Crises
  (d) Recommendations for Education
    (i)   Business and Accounting Curricula

(ii) Professional Certification Examinations and Continuing Professional Education

(iii) Five-Year Accounting Programs and Corporate Initiatives

§A.2 AICPA SAS 53—Errors and Irregularities (U.S.)

(a) Definition of Errors and Irregularities

(b) The Auditor's Responsibility to Detect Errors and Irregularities

(c) Consideration of the Possibility of Material Misstatements in Audit Planning

    (i) Consideration of Audit Risk at the Financial Statement Level

    (ii) The Auditor's Response to Risk at the Financial Statement Level

    (iii) The Auditor's Consideration of Audit Risk at the Balance or Class Level

(d) Professional Skepticism

    (i) Professional Skepticism in Audit Planning

    (ii) Professional Skepticism in Performance of the Audit

(e) Evaluation of Audit Test Results

(f) The Effect of Irregularities on the Audit Report

(g) Communications Concerning Errors or Irregularities

(h) Responsibilities in Other Circumstances

(i) Effective Date

(j) Appendix

    (i) Characteristics of Errors and Irregularities

    (ii) Materiality

    (iii) Level of Involvement

    (iv) Concealment

    (v) Internal Control Structure

    (vi) Financial Statement Effect

    (vii) Summary

§A.3 AICPA SAS 54—Illegal Acts (U.S.)

(a) Definition of Illegal Acts

    (i) Dependence on Legal Judgment

    (ii) Relation to Financial Statements

(b) The Auditor's Consideration of the Possibility of Illegal Acts

    (i) Audit Procedures in the Absence of Evidence Concerning Possible Illegal Acts

(ii)   Specific Information Concerning Possible Illegal Acts

(iii) Audit Procedures in Response to Possible Illegal Acts

(c) The Auditor's Response to Detected Illegal Acts

    (i)   The Auditor's Consideration of Financial Statement Effect

    (ii) Implications for Audit

    (iii) Communication With the Audit Committee

    (iv) Effect on the Auditor's Report

(d) Other Considerations in an Audit in Accordance With Generally Accepted Auditing Standards

(e) Responsibilities in Other Circumstances

(f) Effective Date

(g) Illegal Acts By Clients: Auditing Interpretations of SAS 54

    (i)   Consideration of the Internal Control Structure in a Financial Statement Audit and the Foreign Corrupt Practices Act

    (ii) Material Weaknesses in the Internal Control Structure and the Foreign Corrupt Practices Act

§A.1 Treadway Commission Report Summary

(The following summary of recommendations has been reprinted from the report of the National Commission on Fraudulent Financial Reporting, October 1987). This summary is a synopsis of the organization and content of the Commission's recommendations, which appear in Chapters Two through Five of the report. The Commission urges readers to consider the recommendations along with the accompanying text, which explains, adds guidance, and in certain cases makes ancillary recommendations.

(a) Recommendations for the Public Company

Prevention and earlier detection of fraudulent financial reporting must start with the entity that prepares financial reports. Thus the first focus of the Commission's recommendations is the public company. These recommendations, taken together, will improve a company's overall financial reporting process and increase the likelihood of preventing fraudulent financial reporting and detecting it earlier when it occurs. For some companies, implementing these recommendations will require little or even no change from current practices; for other companies, it will mean adding or improving a recommended practice. Whether it means adding or improving a practice, the benefits justify the costs. The Commission's recommendations for the public company deal with (1) the tone set by top management, (2) the internal accounting and audit functions, (3) the audit committee, (4) management and audit committee reports, (5) the practice of seeking second opinions from independent public accountants, and (6) quarterly reporting.

(i) The Tone at the Top. The first three recommendations focus on an element within the company of overriding importance in preventing fraudulent financial reporting: the tone set by top management that influences the corporate environment within which financial reporting occurs. To set the right tone, top management must identify and assess the factors that could lead to fraudulent financial reporting; all public companies should maintain internal controls that provide reasonable assurance that fraudulent financial reporting will be prevented or subject to early detection-this is a broader concept than internal accounting controls-and all public companies should develop and enforce effective, written codes of corporate conduct. As a part of its ongoing assessment of the effectiveness of internal controls, a company's audit committee should annually review the program that management establishes to monitor compliance with the code. The Commission also recommends that its sponsoring organizations cooperate in developing additional, integrated guidance on internal controls.

(ii) Internal Accounting and Audit Functions. The Commission's recommendations turn next to the ability of the participants in the financial reporting process within the company to prevent or detect fraudulent financial reporting. The internal accounting function must be designed to fulfill the financial reporting responsibilities the corporation has undertaken as a public company. Moreover, all public companies must have an effective and objective internal audit function. The internal auditor's qualifications, staff, status within the company, reporting lines, and relationship with the audit committee of the board of directors must be adequate to ensure the internal audit function's effectiveness and objectivity. The internal auditor should consider his audit findings in the context of the company's financial

statements and should, to the extent appropriate, coordinate his activities with the activities of the independent public accountant.

(iii) The Audit Committee. The audit committee of the board of directors plays a role critical to the integrity of the company's financial reporting. The Commission recommends that all public companies be required to have audit committees composed entirely of independent directors. To be effective, audit committees should exercise vigilant and informed oversight of the financial reporting process, including the company's internal controls. The board of directors should set forth the committee's duties and responsibilities in a written charter. Among other things, the audit committee should review management's evaluation of the independence of the public accountant and management's plans for engaging the company's independent public accountant to perform management advisory services. The Commission highlights additional important audit committee duties and responsibilities in the course of discussing other recommendations affecting public companies.

(iv) Management and Audit Committee Reports. Users of financial statements should be better informed about the roles management and the audit committee play in the company's financial reporting process. The Commission recommends a management report that acknowledges that the financial statements are the company's and that top management takes responsibility for the company's financial reporting process. The report should include management's opinion on the effectiveness of the company's internal controls. The Commission also recommends a letter from the chairman of the audit committee that describes the committee's activities. Both of these communications should appear in the annual report to stockholders.

(v) Seeking a Second Opinion and Quarterly Reporting. Finally, the Commission's recommendations for the public company focus on two opportunities to strengthen the integrity of the financial reporting process. Management should advise the audit committee when it seeks a second opinion on a significant accounting issue, explaining why the particular accounting treatment was chosen. The Commission also recommends additional public disclosure in the event of a change in independent public accountants. Furthermore, the Commission recommends audit committee oversight of the quarterly reporting process.

(b) Recommendations for the Independent Public Accountant.

The independent public accountant's role, while secondary to that of management and the board of directors, is crucial in detecting and deterring fraudulent financial reporting. To ensure and improve the effectiveness of the independent public accountant, the Commission recommends changes in auditing standards, in procedures that enhance audit quality, in the independent public accountant's communications about his role, and in the process of setting auditing standards. On February 14, 1987, the Auditing Standards Board (ASB) exposed for comment a series of proposed auditing standards that address many issues the Commission considered. The Commission commends the ASB for its efforts in these exposure drafts, some of which are responsive to Commission concerns.

(i) Responsibility for Detection and Improved Detection Capabilities. Generally Accepted Auditing Standards (GAAS) should be changed to recognize better the independent public accountant's responsibility for detecting fraudulent financial reporting. The standards should restate this responsibility to require the independent public accountant to take affirmative steps to assess the potential for fraudulent financial reporting and design tests to provide reasonable assurance of detection. Among the affirmative steps recommended is assessment of the company's overall control environment along with improved guidance for identifying risks and designing audit tests. In addition, the independent public accountant should be required to make greater use of analytical review procedures, to identify areas with a high risk of fraudulent financial reporting. The independent public accountant also should be required to review quarterly financial data before its release, to improve the likelihood of timely detection of fraudulent financial reporting.

(ii) Audit Quality. Improved audit quality increases the likelihood of detecting fraudulent financial reporting. In this regard, the Commission makes three recommendations. The first two are designed to improve two aspects of the profession's existing quality assurance program. Peer review should be strengthened by adding reviews, in each office reviewed, of all first-year audits performed for public company clients that were new to the

firm. Concurring, or second partner, review should be enhanced by adding more explicit guidance as to timing and qualifications. In the third recommendation, the Commission encourages greater sensitivity on the part of public accounting firms to pressures within the accounting firm that may adversely impact audit quality.

(iii) Communications by the Independent Public Accountant. Independent public accountants need to communicate better to those who rely on their work. The auditor's standard report can and should convey a clearer sense of the independent public accountant's role, which does not include guaranteeing the accuracy of the company's financial statements. The standard audit report should explain that an audit is designed to provide reasonable, but not absolute, assurance that the financial statements are free of material misstatements arising as a result of fraud or error. It also should describe the extent to which the independent public accountant has reviewed and evaluated the system of internal accounting control. These two steps will promote a better appreciation of an audit and its purpose and limitations and underscore management's primary responsibility for financial reporting.

(iv) Change in the Process of Setting Audit Standards. Finally, the Commission recommends that the process of setting auditing standards be improved by reorganizing the AICPA's Auditing Standards Board (ASB). The Commission believes that the setting of auditing standards should involve knowledgeable persons whose primary concern is with the use of auditing products as well as practicing independent public accountants. Such individuals would have particular sensitivity to the operating implications of auditing standards and to emerging policy issues concerning these standards. The recommendation contemplates a smaller ASB, composed of equal numbers of practitioners and qualified persons not presently engaged in public accounting and led by two full-time officers, that would look beyond the technical aspects of auditing and set an agenda reflecting a broad range of needs, serving public and private interests. The agenda would be implemented by auditing standards of continuing high technical quality, and the ASB would adopt these standards on the basis of their technical quality and their addressing these public and private needs.

(c) Recommendations for the SEC and Others to Improve the Regulatory and Legal Environment.

Strong and effective deterrence is essential in reducing the incidence of fraudulent financial reporting. While acknowledging the SEC's significant efforts and achievements in deterring such fraud, the Commission concludes that the public and private-sector bodies whose activities shape the regulatory and law enforcement environment can and should provide stronger deterrence. The Commission's recommendations for increased deterrence involve new SEC sanctions, greater criminal prosecution, improved regulation of the public accounting profession, adequate SEC resources, improved federal regulation of financial institutions, and improved oversight by state boards of accountancy. In addition, the Commission makes two final recommendations in connection with the perceived insurance and liability crises.

(i) New SEC Sanctions and Greater Criminal Prosecutions. The range of sanctions available to be imposed on those who violate the law through fraudulent financial reporting should be expanded. Congress should give the SEC additional enforcement tools so that it can impose fines, bring cease and desist proceedings, and bar or suspend individual perpetrators from serving as corporate officers or directors, while preserving the full range of due process protections traditionally accorded to targets of enforcement activities. Moreover, with SEC support and assistance, criminal prosecution for fraudulent financial reporting should be made a higher priority.

(ii) Improved Regulation of the Public Accounting Profession. Another regulatory function, the regulation of the public accounting profession, seeks to reduce the incidence of fraudulent financial reporting through ensuring audit quality and thereby enhancing early detection and prevention of such fraud. The Commission studied the existing regulation and oversight, which includes the profession's quality assurance program, and concluded that additional regulation-particularly a statutory self-regulatory organization-is not necessary, provided two key elements are added to the present system. The first element is mandatory membership: all public accounting firms that audit public companies must belong to a professional organization that has peer review and independent oversight functions and is approved by the SEC. The SEC should provide the second element:

enforcement actions to impose meaningful sanctions when a firm fails to remedy deficiencies cited by a quality assurance program approved by the SEC.

(iii) Adequate SEC Resources. The Commission directs many recommendations to the SEC, the agency with primary responsibility to administer the federal securities laws. In that regard, the SEC must have adequate resources to perform its existing functions, as well as additional functions, that help prevent, detect and deter fraudulent financial reporting.

(iv) Improved Federal Regulation of Financial Institutions. Federal regulatory agencies, other than the SEC, have responsibility for financial reporting by certain public companies that are banks and savings and loans. The Commission recommends that these other agencies adopt measures patterned on the Commission's recommendations for the SEC. To enhance efforts to detect fraudulent financial reporting within financial institutions, the Commission also recommends that these federal agencies and the public accounting profession provide for the regulatory examiner and the independent public accountant to have access to each others' information about examined financial institutions.

(v) Improved Oversight by State Boards of Accountancy. State boards of accountancy can and should play an enhanced role in their oversight of the independent public accountant. The Commission recommends that these boards implement positive enforcement programs to review on a periodic basis the quality of services rendered by the independent public accountants they license.

(vi) Insurance and Liability Crises. Finally, the Commission's study of fraudulent financial reporting unavoidably has led to certain topics beyond its charge or ability to address. The perceived liability and insurance crises and the tort reform movement have causes and implications far beyond the financial reporting system. They are truly national issues, touching every profession and business, affecting financial reporting as well. Those charged with responding to the various tort reform initiatives should consider the implications for long-term audit quality and the independent public accountant's detection of fraudulent financial reporting. Moreover, the SEC should reconsider its long-standing position, insofar as it applies to independent directors, that corporate indemnification of officers and direc-

tors for securities law liabilities is against public policy and therefore unenforceable.

(d) Recommendations for Education.

Education can influence present or future participants in the financial reporting system by providing knowledge, skills, and ethical values that potentially may help prevent, detect, and deter fraudulent financial reporting. To encourage educational initiatives toward this end, the Commission recommends changes in the business and accounting curricula as well as in professional certification examinations and continuing professional education.

(i) Business and Accounting Curricula. The complexity and serious nature of fraudulent financial reporting led the Commission to conclude that any initiatives encouraged by its recommendations should permeate the undergraduate and graduate business and accounting curricula. The Commission first recommends that business and accounting students gain knowledge and understanding of the factors that cause fraudulent financial reporting and of the strategies that can lead to a reduction in its incidence. To enable students to deal with risks of such fraud in the future at public companies, the Commission recommends that business and accounting curricula convey a deeper understanding of the function and the importance of internal controls and the overall control environment within which financial reporting takes place. Students should realize that practices aimed at reducing fraudulent financial reporting are not simply defensive measures, but also make good business sense.

In addition, part of the knowledge students acquire about the financial reporting system should be an understanding of the complex regulatory and law enforcement framework that government and private-sector bodies provide to safeguard that system and to protect the public interest. As future participants in that system, students should gain a sense of what will be expected of them legally and professionally when they are accountable to the public interest.

The Commission recommends that the business and accounting curricula also foster the development of skills that can help prevent, detect, and deter such fraud. Analytical reasoning, problem solving, and the exercise of sound judgment are some of the skills that will enable students to grapple successfully in the future with warning signs or novel situations they will encounter in the financial reporting process.

Furthermore, the ethical dimension of financial reporting should receive more emphasis in the business and accounting curricula. The curricula should integrate the development of ethical values with the acquisition of knowledge and skills. Unfortunately, the lack of challenging case studies based on actual incidents of fraudulent financial reporting is a current obstacle to reform. The Commission therefore recommends that business schools give their faculty a variety of incentives and opportunities to develop personal competence and suitable classroom materials for teaching about fraudulent financial reporting. Business school faculty reward systems should acknowledge and reward faculty who develop such competence and materials.

(ii) Professional Certification Examinations and Continuing Professional Education. The Commission makes two additional recommendations relating to education. Both professional certification examinations and continuing professional education should emphasize the knowledge, skills, and ethical values that further the understanding of fraudulent financial reporting and promote a reduction in the incidence of such fraud.

(iii) Five-Year Accounting Programs and Corporate Initiatives. The Commission makes no recommendation with regard to the much-discussed proposal to expand the undergraduate accounting curriculum from 4 to 5 years. Rather, the Commission offers a number of observations based on its research and deliberations. Similarly, the Commission outlines some of the numerous opportunities for public companies to educate their directors, management, and employees about the problem of fraudulent financial reporting.

§A.2 AICPA SAS 53—Errors and Irregularities (U.S.)

(The following has been reprinted from AICPA Professional Standards, published by the American Institute of Certified Public Accountants, January 1991).

01. This section provides guidance on the independent auditor's responsibility for the detection of errors and irregularities in an audit of financial statements in accordance with generally accepted auditing standards. It

describes factors that influence the auditor's ability to detect errors and irregularities and explains how the exercise of due care should give appropriate consideration to the possibility of errors or irregularities. It also provides guidance on the auditor's responsibility to communicate detected matters both within and outside the entity whose financial statements are under audit.

(a) Definition of Errors and Irregularities

02. The term *errors* refers to unintentional misstatements or omissions of amounts or disclosures in financial statements. Errors may involve:

- Mistakes in gathering or processing accounting data from which financial statements are prepared;

- Incorrect accounting estimates arising from oversight or misinterpretation of facts; or

- Mistakes in the application of accounting principles relating to amount, classification, manner of presentation, or disclosure.

03. The term *irregularities* refers to intentional misstatements or omissions of amounts or disclosures in financial statements. Irregularities include fraudulent financial reporting undertaken to render financial statements misleading, sometimes called management fraud, and misappropriation of assets, sometimes called defalcations. Irregularities may involve such acts as the following:

- Manipulation, falsification, or alteration of accounting records or supporting documents from which financial statements are prepared;

- Misrepresentation or intentional omission of events, transactions, or other significant information; or

- Intentional misapplication of accounting principles relating to amounts, classification, manner of presentation, or disclosure.

04. The primary factor that distinguishes errors from irregularities is whether the underlying cause of a misstatement in financial statements is intentional or unintentional. Intent, however, is often difficult to deter-

mine, particularly in matters involving accounting estimates or the application of accounting principles. For example, an unreasonable accounting estimate may result from unintentional bias or may be an intentional attempt to misstate the financial statements.

(b) The Auditor's Responsibility to Detect Errors and Irregularities

05. The auditor should assess the risk that errors and irregularities may cause the financial statements to contain a material misstatement. Based on that assessment, the auditor should design the audit to provide reasonable assurance of detecting errors and irregularities that are material to the financial statements.

06. The auditor's assessment of the risk of material misstatement of the financial statements requires the auditor to understand the characteristics of errors and irregularities that are discussed in paragraph 34 and the complex interaction of those characteristics. Based on that understanding, the auditor designs and performs appropriate audit procedures and evaluates the results.

07. Because of the characteristics of irregularities, particularly those involving forgery and collusion, a properly designed and executed audit may not detect a material irregularity. For example, generally accepted auditing standards do not require that an auditor authenticate documents, nor is the auditor trained to do so. Also, audit procedures that are effective for detecting a misstatement that is unintentional may be ineffective for a misstatement that is intentional and is concealed through collusion between client personnel and third parties or among management or employees of the client.

08. The auditor should exercise (a) due care in planning, performing, and evaluating the results of audit procedures, and (b) the proper degree of professional skepticism to achieve reasonable assurance that material errors or irregularities will be detected. Since the auditor's opinion on the financial statements is based on the concept of reasonable assurance, the auditor is not an insurer and his report does not constitute a guarantee. Therefore, the subsequent discovery that a material misstatement exists in the financial statements does not, in and of itself, evidence inadequate planning, performance, or judgment on the part of the auditor.

(c) Consideration of the Possibility of Material Misstatements in Audit Planning

09. In developing an audit plan, the auditor should consider factors influencing audit risk that relate to several or all account balances and obtain an understanding of the internal control structure. These matters often have effects pervasive to the financial statements taken as a whole and also influence the auditor's consideration of risk at the account balance or class-of-transactions level.

(i) Consideration of Audit Risk at the Financial Statement Level

10. An assessment of the risk of material misstatements should be made during planning. The auditor's understanding of the internal control structure should either heighten or mitigate the auditor's concern about the risk of material misstatements. The factors considered in assessing risk should be considered in combination to make an overall judgment; the presence of some factors in isolation would not necessarily indicate increased risk. Factors such as those listed below may be considered.

- Management Characteristics
  - —Management operating and financing decisions are dominated by a single person.
  - —Management's attitude toward financial reporting is unduly aggressive.
  - —Management (particularly senior accounting personnel) turnover is high.
  - —Management places undue emphasis on meeting earnings projections.
  - —Management's reputation in the business community is poor.
- Operating and Industry Characteristics
  - —Profitability of entity relative to its industry is inadequate or inconsistent.
  - —Sensitivity of operating results to economic factors (inflation, interest rates, unemployment, etc.) is high.
  - —Rate of change in entity's industry is rapid.
  - —Direction of change in entity's industry is declining with many business failures.

—Organization is decentralized without adequate monitoring.

—Internal or external matters that raise substantial doubt about the entity's ability to continue as a going concern are present. (See section 341, *The Auditor's Consideration of an Entity's Ability to Continue as a Going Concern.*).

- Engagement Characteristics

—Many contentious or difficult accounting issues are present.

—Significant difficult-to-audit transactions or balances are present.

—Significant and unusual related party transactions not in the ordinary course of business are present.

—Nature, cause (if known), or the amount of known and likely misstatements detected in the audit of prior period's financial statements is significant.

—It is a new client with no prior audit history or sufficient information is not available from the predecessor auditor.

11. The size, complexity, and ownership characteristics of the entity have a significant influence on the risk factors considered to be important. For example, for a large entity, the auditor would ordinarily give consideration to factors that constrain improper conduct by senior management, such as the effectiveness of the board of directors, the audit committee or others with equivalent authority and responsibility, and the internal audit function. Consideration would also be given to the measures taken to enforce a formal code of conduct and the effectiveness of the budgeting or responsibility reporting system. For a small entity some of these matters might be considered inapplicable or unimportant, particularly if the auditor's past experience with the entity has been that effective owner–manager or trustee involvement creates a good control environment.

12. The auditor should assess the risk of management misrepresentation by reviewing information obtained about risk factors and the internal control structure. Matters such as the following may be considered:

- Are there known circumstances that may indicate a management predisposition to distort financial statements, such as frequent disputes about aggressive application of accounting principles that increase earnings, evasive responses to audit inquiries, or excessive emphasis on meeting quantified targets that must be achieved to receive a substantial portion of management compensation?

- Are there indications that management has failed to establish policies and procedures that provide reasonable assurance of reliable accounting estimates, such as personnel who develop estimates appearing to lack necessary knowledge and experience, supervisors of these personnel appearing careless or inexperienced, or there is a history of unreliable or unreasonable estimates?

- Are there conditions that indicate lack of control of activities, such as constant crisis conditions in operating or accounting areas, disorganized work areas, frequent or excessive back orders, shortages, delays, or lack of documentation for major transactions?

- Are there indications of a lack of control over computer processing, such as a lack of controls over access to applications that initiate or control the movement of assets (for example, a demand deposit application in a bank), high levels of processing errors, or unusual delays in providing processing results and reports?

- Are there indications that management has not developed or communicated adequate policies and procedures for security of data or assets, such as not investigating employees in key positions before hiring, or allowing unauthorized personnel to have ready access to data or assets?

13. The auditor should consider the effect of the matters described in paragraphs 10 to 12 on the overall audit strategy and the expected conduct and scope of the audit.

(ii) The Auditor's Response to Risk at the Financial Statement Level

14. The auditor's overall judgment about the level of risk in an engagement may affect engagement staffing, extent of supervision, overall strategy for expected conduct and scope of audit, and degree of professional skepticism applied. Thus, the auditor's assessment of risk may affect audit planning in one or more of the following ways. The experience and training of personnel assigned significant engagement responsibilities should be commensurate with the auditor's assessment of the level of risk for the engagement. Ordinarily, higher risk requires more experienced personnel or more extensive supervision by the auditor with final responsibility for the engagement during both the planning and the conduct of the engagement. Higher risk may cause the auditor to expand the extent of procedures applied, apply procedures closer to or as of the balance sheet date, particu-

larly in critical audit areas, or modify the nature of procedures to obtain more persuasive evidence. Higher risk will also ordinarily cause the auditor to exercise a heightened degree of professional skepticism in conducting the audit (see paragraphs 16 to 21).

(iii) The Auditor's Consideration of Audit Risk at the Balance or Class Level

15. The following matters are examples of factors that may influence the auditor's consideration of risk of material misstatement related to particular assertions at the balance or class level:

- Effect of risk factors identified at the financial statement or engagement level on the particular account balance or transaction class;

- Complexity and contentiousness of accounting issues affecting balance or class;

- Frequency or significance of difficult-to-audit transactions affecting balance or class;

- Nature, cause, and amount of known and likely misstatements detected in the balance or class in the prior audit;

- Susceptibility of related assets to misappropriation;

- Competence and experience of personnel assigned to processing data that affect the balance or class;

- Extent of judgment involved in determining the total balance or class;

- Size and volume of individual items constituting the balance or class; and

- Complexity of calculations affecting the balance or class.

(d) Professional Skepticism

16. An audit of financial statements in accordance with generally accepted auditing standards should be planned and performed with an attitude of professional skepticism. The auditor neither assumes that management is dishonest nor assumes unquestioned honesty. Rather, the auditor recognizes that conditions observed and evidential matter obtained, including information from prior audits, need to be objectively evaluated to

determine whether the financial statements are free of material misstatement.

17. Management integrity is important because management can direct subordinates to record transactions or conceal information in a manner that can materially misstate financial statements. When approaching difficult-to-substantiate assertions, the auditor should recognize the increased importance of his consideration of factors that bear on management integrity. A presumption of management dishonesty, however, would be contrary to the accumulated experience of auditors. Moreover, if dishonesty were presumed, the auditor would potentially need to question the genuineness of all records and documents obtained from the client and would require conclusive rather than persuasive evidence to corroborate all management representations. An audit conducted on these terms would be unreasonably costly and impractical.

(i) Professional Skepticism in Audit Planning

18. Whenever the auditor has reached a conclusion that there is significant risk of material misstatement of the financial statements, the auditor reacts in one or more ways. The auditor should consider this assessment in determining the nature, timing, or extent of procedures, assigning staff, or requiring appropriate levels of supervision. The auditor may identify specific transactions involving senior management and confirm the details with appropriate external parties and review in detail all material accounting entries prepared or approved by senior management.

19. The auditor should consider whether accounting policies are acceptable in the circumstances. However, when the auditor has reached a conclusion that there is significant risk of intentional distortion of financial statements, the auditor should recognize that management's selection and application of significant accounting policies, particularly those related to revenue recognition, asset valuation, and capitalization versus expensing, may be misused. Increased risk of intentional distortion of the financial statements should cause greater concern about whether accounting principles that are otherwise generally accepted are being used in inappropriate circumstances to create a distortion of earnings. For example, management might use the percentage of completion method in circumstances that do not justify its use to misstate operating results.

20. When evaluation at the financial statement level indicates significant risk, the auditor requires more or different evidence to support material transactions than would be the case in the absence of such risk. For exam-

ple, the auditor may perform additional procedures to determine that sales are properly recorded, giving consideration to the possibility that the buyer has a right to return the product. Transactions that are both large and unusual, particularly at year-end, should be selected for testing.

(ii) Professional Skepticism in Performance of the Audit

21. In performing procedures and gathering evidential matter, the auditor continually maintains an attitude of professional skepticism. The performance of auditing procedures during the audit may result in the detection of conditions or circumstances that should cause the auditor to consider whether material misstatements exist. If a condition or circumstance differs adversely from the auditor's expectation, the auditor needs to consider the reason for such a difference. Examples of such conditions or circumstances are as follows:

- Analytical procedures disclose significant differences from expectations;

- Significant unreconciled differences between reconciliations of a control account and subsidiary records or between a physical count and a related account are not appropriately investigated and corrected on a timely basis;

- Confirmation requests disclose significant differences or yield fewer responses than expected;

- Transactions selected for testing are not supported by proper documentation or are not appropriately authorized;

- Supporting records or files that should be readily available are not promptly produced when requested; and

- Audit tests detect errors that apparently were known to client personnel, but were not voluntarily disclosed to the auditor.

When such conditions or circumstances exist, the planned scope of audit procedures should be reconsidered. As the number of differences from expectations or the frequency with which the auditor is unable to obtain satisfactory explanations increases, the auditor should consider whether the assessment of the risk of material misstatement of the financial statements made in the planning stage of the engagement is still appropriate.

(e) Evaluation of Audit Test Results

22. The auditor should evaluate the significance of differences between the accounting records and the underlying facts and circumstances detected by the application of auditing procedures. The auditor should consider both the quantitative and qualitative aspects of these matters and whether they are indicative of an error or an irregularity. Often a particular matter considered in isolation cannot be identified as an error or irregularity; nevertheless, this evaluation is important. Because irregularities are intentional, they have implications beyond their direct monetary effect and the auditor needs to consider the implications for other aspects of the audit.

23. The auditor's objective is to reach a conclusion on whether the financial statements, taken as a whole, are materially misstated. The auditor should accumulate potential audit adjustments during the audit and summarize and evaluate the combined effect. In this regard, the auditor may designate an amount below which potential audit adjustments need not be accumulated. This amount would be set so that any such adjustments, either individually or when aggregated with other adjustments, would not be material to the financial statements.

24. If the auditor has determined that an audit adjustment is, or may be, an irregularity, but has also determined that the effect on the financial statements could not be material, the auditor should:

a. Refer the matter to an appropriate level of management that is at least one level above those involved.

b. Be satisfied that, in view of the organizational position of the likely perpetrator, the irregularity has no implications for other aspects of the audit or that those implications have been adequately considered.

For example, irregularities involving misappropriation of cash from a small imprest fund would normally be of little significance because both the manner of operating the fund and its size would tend to establish a limit on the amount of loss and the custodianship of such a fund is normally entrusted to a relatively low-level employee.

25. If the auditor has determined that an audit adjustment is, or may be, an irregularity and has either determined that the effect could be material or has been unable to evaluate potential materiality, the auditor should:

a. Consider the implications for other aspects of the audit.

b. Discuss the matter and the approach to further investigation with an appropriate level of management that is at least one level above those involved.

c. Attempt to obtain sufficient competent evidential matter to determine whether, in fact, material irregularities exist and, if so, their effect.

d. If appropriate, suggest that the client consult with legal counsel on matters concerning questions of law.

(f) The Effect of Irregularities on the Audit Report

26. If the auditor has concluded that the financial statements are materially affected by an irregularity, the auditor should insist that the financial statements be revised and, if they are not, express a qualified or an adverse opinion on the financial statements, disclosing all substantive reasons for his opinion.

27. If the auditor is precluded from applying necessary procedures, or if, after the application of extended procedures, the auditor is unable to conclude whether possible irregularities may materially affect the financial statements, the auditor should:

a. Disclaim or qualify an opinion on the financial statements.

b. Communicate his findings to the audit committee or the board of directors.

If the client refuses to accept the auditor's report as modified for the circumstances described above, the auditor should withdraw from the engagement and communicate the reason for the withdrawal to the audit committee or board of directors. Whether the auditor concludes that withdrawal from the engagement is appropriate in other circumstances depends on the diligence and cooperation of senior management and the board of directors in investigating the circumstances and taking appropriate remedial action. For example, if the auditor is precluded by the client from obtaining reasonably available evidential matter, withdrawal ordinarily would be appropriate. However, because of the variety of circumstances that may arise, it is not possible to describe all those circumstances when withdrawal would be appropriate.

(g) Communications Concerning Errors or Irregularities

28. For the audit committee to make the informed judgments necessary to fulfill its responsibility for the oversight of financial reporting, the auditor should assure himself that the audit committee is adequately informed about any irregularities of which the auditor becomes aware during the audit unless those irregularities are clearly inconsequential. For example, a minor defalcation by an employee at a low level in the organization might be considered inconsequential. However, irregularities involving senior management of which the auditor becomes aware should be reported directly to the audit committee. Irregularities that are individually immaterial may be reported to the audit committee on an aggregate basis, and the auditor may reach an understanding with the audit committee on the nature and amount of reportable irregularities.

29. Disclosure of irregularities to parties other than the client's senior management and its audit committee or board of directors is not ordinarily part of the auditor's responsibility, and would be precluded by the auditor's ethical or legal obligation of confidentiality unless the matter affects his opinion on the financial statements. The auditor should recognize, however, that in the following circumstances a duty to disclose outside the client may exist:

a. When the entity reports an auditor change under the appropriate securities law on Form 8-K.

b. To a successor auditor when the successor makes inquiries in accordance with section 315, Communications Between Predecessor and Successor Auditors.

c. In response to a subpoena.

d. To a funding agency or other specified agency in accordance with requirements for the audits of entities that receive financial assistance from a government agency.

Because potential conflicts with the auditor's ethical and legal obligations for confidentiality may be complex, the auditor may wish to consult with legal counsel before discussing irregularities with parties outside the client.

(h) Responsibilities in Other Circumstances

30. This section describes the auditor's responsibilities to detect and report errors and irregularities in an audit of a complete set of financial statements made in accordance with generally accepted auditing standards. In other engagements, the auditor's responsibilities may be more extensive or more restricted, depending on the terms of the engagement.

31. The auditor may accept an engagement that necessitates a more extensive responsibility to detect or report irregularities. For example, in an audit in accordance with Standards for Audit of Governmental Organizations, Programs, Activities, and Functions, 1981 Revision, issued by the U.S. General Accounting Office, the auditor should be aware that such standards go beyond generally accepted auditing standards as they relate to notification when the audit indicates that irregularities may exist. These standards require the auditor not only to promptly report instances of irregularities to the audited entity's management, but also to report the matter to the funding agency or other specified agency.

32. When an examination does not encompass a complete set of financial statements or a complete individual financial statement, or when the scope is less extensive than an audit in accordance with generally accepted auditing standards, the auditor's ability to detect material misstatements may be considerably reduced. For example, in an engagement to report on specified elements, accounts, or items of financial statements, the auditor's procedures focus on the specific element, account, or item and the special purpose of the engagement. In these circumstances, the auditor's assessment of risk at the financial statement level and other aspects of the examination that relate to the entity and its financial statements taken as a whole is necessarily more restricted.

(i) Effective Date

33. This section is effective for audits of financial statements for periods beginning on or after January 1, 1989. Early application of the provisions of this section is permissible.

(j) Appendix

(i) Characteristics of Errors and Irregularities

1. Characteristics of errors and irregularities that are relevant because of their potential influence on the auditor's ability to detect such matters are materiality of the effect on financial statements, level of management or employees involved, extent and skillfulness of any concealment, relationship to established specific control procedures, and the specific financial statements affected.

(ii) Materiality

2. Section 312, Audit Risk and Materiality in Conducting an Audit, paragraph 04, states that "financial statements are materially misstated when they contain errors or irregularities whose effect, individually or in the aggregate, is important enough to cause them not to be presented fairly in conformity with generally accepted accounting principles." Section 312.13 also states: "The auditor generally plans the audit primarily to detect errors that he believes could be large enough, individually or in the aggregate, to be quantitatively material to the financial statements." As used in section 312, the term errors refers to both errors and irregularities.

3. In planning the audit, the auditor is concerned with matters that could be material to the financial statements. An audit in accordance with generally accepted auditing standards may detect errors or irregularities that are not material to the financial statements, but such an audit can provide no assurance of detecting immaterial errors or irregularities. In this regard, there is no important distinction between errors and irregularities. There is a distinction, however, in the auditor's response to detected matters. Generally, an isolated, immaterial error in processing accounting data or applying accounting principles is not significant to the audit. In contrast, detection of an irregularity requires consideration of the implications for the integrity of management or employees and the possible effect on other aspects of the audit.

(iii) Level of Involvement

4. An irregularity may be caused by an employee or by management and, if by management, by a relatively high or low level of management. The experience of auditors indicates that the level of involvement often

combines with other characteristics in ways that have an influence on the auditor's ability to detect.

5. Defalcations by employees are often immaterial in amount and concealed in a manner that does not misstate net assets or net income. This type of irregularity can be more efficiently and effectively dealt with by an effective internal control structure and fidelity bonding of employees.

6. Material irregularities perpetrated by senior levels of management, including an owner-manager of a small business, are infrequent, but when they do occur they often engender widespread attention. These irregularities may not be susceptible to prevention or detection by specific control procedures because senior management is above the controls that deter employees or may override these controls with relative ease. Culture, custom, and the corporate governance system inhibit irregularities by senior management, but are not infallible deterrents. For this reason, an audit in accordance with generally accepted auditing standards necessarily gives due consideration to factors that bear on management integrity and the control environment.

(iv) Concealment

7. Concealment is any attempt by the perpetrator of an irregularity to reduce the likelihood of detection. Concealment usually involves manipulation of accounting records or supporting documents to disguise the fact that the accounting records are not in agreement with the underlying facts and circumstances. Concealment can be skillful and elaborate or clumsy and limited. The auditor's ability to detect a concealed irregularity depends on the skillfulness of the perpetrator, the frequency and extent of manipulation, and the relative size of individual amounts manipulated.

8. Forgery may be used to create false signatures, other signs of authenticity, or entire documents. Collusion may result in falsified confirmations or other evidence of validity. Also, unrecorded transactions are normally more difficult to detect than concealment achieved by manipulation of recorded transactions. However, the effect of concealment on the ability to detect an irregularity is dependent on the particular circumstances. For example, an attempt to mislead users of financial statements by recording large, fictitious revenue transactions late in the period without supporting documentation would be more readily detected than fictitious revenue

transactions spread throughout the period, individually immaterial in amount, and supported by legitimate-appearing invoices and shipping documents. Moreover, both of these irregularities might be extremely difficult, if not impossible, to detect if collusion of customers is added to the concealment scheme.

(v) Internal Control Structure

9. A lack of control procedures could permit an error or irregularity to occur repeatedly and the repeated occurrence could accumulate to a material amount. However, the auditor may not detect an error or irregularity that results from a nonrecurring breakdown of a specific control procedure because a rare item permitted by temporary conditions may not come to light in the performance of analytical or other procedures.

10. Irregularities may also be perpetrated or concealed by circumvention of specific control procedures or may be perpetrated by a level of management above specific control procedures. These types of irregularities are generally more difficult for an auditor to detect. However, the auditor should consider whether there are circumstances or factors that indicate a higher risk of these types of irregularities and modify auditing procedures accordingly.

(vi) Financial Statement Effect

11. Other matters remaining equal, errors or irregularities that involve overstatement will generally be more readily detected than those that involve understatement because the audit evidence available is more reliable for detecting such errors or irregularities. Also, misstatements that are charged to the income statement are less likely to be detected than those that are concealed in the balance sheet, because the process of comparing recorded accountability with the existing assets should detect significant errors concealed in the balance sheet.

(vii) Summary

12. The foregoing discussion considers characteristics of errors and irregularities individually and explains the effect an individual characteristic tends to have on the auditor's detection ability. However, these characteristics may interact in particular circumstances in ways that also affect the auditor's ability to detect a specific error or irregularity.

§A.3 AICPA SAS 54—Illegal Acts (U.S.)

(The following has been reprinted from AICPA Professional Standards, published by the American Institute of Certified Public Accountants, January 1991).

01. This section prescribes the nature and extent of the consideration an independent auditor should give to the possibility of illegal acts by a client in an audit of financial statements in accordance with generally accepted auditing standards. The section also provides guidance on the auditor's responsibilities when a possible illegal act is detected.

(a) Definition of Illegal Acts

02. The term illegal acts, for purposes of this section, refers to violations of laws or governmental regulations. Illegal acts by clients are acts attributable to the entity whose financial statements are under audit or acts by management or employees acting on behalf of the entity. Illegal acts by clients do not include personal misconduct by the entity's personnel unrelated to their business activities.

(i) Dependence on Legal Judgment

03. Whether an act is, in fact, illegal is a determination that is normally beyond the auditor's professional competence. An auditor, in reporting on financial statements, presents himself as one who is proficient in accounting and auditing. The auditor's training, experience, and understanding of the client and its industry may provide a basis for recognition that some client acts coming to his attention may be illegal. However, the determination as to whether a particular act is illegal would generally be based on the advice of an informed expert qualified to practice law or may have to await final determination by a court of law.

(ii) Relation to Financial Statements

04. Illegal acts vary considerably in their relation to the financial statements. Generally, the further removed an illegal act is from the events and transactions ordinarily reflected in financial statements, the less likely the auditor is to become aware of the act or to recognize its possible illegality.

05. The auditor considers laws and regulations that are generally recognized by auditors to have a direct and material effect on the determination

317

of financial statement accounts. For example, tax laws affect accruals and the amount recognized as expense in the accounting period; applicable laws and regulations may affect the amount of revenue accrued under government contracts. However, the auditor considers such laws or regulations from the perspective of their known relation to audit objectives derived from financial statements assertions rather than from the perspective of legality *per se*. The auditor's responsibility to detect and report misstatements resulting from illegal acts having a direct and material effect on the determination of financial statement amounts is the same as that for errors and irregularities as described in section 316, The Auditor's Responsibility to Detect and Report Errors and Irregularities.

06. Entities may be affected by many other laws or regulations, including those related to securities trading, occupational safety and health, food and drug administration, environmental protection, equal employment, and price-fixing or other antitrust violations. Generally, these laws and regulations relate more to an entity's operating aspects than to its financial and accounting aspects, and their financial statement effect is indirect. An auditor ordinarily does not have sufficient basis for recognizing possible violations of such laws and regulations. Their indirect effect is normally the result of the need to disclose a contingent liability because of the allegation or determination of illegality. For example, securities may be purchased or sold based on inside information. While the direct effects of the purchase or sale may be recorded appropriately, their indirect effect, the possible contingent liability for violating securities laws, may not be appropriately disclosed. Even when violations of such laws and regulations can have consequences material to the financial statements, the auditor may not become aware of the existence of the illegal act unless he is informed by the client, or there is evidence of a governmental agency investigation or enforcement proceeding in the records, documents or other information normally inspected in an audit of financial statements.

(b) The Auditor's Consideration of the Possibility of Illegal Acts

07. As explained in paragraph 05, certain illegal acts have a direct and material effect on the determination of financial statement amounts. Other illegal acts, such as those described in paragraph 06, may, in particular circumstances, be regarded as having material but indirect effects on financial statements. The auditor's responsibility with respect to detecting, con-

sidering the financial statement effects of, and reporting these other illegal acts is described in this section. These other illegal acts are hereinafter referred to simply as illegal acts. The auditor should be aware of the possibility that such illegal acts may have occurred. If specific information comes to the auditor's attention that provides evidence concerning the existence of possible illegal acts that could have a material indirect effect on the financial statements, the auditor should apply audit procedures specifically directed to ascertaining whether an illegal act has occurred. However, because of the characteristics of illegal acts explained above, an audit made in accordance with generally accepted auditing standards provides no assurance that illegal acts will be detected or that any contingent liabilities that may result will be disclosed.

(i) Audit Procedures in the Absence of Evidence Concerning Possible Illegal Acts

08. Normally, an audit in accordance with generally accepted auditing standards does not include audit procedures specifically designed to detect illegal acts. However, procedures applied for the purpose of forming an opinion on the financial statements may bring possible illegal acts to the auditor's attention. For example, such procedures include reading minutes; inquiring of the client's management and legal counsel concerning litigation, claims, and assessments; performing substantive tests of details of transactions or balances. The auditor should make inquiries of management concerning the client's compliance with laws and regulations. Where applicable, the auditor should also inquire of management concerning:

- The client's policies relative to the prevention of illegal acts; and

- The use of directives issued by the client and periodic representations obtained by the client from management at appropriate levels of authority concerning compliance with laws and regulations.

The auditor also ordinarily obtains written representations from management concerning the absence of violations or possible violations of laws or regulations whose effects should be considered for disclosure in the financial statements or as a basis for recording a loss contingency. (See section 333, Client Representations.) The auditor need perform no further procedures in this area absent specific information concerning possible illegal acts.

(ii) Specific Information Concerning Possible Illegal Acts

09. In applying audit procedures and evaluating the results of those procedures, the auditor may encounter specific information that may raise a question concerning possible illegal acts, such as the following:

- Unauthorized transactions, improperly recorded transactions, or transactions not recorded in a complete or timely manner in order to maintain accountability for assets;

- Investigation by a governmental agency, an enforcement proceeding, or payment of unusual fines or penalties;

- Violations of laws or regulations cited in reports of examinations by regulatory agencies that have been made available to the auditor;

- Large payments for unspecified services to consultants, affiliates, or employees;

- Sales commissions or agents' fees that appear excessive in relation to those normally paid by the client or to the services actually received;

- Unusually large payments in cash, purchases of bank cashiers' checks in large amounts payable to bearer, transfers to numbered bank accounts, or similar transactions;

- Unexplained payments made to government officials or employees; and

- Failure to file tax returns or pay government duties or similar fees that are common to the entity's industry or the nature of its business.

(iii) Audit Procedures in Response to Possible Illegal Acts

10. When the auditor becomes aware of information concerning a possible illegal act, the auditor should obtain an understanding of the nature of the act, the circumstances in which it occurred, and sufficient other information to evaluate the effect on the financial statements. In doing so, the auditor should inquire of management at a level above those involved, if possible. If management does not provide satisfactory information that there has been no illegal act, the auditor should:

a. Consult with the client's legal counsel or other specialists about the application of relevant laws and regulations to the circumstances and the possible effects on the financial statements. Arrangements for such consultation with client's legal counsel should be made by the client.

b. Apply additional procedures, if necessary, to obtain further understanding of the nature of the acts.

11. The additional audit procedures considered necessary, if any, might include procedures such as the following:

a. Examine supporting documents, such as invoices, canceled checks, and agreements and compare with accounting records.

b. Confirm significant information concerning the matter with the other party to the transaction or with intermediaries, such as banks or lawyers.

c. Determine whether the transaction has been properly authorized.

d. Consider whether other similar transactions or events may have occurred, and apply procedures to identify them.

(c) The Auditor's Response to Detected Illegal Acts

12. When the auditor concludes, based on information obtained and, if necessary, consultation with legal counsel, than an illegal act has or is likely to have occurred, the auditor should consider the effect on the financial statements as well as the implications for other aspects of the audit.

(i) The Auditor's Consideration of Financial Statement Effect

13. In evaluating the materiality of an illegal act that comes to his attention, the auditor should consider both the quantitative and qualitative materiality of the act. For example, section 312, Audit Risk and Materiality in Conducting an Audit, paragraph 07, states that "an illegal payment of an otherwise immaterial amount could be material if there is a reasonable possibility that it could lead to a material contingent liability or a material loss of revenue."

14. The auditor should consider the effect of an illegal act on the amounts presented in financial statements including contingent monetary effects, such as fines, penalties and damages. Loss contingencies resulting from illegal acts that may be required to be disclosed should be evaluated in the same manner as other loss contingencies. Examples of loss contingencies that may arise from an illegal act are: threat of expropriation of assets, enforced discontinuance of operations in another country, and litigation.

15. The auditor should evaluate the adequacy of disclosure in the financial statements of the potential effects of an illegal act on the entity's operations. If material revenue or earnings are derived from transactions involving illegal acts, or if illegal acts create significant unusual risks associated with material revenue or earnings, such as loss of a significant business relationship, that information should be considered for disclosure.

(ii) Implications for Audit

16. The auditor should consider the implications of an illegal act in relation to other aspects of the audit, particularly the reliability of representations of management. The implications of particular illegal acts will depend on the relationship of the perpetration and concealment, if any, of the illegal act to specific control procedures and the level of management or employees involved.

(iii) Communication With the Audit Committee

17. The auditor should assure himself that the audit committee, or others with equivalent authority and responsibility, is adequately informed with respect to illegal acts that come to the auditor's attention. The auditor need not communicate matters that are clearly inconsequential and may reach agreement in advance with the audit committee on the nature of such matters to be communicated. The communication should describe the act, the circumstances of its occurrence, and the effect on the financial statements. Senior management may wish to have its remedial actions communicated to the audit committee simultaneously. Possible remedial actions include disciplinary action against involved personnel, seeking restitution, adoption of preventive or corrective company policies, and modifications of specific control procedures. If senior management is involved in an illegal act, the auditor should communicate directly with the audit committee. The communication may be oral or written. If the communication is oral, the auditor should document it.

(iv) Effect on the Auditor's Report

18. If the auditor concludes that an illegal act has a material effect on the financial statements, and the act has not been properly accounted for or

322

disclosed, the auditor should express a qualified opinion or an adverse opinion on the financial statements taken as a whole, depending on the materiality of the effect on the financial statements.

19. If the auditor is precluded by the client from obtaining sufficient competent evidential matter to evaluate whether an illegal act that could be material to the financial statements has, or is likely to have, occurred, the auditor generally should disclaim an opinion on the financial statements.

20. If the client refuses to accept the auditor's report as modified for the circumstances described in paragraphs 18 and 19, the auditor should withdraw from the engagement and indicate the reasons for withdrawal in writing to the audit committee or board of directors.

21. The auditor may be unable to determine whether an act is illegal because of limitations imposed by the circumstances rather than by the client or because of uncertainty associated with interpretation of applicable laws or regulations or surrounding facts. In these circumstances, the auditor should consider the effect on his report.

(d)   Other Considerations in an Audit in Accordance With Generally Accepted Auditing Standards

22. In addition to the need to withdraw from the engagement, as described in paragraph 20, the auditor may conclude that withdrawal is necessary when the client does not take the remedial action that the auditor considers necessary in the circumstances even when the illegal act is not material to the financial statements. Factors that should affect the auditor's conclusion include the implications of the failure to take remedial action, which may affect the auditor's ability to rely on management representations, and the effects of continuing association with the client. In reaching a conclusion on such matters, the auditor may wish to consult with his own legal counsel.

23. Disclosure of an illegal act to parties other than the client's senior management and its audit committee or board of directors is not ordinarily part of the auditor's responsibility, and such disclosure would be precluded by the auditor's ethical or legal obligation of confidentiality, unless the matter affects his opinion on the financial statements. The auditor should recognize, however, that in the following circumstances a duty to notify parties outside the client may exist:

a. When the entity reports an auditor change under the appropriate securities law on Form 8-K.

b. To a successor auditor when the successor makes inquiries in accordance with section 315, Communications Between Predecessor and Successor Auditors.

c. In response to a subpoena.

d. To a funding agency or other specified agency in accordance with requirements for the audits of entities that receive financial assistance from a government agency.

Because potential conflicts with the auditor's ethical and legal obligations for confidentiality may be complex, the auditor may wish to consult with legal counsel before discussing illegal acts with parties outside the client.

(e) Responsibilities in Other Circumstances

24. An auditor may accept an engagement that entails a greater responsibility for detecting illegal acts than that specified in this section. For example, a governmental unit may engage an independent auditor to perform an audit in accordance with the Single Audit Act of 1984. In such an engagement, the independent auditor is responsible for testing and reporting on the governmental unit's compliance with certain laws and regulations applicable to Federal financial assistance programs. Also, an independent auditor may undertake a variety of other special engagements. For example, a corporation's board of directors or its audit committee may engage an auditor to apply agreed-upon procedures and report on compliance with the corporation's code of conduct under the attestation standards.

(f) Effective Date

25. This section is effective for audits of financial statements for periods beginning on or after January 1, 1989. Early application of the provisions of this section is permissible.

(g)   Illegal Acts By Clients: Auditing Interpretations of SAS 54

(i) Consideration of the Internal Control Structure in a Financial Statement Audit and the Foreign Corrupt Practices Act

01. Question: The second standard of field work requires the auditor to obtain a sufficient understanding of the internal control structure to plan the audit and to determine the nature, timing, and extent of tests to be performed. Is the auditor of an entity subject to the Securities Exchange Act of 1934 required, because of the Foreign Corrupt Practices Act of 1977 and the provisions of section 317, to expand his consideration of the internal control structure beyond that which is required by the second standard of field work?

02. Interpretation: No. There is nothing in the Act or the related legislative history that purports to alter the auditor's duty to his client or the purpose of his consideration of the internal control structure. The Act creates express new duties only for companies subject to the Securities Exchange Act of 1934, not for auditors. Issue Date: October, 1978.

(ii) Material Weaknesses in the Internal Control Structure and the Foreign Corrupt Practices Act

03. Question: What course of action should be followed by the auditor of an entity subject to the internal accounting control provision of the Foreign Corrupt Practices Act of 1977 to comply with section 317 when a material weakness in the internal control structure comes to his attention?

04. Interpretation: The standards applied by an auditor in determining a material weakness in the internal control structure may differ from the standards for determining a violation of the Act. Nevertheless, a specific material weakness may ultimately be determined to be a violation and, hence, an illegal act. Therefore, the auditor should inquire of the client's management and consult with the client's legal counsel as to whether the material weakness is a violation of the Act.

05. In consultation with management and legal counsel, consideration should be given to corrective action taken or in process. If management has concluded that corrective action for a material weakness is not practicable, consideration should be given to the reasons underlying that conclusion, including management's evaluation of the costs of correction in relation to the expected benefit to be derived. If it is determined that there

has been a violation of the Act and appropriate consideration is not given to the violation, the auditor should consider withdrawing from the current engagement or dissociating himself from any future relationship with the client (see section 317.22).

06. A violation of the internal accounting control provision of the Act would not, in and of itself, have a direct effect on amounts presented in audited financial statements. However, the contingent monetary effect on an entity ultimately determined to have willfully violated the internal accounting control provision of the Act could be fines of up to $10,000 for the violation. The auditor should consider the materiality of such contingent monetary effect in relation to the audited financial statements taken as a whole. Other loss contingencies, as defined by FASB Statement No. 5 (AC section C59), ordinarily would not result from a weakness in the internal control structure which gives rise to such a violation of the Act.

Issue Date: October, 1978.

Index

A

Accidents:
casualty insurance frauds, 158–159
computer security system and, 87–88

Accounting procedures:
forensic accounting skills and attributes,
234–235
high fraud/low fraud environments and,
27
internal controls and "fraudproofing,"
33–34

Acquisition and payment cycle, 126–132
detection, 130
financial statement accounts, 126–127
functions, 126
operation of cycle, 126
perpetration, 127–129
prevention, 131–132

Advance fee fraud, bank fraud, 170–171

AICPA. See American Institute of Certified
Public Accountants (AICPA) American
Institute of Certified Public Accountants
(AICPA) SAS 53—Errors and
Irregularities (U.S.), 301–316
auditor's responsibility, 303
audit planning material misstatements,
304–307
audit report irregularities, 311
audit test results evaluation, 310–311
communications of errors or irregularities,
312
definitions, 302–303
effective date, 313

professional skepticism, 304–309

American Institute of Certified Public
Accountants (AICPA) SAS 54—Illegal
Acts (U.S.), 317–326
auditor's consideration, 318–321
auditor's response to acts, 321–323
definitions, 317–318
effective date, 324
generally accepted auditing standards,
323–324
illegal acts by clients, auditing
interpretations, 325–326

Antitrust violations, commercial crime, 219

Approvals:
inventory and warehousing cycle crime
prevention, 138
payroll and personnel cycle crime
prevention, 135
sales and collection cycle crime
prevention, 126
supervision, internal controls and
"fraudproofing," 35–36

Arson, property insurance fraud, 160

Asset misappropriation (internal), 119–144
acquisition and payment cycle, 126–132
detection, 130
financial statement accounts, 126–127
functions, 126
operation of cycle, 126
perpetration, 127–129
prevention, 131–132
capital acquisition and repayment cycle,
139–140
cash misappropriation, 140–143

Index

Asset misappropriation (internal) (*continued*)
  cash misappropriation (*continued*)
    detection and prevention, 142–143
    perpetration, 140–141
  classification of fraud, 121–122
  inventory and warehousing cycle,
      136–138
    detection, 137–138
    financial statement accounts, 136
    functions, 136
    operation of cycle, 136
    perpetration, 136–137
    prevention, 138
  overview of, 10
  payroll and personnel cycle, 132–136
    detection, 134–135
    financial statement accounts, 133
    functions, 132–133
    operation of cycle, 132
    perpetration, 133–134
    prevention, 135–136
  sales and collection cycle, 122–126
    detection, 123–125
    perpetration, 122–123
    prevention, 125–126
Assignment, fidelity insurance policy clause,
    75
Attorneys, lawyer crime, commercial crime,
    220. *See also* Law
Audit controls:
  asset misappropriation (internal), cash
      misappropriation, 142–143
  high fraud/low fraud environments and,
      27
  internal controls and "fraudproofing,"
      36–37
Audit skills, forensic accounting skills and
    attributes, 234–235
Awareness. *See* Vigilance

B

Back–up, operational failure recovery,
    108–109
Balance sheet. *See also* Financial statement
    accounts; Income statement
  acquisition and payment cycle, 126–127
  capital acquisition and repayment cycle
      crimes, 139
  inventory and warehousing cycle crime,
      136

payroll and personnel cycle crime, 133
Bank deposit theft, perpetration, 141
Bankers Blanket Bond, described, 65–66
Bank fraud:
  advance fee fraud, 170–171
  bribery, 165–166
  check frauds, 166–169
  commercial real estate fraud, 164–165
  loan fraud, 162–164
  money laundering, 171–172
  money transfer fraud, 169–170
  overview, 161–162
Banking industry:
  computer crime in, 198
  defininitions, 161
  losses in, 18
Banking premises, fidelity insurance policy
    definition, 68
Bankruptcy fraud, finance–related fraud, 148
Bank statements, asset misappropriation
    (internal), cash misappropriation,
    142–143
Benefit programs, government frauds, 156
Bernoulli Box, 107
Bids and bidding:
  acquisition and payment cycle crime
      detection, 130
  government frauds, contracts, 156
Billings, casualty insurance frauds, 159
Bond period; territory discovery, fidelity
    insurance policy clause, 70
Books and records, fidelity insurance policy
    clause, 71
Bribery:
  bank fraud, 165–166
  organizational bribegiving, commercial
      crime, 218–219
Brokers Blanket Bond, described, 66–67
Bundling and unbundling claims, health
    insurance frauds, 160
Buyers, acquisition and payment cycle crime
    perpetration, 127–129

C

Cancellation as to any employee, fidelity
    insurance policy clause, 74–75

Index

Cancellation of bond or insuring agreement, fidelity insurance policy clause, 75

Capital acquisition and repayment cycle, 139–140

Card access devices, computer security system, 98

Cash misappropriation, 140–143
 detection and prevention, 142–143
 perpetration, 140–141

Casualty insurance frauds, 158–159

Catastrophic opportunity levels, generic risk factors, 22

Catastrophic risk, risk financing concepts, 62

Chain referral schemes, individual and small business fraud, 151–152

Charity and religious frauds, individual and small business fraud, 154

Check frauds, bank fraud, 166–169

Civil actions, forensic accounting services, 242–244

Clients, conflict of interest, 49

Code of Business Conduct sample, 47–53
 Company Funds, 51
 Company Records, 51–52
 Compliance with Laws and Regulations, 48
 Conflict of Interest, 48–51
 Dealing with Outside Persons and Organizations, 52
 Political Activity, 51
 Privacy and Confidentiality, 52–53
 Prompt Communications, 52
 Purpose, 47–48

Codes of business ethics and conduct:
 acquisition and payment cycle crime prevention, 131–132
 environmental factors and, 46
 moral character (greed factor) and, 24

Collusion, health insurance frauds, 160

Commercial crime, 205–228
 causes of, 212–214
 characteristics of, 210–212
 definitions, 206–208
 extent of, 209
 forms of, 214–221
  antitrust violations, 219
  bribery, organizational bribegiving, 218–219

  environmental, occupational, and public health and safety, 220–221
  false advertising, 215
  industrial espionage and trade secret theft, 215–216
  insider trading, 217
  lawyer crime, 220
  securities fraud, 217–218
 overview of, 10
 prevention of, 221–227
  deterrence concepts, 221–223
  ethics, 225
  formal deterrence, 223–224
  informal deterrence, 224–225
  strategy for, 225–226
 responsibility for, 209–210
 victims of, 208–209

Commercial real estate fraud, bank fraud, 164–165

Common sense, motivation (need factor) and, 26

Communication(s):
 Code of Business Conduct sample, 52
 of findings, forensic accounting five–step investigative approach, 246
 security for, computer security system, 99, 101–102
 skills in, forensic accounting skills and attributes, 238

Company funds, Code of Business Conduct sample, 51

Company records, Code of Business Conduct sample, 51–52

Computer analysis. See also Computer crime; Computer security
 asset misappropriation (internal), cash misappropriation, 143
 information technology expertise and, forensic accounting, skills and attributes, 238–239
 inventory and warehousing cycle crime detection, 137–138
 investigative software packages, forensic accounting tools, 241–242

Computer crime, 173–204. See also Computer security
 categorization of, 177
 environmental factors, 189–196
  discouraging factors, 192–194
  enhancing factors, 191–192
  improvement recommendations, 196

Computer crime (*continued*)
  environmental factors (*continued*)
    security countermeasures, 194–195
  examples of, 197–201
  history and evolution of, 176–177
  losses from, 18
  nature and extent of, 177–183
    common forms, 180–181
    trends in, 181–183
    typology, 179–180
  overview of, 10, 174–176
  personality profile of criminal, 183–189

Computer room construction, computer
    security system, 95

Computer security, 83–115. *See also*
    Computer crime
  checklist for, 90–94
  computer vital functions, 85–86
  concerns, 86–87
  logical security, 99–107
    communication security, 99, 101–102
    computer operations, 106–107
    data security, 102–105
    microcomputers, 107
    software integrity, 105–106
  management responsibility, 113–114
  overview of, 9, 20
  physical security, 94–98
    access, 94
    computer room accesss, 98
    computer room construction, 95
    electrical power reliability, 96–97
    environmental control, 97
    fire detection and suppression system,
      95–96
    generally, 95
    microcomputer security, 98
    water protection, 96
  policing, 114–115
  policy, standards, guidelines, and
    procedures, 114
  security function, 114–115
  system for, 87–90
  system recovery, 107–113
    disaster recovery plans, 109–111
    insurance, 111, 113
    microcomputer, 113
    operational failures, 108–109
    overview of, 107–108

Confidentiality:
  Code of Business Conduct sample, 52–53

computer security concerns, 86

Conflict of interest, Code of Business
    Conduct sample, 48–51

Contamination, environmental, computer
    security system, 97

Contracts, government frauds, 156–157

Controlled destruction, data security, 105

Corporate mission statement, moral
    character (greed factor) and, 24

Correspondence schools, individual and
    small business fraud, 154–155

Cost inflation, government frauds, contracts,
    156–157

Counterfeit paper currency:
  Bankers Blanket Bond, 67
  Dishonesty, Destruction, and
    Disappearance bonds (3–D), 65

Coupon redemption frauds, individual and
    small business fraud, 153

Credit fraud, finance–related fraud, 148

Criminal actions:
  forensic accounting services, 242–244
  fraud definition and, 4

Crisis management, 231–247. *See also*
    Forensic accounting
  five–step investigative approach, 244–247
  forensic and investigative accounting
    defined, 232–233
  fraud and, 11
  overview of, 232
  services categorized, 242–244
  skills and attributes of forensic
    accountant, 233–239
  tools of forensic accountant, 239–242

Critical skepticism: AICPA SAS 53—
    Errors and Irregularities (U.S.),
    304–309
  forensic accounting skills and attributes,
    236–237

Culture, commercial crime and, 206–207

Custodian, fidelity insurance policy
    definition, 68

Cycle, fraud classification and, 122. *See
    also* Acquisition and payment cycle;
    Capital acquisition and repayment
    cycle; Payroll and personnel cycle;
    Sales and collection cycle

Cypher locks, computer security system, 98

Index

D

Data diddling, computer crime, 179

Data encryption, data security, 102

Data file, operational failure recovery, 108–109

Data security, computer security, 102–105. *See also* Computer security

Debt consolidation schemes, finance–related fraud, 149

Deception. *See* Criminal actions

Destruction, data security, 105

Detection:
  acquisition and payment cycle, 130
  capital acquisition and repayment cycle crimes, 139–140
  cash misappropriation, 142–143
  computer crime, 193–194
  inventory and warehousing cycle crime, 137–138
  payroll and personnel cycle crime, 134–135
  sales and collection cycle, 123–125

Detection controls, computer security system and, 88

Dial-up security, computer security system, 101–102

Differential association theory, commercial crime causation, 212–214

Diffusion of harm, commercial crime characteristic, 211–212

Diploma mills, individual and small business fraud, 154

Directorships, conflict of interest, 49

Directory advertising schemes, individual and small business fraud, 153

Disaster recovery plans, operational failure recovery, 109–111

Discovery. *See* Likelihood of discovery

Dishonesty, Destruction, and Disappearance bonds (3–D), described, 64–65

Distribution control, data security, 105

Documentation:
  acquisition and payment cycle crime prevention, 131
  payroll and personnel cycle crime prevention, 135
  sales and collection cycle crime, 125

Documents, data security, 104–105

Double indemnity, life insurance frauds, 158

Drug marketing (pharmaceutical industry), commercial crime, 220–221

Drugs (illicit), money laundering, bank fraud, 171–172

E

Economic need. *See* Motivation (need factor)

Education, ethics, 225

Electrical power reliability, computer security system, 96–97

Embezzlement, lawyer crime, commercial crime, 220

Employee(s):
  fidelity insurance policy definition, 68
  hiring practices
    environmental factors and, 47
    moral character (greed factor) and, 25
  relations with, environmental factors and, 47

Employee assistance programs, motivation (need factor) and, 26

Employee testing and screening programs:
  computer crime, 192
  high fraud/low fraud environments and, 27
  motivation (need factor) and, 26
  sales and collection cycle crime, 125

Encryption, data security, 102

Enforcement:
  commercial crime prevention, 223
  environmental factors and, 46–47

Entertainment, conflict of interest, 50

Environmental factors, 45–58
  checklist for, 53–58
  Code of Business Conduct sample, 47–53
    Company Funds, 51
    Company Records, 51–52
    Compliance with Laws and Regulations, 48
    Conflict of Interest, 48–51
    Dealing with Outside Persons and Organizations, 52
    Political Activity, 51
    Privacy and Confidentiality, 52–53
    Prompt Communications, 52
    Purpose, 47–48
  commercial crime prevention, 225

Environmental factors (*continued*)
 computer crime and, 188–189
 computer security system, 97, 189–196
  contamination, 97
  discouraging factors, 192–194
  enhancing factors, 191–192
  improvement recommendations, 196
  security countermeasures, 194–195
 generally, 46–47
  employee hiring and employee
   relations, 47
  enforcement, 46–47
  tone setting, 46
 high fraud/low fraud environments, 27–31
 motivation (need factor) and, 25
Environmental pollution (ecological),
 commercial crime, 220–221
Ethics, 9, 20, 239. *See also* Code of
 Business Conduct sample; Codes of
 business ethics and conduct;
 Environmental factors
Exclusions, fidelity insurance policy clause,
 69
Expense accounts, environmental factors
 and, 46
External audits, internal controls and
 "fraudproofing," 37
External perpetrators, 145–172
 bank fraud, 161–172
  advance fee fraud, 170–171
  bribery, 165–166
  check frauds, 166–169
  commercial real estate fraud, 164–165
  loan fraud, 162–164
  money laundering, 171–172
  money transfer fraud, 169–170
  overview, 161–162
 government frauds, 155–157
  benefit programs, 156
  contracts, 156–157
  income tax frauds, 155–156
 individuals and small businesses, 148–155
  chain referral schemes, 151–152
  charity and religious frauds, 154
  coupon redemption frauds, 153
  directory advertising schemes, 153
  finance–related fraud, 148–149
  land frauds, 150–151
  merchandise swindles, 152–153
  personal improvement frauds, 154–155
  property improvement schemes,
   149–150

insurance fraud, 157–161
 casualty insurance frauds, 158–159
 definitions, 157–158
 health insurance frauds, 160
 life insurance fraud, 158
 mortgage insurance frauds, 161
 personal injury insurance frauds,
  160–161
 property insurance frauds, 159–160
overview of, 10, 147

F

False advertising, commercial crime, 215
False instrument for filing, insurance fraud
 and, 158
Favors, conflict of interest, 50
Fidelity insurance policies, 63–75. *See also*
 Risk financing clauses in assignment,
  75
 bond period; territory discovery, 70
 books and records, 71
 cancellation as to any employee, 74–75
 cancellation of bond or insuring
  agreement, 75
 definitions, 67–69
 exclusions, 69
 limit of liability under current bond and
  prior insurance, 74
 limits of liability, 73
 loss caused by unidentifiable
  employees, 71
 loss–notice–proof–action against
  underwriter, 72
 loss under prior bond or policy, 70
 no benefit to bailee, 75
 other insurance, 74
 ownership of property; interests
  covered, 71
 prior fraud, dishonety, or cancellation,
  71
 recoveries, 73
 subrogation, 74
 valuation–payment–replacement, 72
 types of, 63–67
  Bankers Blanket Bond, 65–66
  bonds, generally, 66–67
  Brokers Blanket Bond, 66–67
  Dishonesty, Destruction, and
   Disappearance bonds (3–D), 64–65
  generally, 63–64

Filings, offering a false instrument for
filing, insurance fraud and, 158

Finance–related fraud, 148–149
bankruptcy fraud, 148
credit fraud, 148
debt consolidation schemes, 149
security fraud, 149

Financial benefit, fraud definition and, 5

Financial institutions. *See* Banking industry

Financial statement accounts. *See also*
Balance sheet; Income statement
acquisition and payment cycle, 126–127
AICPA SAS 54—Illegal Acts (U.S.),
317–318
capital acquisition and repayment cycle
crime, 139
inventory and warehousing cycle crime,
136
payroll and personnel cycle crime, 133

Fire detection and suppression system,
computer security system, 95–96

Forensic accounting. *See also* Crisis
management defined, 232–233
five–step investigative approach, 244–247
communication of findings, 246
financial analysis and synthesis, 246
issues identification, 245
issues investigation, 246
presentation of evidence, 247
skills and attributes, 233–239
accounting and audit skills, 234–235
communication skills, 238
computer and information technology
expertise, 238–239
ethics and, 239
fraud expertise, 235–236
investigative mentality and skepticism,
236–237
law and rules of evidence expertise,
236
psychology and motivation expertise,
237–238
tools of, 239–242
information gathering techniques, 240
interview techniques, 239–240
investigative software packages,
241–242
private investigators, 240–241

Forgery:
Bankers Blanket Bond, 66
Brokers Blanket Bond, 66

check frauds, 168
Dishonesty, Destruction, and
Disappearance bonds (3–D), 65

Fraud. *See also entries under specific types
of frauds*
crisis management and, 11
defined, 4–5
forensic accounting skills and attributes,
235–236
fraudulent billings, casualty insurance
frauds, 159
government frauds, 155–157
magnitude of threat, 5
source of threat, 7–8

Fraud awareness. *See* Vigilance

Fraud prevention. *See* Prevention

Fraudproofing. *See* Internal controls and
"fraudproofing"

G

Generic risk factors:
described, 21–23
individual factors versus, 18–19

Ghost employees, payroll and personnel
cycle crime detection, 134

Gifts:
acquisition and payment cycle crime
prevention, 131–132
conflict of interest, 50

GONE theory, risk factor classification
system, 20–21

Government frauds, 155–157
benefit programs, 156
contracts, 156–157
income tax frauds, 155–156

Grand larceny, insurance fraud and, 157

Greed factor. *See* Moral character (greed
factor)

Guidelines, computer security, 114

H

Hackers, 101–102, 180

Health insurance frauds, 160

High fraud/low fraud environments. *See*
Environmental factors

Index

Hiring practices. *See also* Employees
  environmental factors and, 47
  moral character (greed factor) and, 25
Homicide, life insurance frauds, 158
Honesty:
  common perceptions of, 17
  integrity and, 6
Humidity control, computer security system, 97

I

Identification, commercial crime
  responsibility and, 210
Illicit drugs, money laundering, bank fraud, 171–172
Imputation, commercial crime responsibility and, 210
Income statement. *See also* Balance sheet; Financial
  statement accounts
  acquisition and payment cycle, 127
  capital acquisition and repayment cycle crimes, 139
  inventory and warehousing cycle crime, 136
  payroll and personnel cycle crime, 133
Income tax frauds, government frauds, 155–156
Independent verification. *See* Verification
Individual(s) and small business(es) fraud, 148–155
  chain referral schemes, 151–152
  charity and religious frauds, 154
  coupon redemption frauds, 153
  directory advertising schemes, 153
  finance–related fraud, 148–149
  land frauds, 150–151
  merchandise swindles, 152–153
  personal improvement frauds, 154–155
  property improvement schemes, 149–150
Individual risk factors, 23–27
  generic factors versus, 18–19
  moral character (greed factor), 23–25
  motivation (need factor), 25–26
  profiles of perpetrators, 26–27
Industrial espionage, commercial crime, 215–216
Information gathering techniques, forensic
  accounting tools, 240

Information integrity, computer security
  concerns, 87
Information technology expertise, computer
  analysis and,
  forensic accounting, skills and
    attributes, 238–239
Injury, personal injury insurance fraud, 160–161
Input tampering, computer crime, 179
Insider trading, commercial crime, 217
Insurance, operational failure recovery, 111, 113
Insurance fraud, 157–161
  casualty insurance frauds, 158–159
  definitions, 157–158
  health insurance frauds, 160
  life insurance fraud, 158
  mortgage insurance frauds, 161
  personal injury insurance frauds, 160–161
  property insurance frauds, 159–160
Insurance industry, computer crime in, 198–199
Integrity:
  fraud and, 5
  honesty and, 6
Intent, commercial crime responsibility and, 210
Interest payments, capital acquisition and
  repayment cycle crimes, 139–140
Internal asset misappropriation (internal).
  See Asset misappropriation (internal)
Internal audits, internal controls and
  "fraudproofing,' 36–37
Internal company activities, conflict of
  interest, 50–51
Internal controls and "fraudproofing,"
  31–37
  audits, 36–37
  description of controls, generally, 31–34
  high fraud/low fraud environments and, 27
  objectives, 31
  risk management policy, 19–20
  supervision, 34–36
Interview techniques, forensic accounting
  tools, 239–240
Inventory and warehousing cycle, 136–138
  detection, 137–138
  financial statement accounts, 136
  functions, 136

Index

operation of cycle, 136
perpetration, 136–137
prevention, 138

Investigative accounting, defined, 232–233

Investigative mentality, forensic accounting skills and attributes, 236–237

Investigative software packages, forensic accounting tools, 241–242

Investments, conflict of interest, 49

J

Job Control Language, computer operations security, 106–107

Job descriptions, internal controls and "fraudproofing," 32–33

K

Key locks, computer security system, 98

Kickbacks:
bank frauds, loans, 164
to customers, sales and collection cycle crime, 123, 124–125

Kiting, check frauds, 166–168

L

Land flip, commercial real estate fraud, 164

Land frauds, individual and small business fraud, 150–151

Law. *See also* Forensic accounting
banking industry and, 161–162
commercial crime responsibility and, 210
compliance, Code of Business Conduct sample, 48
forensic accounting skills and attributes, 236
polygraph, 125

Lawyer crime, commercial crime, 220

Life insurance fraud, 158

Likelihood of discovery, generic risk factors, 22

Limit of liability under current bond and prior insurance,
fidelity insurance policy clause, 74

Limits of liability, fidelity insurance policy clause, 73

Loan fraud, bank fraud, 162–164

Loans, capital acquisition and repayment cycle crimes, 139–140

Logical security. *See* Computer security: logical security

Loss, fidelity insurance policy definition, 69

Loss caused by unidentifiable employees, fidelity insurance policy clause, 71

Loss-notice-proof-action against underwriter, fidelity insurance policy clause, 72

Loss under prior bond or policy, fidelity insurance policy clause, 70

M

Management of risk. *See* Risk management

Management responsibility, computer security, 113–114

Management style, moral character (greed factor) and, 24–25

Merchandise swindles, individual and small business fraud, 152–153

Messenger, fidelity insurance policy definition, 68

Microcomputer:
computer crime and, 177
operational failure recovery, 111, 113
security
computer security system, 98
logical security, 107

Migration of programs, data security, 106

Misappropriation. *See* Asset misappropriation (internal)

Mobile labs, health insurance frauds, 160

Modeling schools, individual and small business fraud, 155

Money, fidelity insurance policy definition, 67

Money laundering, bank fraud, 171–172

Money transfer fraud, bank fraud, 169–170

Moral character (greed factor), individual risk factors, 23–25

Morale, motivation (need factor) and, 25

Mortgage(s), bank frauds, loans, 162–164

Mortgage insurance frauds, insurance fraud, 161

Motivation (need factor):

Motivation (need factor): (*continued*)
computer crime, 186–189, 191
forensic accounting skills and attributes, 237–238
individual risk factors, 25–26

N

Need factor. *See* Motivation (need factor)
Network security features, computer security system, 101
New account frauds, check frauds, 168–169
No benefit to bailee, fidelity insurance policy clause, 75

O

Occupational safety and health laws, commercial crime, 220–221
Off-book fraud, described, 122
Offering a false instrument for filing, insurance fraud and, 158
Off-line data files, data security, 104
Off-line software, data security, 105–106
On-book fraud, described, 122
On-line data files, data security, 102, 104
On-line software libraries, data security, 105
Opportunity, generic risk factors, 21–22
Organizational bribegiving, commercial crime, 218–219
Organizational factors, high fraud/low fraud environments, 27–31
Output tampering, computer crime, 179–180
Outside perpetrators. *See* External perpetrators
Outside persons and organizations, Code of Business Conduct sample, 52
Ownership of property; interests covered, fidelity insurance policy clause, 71

P

Passwords, computer security system, 99, 101, 107, 194
Payroll and personnel cycle, 132–136
detection, 134–135
financial statement accounts, 133

functions, 132–133
operation of cycle, 132
perpetration, 133–134
prevention, 135–136
Performance checks:
inventory and warehousing cycle crime prevention, 138
motivation (need factor) and, 25–26
sales and collection cycle crime, 126
Perpetration:
acquisition and payment cycle, 127–129
capital acquisition and repayment cycle crimes, 139
inventory and warehousing cycle crime, 136–137
payroll and personnel cycle crime, 133–134
sales and collection cycle, 122–123
Perpetrators, profiles of, 26–27, 183–189
Personal improvement frauds, individual and small business fraud, 154–155
Personal injury insurance frauds, 160–161
Personal investments, conflict of interest, 49
Personality:
computer crime profile of criminal, 183–189
profiles of perpetrators, 26–27
Personnel. *See* Employee(s)
Personnel cycle. *See* Payroll and personnel cycle
Petty cash theft, perpetration, 140–141
Pharmaceutical industry, commercial crime, 220–221
Physical access:
computer security system, 94, 98
data security, 104
internal controls and "fraudproofing," 32
inventory and warehousing cycle crime prevention, 138
sales and collection cycle crime, 125
Policing, computer security, 114–115
Policy, computer security, 114
Political activity, Code of Business Conduct sample, 51
Pollution, commercial crime, 220–221
Polygraph, sales and collection cycle crime, 125
Ponzi schemes, individual and small business fraud, 151–152

Index

Premises, fidelity insurance policy
definition, 68
Prevention, 9–10
asset misappropriation (internal)
acquisition and payment cycle, 131–132
capital acquisition and repayment cycle
crimes, 140
cash misappropriation, 142–143
inventory and warehousing cycle crime,
138
payroll and personnel cycle crime,
135–136
sales and collection cycle, 125–126
commercial crime, 221–227
computer crime, 193
computer security system and, 88
overview of, 9
risk management, 15–44. *See also* Risk
management types of fraud and, 10
Printing control, data security, 104–105
Prior fraud, dishonety, or cancellation,
fidelity insurance policy clause, 71
Privacy, Code of Business Conduct sample,
52–53. *See also* Confidentiality
Private investigators, forensic accounting
tools, 240–241
Proactive forensic accounting services,
described, 242
Procedures, computer security, 114
Product substitution:
government frauds, contracts, 157
property improvement scheme fraud, 150
Professional studies and pronouncements,
291–326. *See also* American Institute
of Certified Public Accountants
(AICPA)
AICPA SAS 53—Errors and Irregularities
(U.S.), 301–316
AICPA SAS 54—Illegal Acts (U.S.),
317–326
Treadway Commission Report Summary,
293–301
Programmed network security features,
computer security system, 101
Property improvement schemes, individual
and small business fraud, 149–150
Property insurance frauds, insurance fraud,
159–160
Psychology, forensic accounting skills and
attributes, 237–238

Public health, commercial crime, 220–221
Public relations, conflict of interest, 49
Punishment:
commercial crime prevention, 221–224
generic risk factors, 22–23
Pyramid schemes, individual and small
business fraud, 151–152

R

Rationalization:
commercial crime characteristic, 212
fraud and, 17–18
Reconciliations, asset misappropriation
(internal), cash misappropriation,
142–143
Records. *See* Books and records
Recoveries, fidelity insurance policy clause,
73
Recovery controls, computer security system
and, 88
Religious and charity frauds, individual and
small business fraud, 154
Reperformance, supervision, internal
controls and "fraudproofing," 35–36
Reports, data security, 104–105
Review procedures, supervision, internal
controls and
"fraudproofing," 35–36
Reward systems, motivation (need factor)
and, 25–26, 189
Risk financing, 59–82. *See also* Fidelity
insurance
checklist for, 78–82
concept of, 61–62
fidelity insurance policies, 63–75
clauses in, 67–75
types of, 63–67
historical background of, 62–63
overview of, 9, 20
purchase decision, 77–78
responsibilities of insured, 76–77
Risk management, 15–44
checklist for, 37–44
factors, 20–31
classification systems, 20–21
environments, 27–31
generic factors, 21–23
individual factors, 23–27

Index

Risk management (*continued*)
generally, 9, 16–20
internal controls and "fraudproofing,"
31–37
audits, 36–37
description of controls, generally,
31–34
objectives, 31
supervision, 34–36
policy development and implementation,
19–20
Robbery, fidelity insurance policy definition,
68
Role models:
environmental factors and, 46
moral character (greed factor) and, 24–25
Rules of evidence, forensic accounting skills
and attributes, 236

S

Safe burglary, fidelity insurance policy
definition, 68–69
Sales and collection cycle, 122–126
detection, 123–125
perpetration, 122–123
prevention, 125–126
Screening programs. *See* Employee testing
and screening programs
Secure storage, data security, 105
Securities:
Bankers Blanket Bond, 67
Brokers Blanket Bond, 67
fidelity insurance policy definition, 67
Securities fraud:
commercial crime, 217–218
finance–related fraud, 149
Security function, computer security,
114–115
Sentencing (criminal), commercial crime
prevention, 223–224
Separation of duties:
inventory and warehousing cycle crime
prevention, 138
payroll and personnel cycle crime
prevention, 135
sales and collection cycle crime, 125
Skepticism:
AICPA SAS 53—Errors and Irregularities
(U.S.), 304–309

forensic accounting skills and attributes,
236–237
Small business fraud. *See* Individual(s) and
small business(es) fraud
Smurfs, money laundering fraud, 172
Social values, moral character (greed factor)
and, 23–24
Software back–up, operational failure
recovery, 108–109
Software integrity, computer security
system, 105–106
Software restrictions, data security, 102
Song publishing schemes, individual and
small business fraud, 155
Staged accidents, casualty insurance frauds,
158
Staged death, life insurance frauds, 158
Standards, computer security, 114
Stocks, security fraud, finance–related fraud,
149
Subrogation, fidelity insurance policy
clause, 74
Supervision:
high fraud/low fraud environments and,
27
internal controls and "fraudproofing,"
34–36
Suppliers, conflict of interest, 49
System availability, computer security
concerns, 87
System recovery. *See* Computer security:
system recovery

T

Telephone, dial–up security, computer
security system, 101–102
Temperature control, computer security
system, 97
Testing and screening programs. *See*
Employee testing and screening
programs
Theft:
of assets, sales and collection cycle crime,
123, 124
of cash, sales and collection cycle crime,
122–124
fraud and, 16–18

Index

Throughput tampering, computer crime, 179

Tolerance, commercial crime characteristic, 210–211

Trade secret theft, commercial crime, 215–216

Treadway Commission Report Summary, 293–301

U

Unbundling and bundling claims, health insurance frauds, 160

V

Valuation-payment-replacement, fidelity insurance policy clause, 72

Vanity publishing schemes, individual and small business fraud, 155

Vendors, acquisition and payment cycle crime perpetration, 127–129

Verification, payroll and personnel cycle crime prevention, 135–136

Vigilance:
acquisition and payment cycle crime detection, 130, 131
motivation (need factor) and, 26
supervision, internal controls and "fraudproofing," 34–35

W

Warehousing. *See* Inventory and warehousing cycle

Water protection, computer security system, 96

White-collar crime, definitions, 206, 207–208

Working conditions, motivation (need factor) and, 25

Written codes of business ethics:
environmental factors and, 46
moral character (greed factor) and, 24